Sister Linda

Chicken Soup for the Soul.

Family Caregivers

D0029205

Chicken Soup for the Soul: Family Caregivers
101 Stories of Love, Sacrifice, and Bonding
Joan Lunden, Amy Newmark.

Published by Chicken Soup for the Soul Publishing, LLC   www.chickensoup.com
Copyright © 2012 by Chicken Soup for the Soul Publishing, LLC. All Rights Reserved.
No part of this publication may be reproduced, stored in a retrieval system or transmit-
ted in any form or by any means, electronic, mechanical, photocopying, recording or
otherwise, without the written permission of the publisher.

CSS, Chicken Soup for the Soul, and its Logo and Marks are trademarks of
Chicken Soup for the Soul Publishing LLC.

The publisher gratefully acknowledges the many publishers and individuals who
granted Chicken Soup for the Soul permission to reprint the cited material.

Front cover photo courtesy of iStockphoto.com/bowdenimages (© Mark Bowden).
Back cover photo courtesy of Tom Eccerle.
Interior illustration courtesy of iStockphoto.com/Pobytov (© Stanislav Pobytov).

Cover and Interior Design & Layout by Pneuma Books, LLC
For more info on Pneuma Books, visit www.pneumabooks.com

Distributed to the booktrade by Simon & Schuster. SAN: 200-2442

Publisher's Cataloging-in-Publication Data
(Prepared by The Donohue Group)
Chicken soup for the soul : family caregivers : 101 stories of love, sacrifice,
  and bonding / [compiled by] Joan Lunden [and] Amy Newmark.

  p. ; cm.

  Summary: A collection of 101 personal stories and interviews by family caregivers
and by the recipients of that care, about caregiving for all age groups, but focused on
elder care. Includes stories about caregiving for patients with dementia or Alzheimer's,
interviews by Joan Lunden with experts such as Gail Sheehy, Leeza Gibbons, and
Dr. Alexis Abramson, and lots of tips and advice for developing a caregiving plan in
advance, caregiving and end of life.
  ISBN: 978-1-935096-83-2

  1. Caregivers--Literary collections. 2. Caregivers--Anecdotes. 3. Older people--Care-
-Literary collections. 4. Older people--Care--Anecdotes. 5. Care of the sick--Literary
collections. 6. Care of the sick--Anecdotes. I. Lunden, Joan. II. Newmark, Amy. III.
Title: Family caregivers

PN6071.C28 C45 2012
810.2/02/356/1   2011942713

PRINTED IN THE UNITED STATES OF AMERICA
on acid∞free paper
21 20 19 18 17 16 15 14 13 12   02 03 04 05 06 07 08 09 10

Chicken Soup for the Soul.

Family Caregivers

101 Stories of Love, Sacrifice, and Bonding

Joan Lunden
Amy Newmark

Chicken Soup for the Soul Publishing, LLC
Cos Cob, CT

Chicken Soup
for the Soul

www.chickensoup.com

Contents

❸

~Finding Joy~

❹

~Acceptance~

❺

~Laughter Is the Best Medicine~

❻

~Perseverance~

❼

~Blessings~

❽

~Saying Goodbye~

Introduction

I am a caregiver for my mom Gladyce who is 93 years old, so family caregiving is a subject that is very close to my heart, one that I live every day. Statistics tell us that there are about 46 million Americans, like me, who are providing care to a loved one. However many of us don't identify ourselves as such and therefore we don't always recognize that we are dealing with caregiver issues. In fact, it was only as I sat down to write my story for this book that I truly realized that I first became a caregiver 30 years ago when my brother Jeff began to need my assistance due to his diabetes.

My brother and I grew up in Sacramento, California, where my dad was a cancer surgeon and my mother was a stay-at-home mom. My dad was also an avid private pilot and flew around the country speaking at medical conventions and assisting other doctors with difficult surgeries. When I was 14 years old my dad was returning home from a cancer convention when his plane crashed and he was killed. My mom's world was turned upside down; she suddenly became a single parent to two young teenagers. My mom went to work as a real estate agent to take care of my brother and me. When I was in my twenties I moved east to New York City to work as a television journalist for ABC-TV. My mom and my brother remained in our hometown of Sacramento.

A few years after I left California, my brother's health started failing—he was diagnosed with Type II diabetes. When a person develops Type II diabetes at a young age it can ravage their body, and by the time my brother was in his thirties he was already suffering from migraines and blurred vision, and he later went through numerous surgeries on his hands and feet as vascular problems set in. He found it impossible to stand for long periods of time and consequently he no longer could hold a job.

So when I was in my early thirties, with my brother in ill health, I found myself financially responsible for the lives of both my mom and my brother much sooner than I ever would have anticipated. The time came when I began to feel the financial burden of keeping both of them living in their own homes; I realized that moving them in together would mean one electric bill each month rather than two. So I bought a condominium for the two of them to live together, handicapped designed to accommodate my brother's needs and also for any future needs for my mom. The home had separate living areas so that they would each have their privacy. I even put in separate thermostats and heating systems since my mom liked her home warm and my brother preferred it cool. For the next few decades they lived comfortably with each other in their hometown where they had their roots and their friends—I would pay the bills and I would travel home for visits. Mom and Jeff took care of each other, and I believe that this living arrangement helped to keep each of them well since they had to worry about the other's health. Then as their health began to slip I hired an in-home aide to come each day to help clean, shop, cook and take them to doctor's appointments.

My brother dealt with the details of their daily life, including all of my mom's health care. Unfortunately we never took the time to sit down and have a family meeting or to make a plan for what would happen when the time came that Mom needed more daily care, or as it happened—that one of them would die. We all know the day will come when we have to step in and deal with the demise of a parent, a spouse, a sibling or another loved one. There is no escaping this aspect of life, yet no one ever wants to talk about it. As adult children we seem to find it difficult to press our parents to talk about their twilight years and their end-of-life issues. However dealing with these issues before crisis hits, while our loved ones are still able to provide us with answers, can make this difficult life event so much easier to manage.

I learned this lesson the hard way five years ago when I got the call that my brother Jeff had died suddenly at age 56 from complications of Type II diabetes. My brother and my mother had become quite comfortable living together and taking care of one another and they enjoyed each other's company. I knew that my mom was beginning to show signs of aging, but what I didn't realize was how seriously my brother's health was deteriorating. He always put on a good face and didn't let on to me that it was becoming increasingly difficult for him to manage their lives. In fact, he had reached the point where he was really not even able to take care of his own health.

When Jeff died, my mother was 88 years old and she was overcome with grief. With my brother gone, everything changed. My 88-year-old mom could never remain living in that condominium all by herself. Mom had also begun to show signs of dementia and was unable to cope with even the simplest of matters. I was left with so many questions and so few answers. Even though my brother's health had been deteriorating terribly, I had no plan in place as to what to do next. I wished that I had talked to my mother and brother about their health, their insurance, their banking, their business affairs, and their end-of-life wishes when they were healthy enough to be able to provide me the information. My mother often feels so helpless, knowing that she simply cannot remember important details about her health or even about our lives growing up.

Frankly, my situation is not all that uncommon. Most of us are not preparing ourselves for the inevitable; we're not doing due diligence, getting ready to take care of older parents or other family members who will require our attention. I think it's fair to say most people are not prepared for the day when it falls to them to be a caregiver. It's usually thrust upon you when one parent dies or your only parent left takes ill. All of a sudden you have to learn how to be a caregiver, instantly.

I'll never forgot when I arrived back home in California following my brother's death, how my mom was just sitting there in shock. You could see the pain in her face and the uncertainty as to what would happen next. I knew immediately that I didn't have any time to waste; I had to spring into action and find all of her important documents. I would have to act for my mother, whose dementia had suddenly worsened because of the shock of my brother's death. But how could I take care of her banking and handle her Social Security checks if I wasn't a signer on her bank account? You know, these are things you need to do and know about ahead of time.

I would ask Mom, "Where's your driver's license?" She would reply, "I don't know, sweetie. I stopped driving quite a long time ago." "Where's your passport, Mom?" Again, "I don't know, honey. I stopped traveling a while ago." "So where's your Social Security card, Mom?" Again, she had no clue. How could it be that I was finding stacks of old mail and newspapers, and books and years of living in every nook and cranny of their condo but not any of the important documents that I needed? After spending hours and hours going through boxes and boxes I figured it out. My brother had long ago stopped keeping any up-to-date financial or medical records.

There I was sifting through hundreds, if not thousands, of papers trying to find Social Security cards, Medicare cards, car titles, bank accounts, insurance policies, etc. When few of them could be found, I literally had to reconstruct my mother's identity in order to get the documents necessary to run her life. I first had to obtain a birth certificate and then a copy of her marriage license from the respective states and then with those in hand, I was finally able to get her a new Social Security card and Medicare card. The bureaucratic red tape was never ending. It took months to track down the details of her life and health, spending many frustrating hours on the phone with government agencies, all while trying to comfort my mother and get her settled into a new living environment. I had always thought that I had everything under control with my mom and brother. Boy was I mistaken. I vowed to use my experience to help others be more prepared for this difficult time.

We all need to know where all those important papers are — mortgages and titles, wills and insurance policies — or you need to know who has all this information. Where is your parents' bank? Are you signed on that account so that you can do their business should something happen to them? Is there is a safety deposit box somewhere? Where's the key and what's the code? When I returned to New York, I conducted my own personal survey, asking everyone I came into contact with if they knew all of this information about their parents, or even their spouse. Again and again I got a bewildered "Not really." I think it's fair to say that most people don't know all this information. And, quite honestly, you should know it about your spouse as well as your parents. The day that a trauma happens is not when you want to learn about this.

Throughout the initial emotional weeks after my brother's death, along with planning a funeral I had to plan a new life for my mom. I needed to find my mom a new home. I started looking at senior assisted-living facilities throughout Sacramento. I had to become an instant expert on which kind of care home would be the best environment for my mom—and then I learned that there are also different levels of care within each facility. I looked at many different places where I thought she might like to live. Mom was incapable of helping with any details or even rendering an opinion, so in the end I had to make the decision for her and of course all of the arrangements and the move.

But that was the easy part, trust me. Then I had to have that difficult conversation that none of us ever wants to have with our parents—the one where we tell them they must leave the comfort of their home and move into a senior facility. It doesn't matter how pretty the place is or how exclusive it is, it means moving out of the home where they feel safe and secure. Needless to say, my mom didn't want to move. (They never do and you can't blame them.) However there comes a time when it's not a matter of, "Gee, what would they like to do?" That decision must be based on where your loved one will be safe and best cared for. That's where many people make a mistake—it really comes down to what's safe. It's always so difficult when that time comes and you have to make that decision. It was so hard; not only had my mom lost one of her children, but I was about to make her leave her home.

I first moved my mom into a fancy-schmancy assisted-living facility. In my mind, it was a beautiful place where my mom belonged. I thought she would be able to go downstairs to the dining room and be a social butterfly with other Sacramento seniors and then retreat to a beautifully decorated one-bedroom apartment where she could entertain friends if she wished. The problem with my well-meaning plan is that I was making arrangements for the mom that I used to know, and not who she had become. My mom now couldn't remember who people were, and she would get frightened when taken downstairs to the dining hall. And for the first time, my mom was afraid of being left alone in an apartment, no matter how pretty it looked. As soon as it would start to get dark, she suffered from sundown syndrome, becoming increasingly frightened as the shadows fell into the darkness of night. She had felt safe and secure living with my brother in a familiar setting all those years, but now here she was in this strange place by herself. I thought I was doing what was the best thing for her, but in the end it didn't work out at all.

Less than a year later, I found myself back in California looking for yet another home where Mom would be happy and safe. I tried to talk my mom into moving back east closer to me; however she still had friends in Sacramento who came to see her. She's a California sunshine gal—all the snow and cold weather back east just wasn't her cup of tea, to use her words. I found another lovely facility that provided a higher level of care—but even with more personal attention my mom still felt scared and lonely. In this new facility, aides were coming in and out throughout the day to assist her with personal care; however over the next year and a half she took a number of falls and would end up in the hospital each time. My mom was having issues with balance, and with each fall the injuries got worse; first it was a broken toe, then it was a broken rib, then it was staples in the back of the head. Every time it happened, I jumped on an airplane and flew back to California.

Finally, about two years ago, when she was back in the hospital for yet another fall, and more staples in the back of her head, her physician told me that she really couldn't go back to where she'd been living—the next fall could be fatal. The doctor recommended that I move her to a small residential care facility, a private home where there would be only a few residents. In this kind of living arrangement, my mom would have her own bedroom but would be constantly watched round the clock, not just checked on occasionally.

Once again I was looking for that perfect place where my mom would be happy and safe. However this search seemed even more difficult to me. In the larger facilities you could see the round-the-clock staffs, and check their schedules. Now I was looking to put my mom into someone's private home—how would I know what they were doing? I wasn't sure where to begin this search. But this time around I was fortunate to secure the help of a "senior advocate," a knowledgeable professional who could answer all my questions and could show me the residential care facilities available in the area. This made all the difference in the world. I highly recommend obtaining the services of a senior advocate or eldercare advisor to help you navigate this journey. This kind of professional can help save you hours of time and stress by narrowing your choices to locations that meet your specific needs. They help families evaluate issues such as care requirements, finances and amenity preferences. Because of my passion for preserving quality of life for our loved ones, I've recently aligned myself with A Place for Mom, our nation's largest senior living referral information service. The Senior Living Advisors at A Place for Mom are kind and knowledgeable, and easy to talk to about any senior care situation. They can answer all of your questions and help you find the appropriate living arrangement for your loved one.

My senior advocate knew I was nervous about putting my mom into a private home with just a few other seniors, but I remember she looked at me as we got out of the car to check on the first home and she said, "I can show you a dozen places, Joan, but if it was my mom—this is where I would want her to live." It was a lovely ranch-style house with six residents, each with their own bedroom. My advocate was there by my side to ask all of the important questions (which I really didn't know) and to unabashedly scrutinize the facility (which I was admittedly reluctant to do myself). The residents were sitting together in the living room chatting and watching TV and talking with the care workers who scurried about tending to their needs and getting lunch ready. The home was impeccably clean and the food being readied in the kitchen smelled yummy. All of my worries began to melt away when I met the owners, James and Rowena Ashley, who were welcoming, warm, knowledgeable and obviously dedicated to their residents.

It has turned out to be a wonderful environment for my mom. They are there with her when she awakens, they get her dressed and they bring to the dining room table for each meal. The residents are all in their nineties, they don't always talk a lot, but they play Bingo and do crafts projects and jigsaw puzzles. My mom is the reigning Bingo champion right now. She's comfortable, happy and safe, and in this kind of residential care facility you can stay right through to hospice care at the end. Therefore residents don't have to get moved around and that's important because every move can be an emotional, mental and physical setback.

One thing that made this last move much easier on my mom was an idea that my daughter Lindsay came up with. She traveled with me to California to help me get my mom resettled. Any move to a new environment can be upsetting to the elderly, so before you move your loved one, take pictures of where everything is located in their current room or apartment. For example, if there's a bookcase with all kinds of memorabilia, photos and books, snap a few pictures. When we moved my mom into her new room, Lindsay literally went back to the shots in her camera and we recreated my mother's room as identical as possible, putting everything on every single shelf exactly where it had been before — and that made such a huge difference for her.

If there is one thing that I could point to that would have made taking on the role of caregiver more manageable, it would definitely have been **asking more questions when I could still get answers**. Oh how I wish I had had a family meeting! Families really need to have these talks, but of course the tendency by most people is to duck the subject. It's like the elephant in the room, isn't it? Yes, it's the elephant in the room and I think we just can't get the words out of our mouths: "Hey, what are we going to do with Mom and Dad when Mom and Dad can't take care of themselves?"

I got thrown into it all, as most of us do. Suddenly, you're in this world where you are expected to understand the difference between senior care and assisted care and nursing homes—and long-term care insurance… it's all so complicated. My top recommendation to everyone is to **call a family meeting**. If you have older parents or a family member who will seemingly require your care any time soon, you need to schedule this meeting. I recommend that you approach this as you would any other serious business meeting. You need an agenda and you need to think through all of the areas that should be discussed before you all sit down together. Where do we think Mom and Dad should be living as they age? Is there anyone they might move in with when the time comes? You have to ask these questions. And you must go right down that checklist. Is there a will in place? Do you have a power of attorney for their health and business? Is there an advanced healthcare directive? Where are these documents? Do your parents have long-term health care insurance? If not, how will you pay for their care? Do you know their end-of-life wishes?

Many times parents are reluctant to have this conversation, and finances can be an especially sensitive topic. You may need to be less direct with those questions as you start out, but it is essential for all adult children to open this line of communication. Don't make the discussion about what "you are going to have to do for them," since no parent wants to feel like a burden. Make the discussion about what "they want to do and how you might be able to help them towards that end."

It is probably best to have an initial family meeting without your parents present, in order for the grown kids to be honest and forthcoming about what they are really willing and able to do. Maybe everyone can't help equally, but talk about what each of you could do. Perhaps one brother is an accountant; he could be in charge of finances. Is there a stay-at-home mom or an empty nester who might be able to help with day-to-day care? Is there a teenager who loves driving around but needs gas money? There's your chauffeur to doctor's appointments and the runner to the drugstore and grocery store for Grandma. Discuss your options, and have a plan in place—it will mean having the information necessary to help your loved ones when they need your help the most and it often means that you will also be protecting yourself. And again, remember that caregiving and all of its responsibilities can be complex and overwhelming; I have found much guidance and emotional support from my senior advocate and also from an Elder Lawyer who has counseled me on my mom's legal affairs.

Something else that I have done that I would highly recommend, is that you sit down with a video camera and **interview and record your parents, grandparents and other relatives**. Construct an interview ahead of time; you can start with your own childhood, ask them what life was like when you were a child. What were you like as a child? And don't forget to ask them what life was like for them when they were young, and what the world was like back then. Ask about when your parents met, courted, got married, and first got pregnant with you — all those things that you will never know unless you ask the questions. This kind of video recording of your family history is priceless.

Make sure that you also ask family members about childhood illnesses or family health issues that might affect your own health risks. Once you have them talking, then you can ask about what their wishes are for their older life. Ask questions like: Where do you hope to live as you get older and need more care? How do you envision your Golden Years? And when the day comes, what kind of funeral do you want? I know, a lot of people say that's morbid. Well, it's really not. It's important to make your parents understand that not addressing those issues can create an incredible emotional and sometimes financial burden for their children.

When I got my mom going on the subject of a funeral, or her Bon Voyage Party as I called it, I was surprised by how much she had to say. My mom, who has always enjoyed being in the spotlight, mapped out a funeral for herself like it was a prime time entertainment special. She even selected the songs she wants sung, and who she wants to perform them (fortunately a family friend). My best friend got her mom to have this discussion, and as it turns out her mom had some very specific requests — including wanting her grandniece to play the flute during the ceremony. It may seem like this would be a terribly awkward subject; however I think you may be surprised if you initiate the conversation, your loved one may welcome this opportunity.

On my many trips back to my hometown to visit my mom, I not only have sat and recorded many conversations with her, but I also arranged to interview family friends and several doctors in Sacramento who were colleagues of my father. They were able to tell me about working with my father in his medical office and next to him in the operating room, as well as about trips they had taken together with my parents. I never got a chance to know my father as an adult; I was only 14 years old when he died, so it's been fascinating to learn more about him. Two of the three doctors I interviewed have since died, so it's a lucky thing I got to have those conversations. These videos are cherished memories that I captured and will treasure forever.

Of all the lessons I've learned through my years of caregiving, I think the most important thing all of us can do, no matter whether we are providing day-to-day care or overseeing the care from afar, is to **keep the love connection going.** Just tell them that you love them again and again and again. You will never say it too much, ever. I try to make sure my mom either hears from me or gets a little something from me often. It can be as simple as sending a magazine with a little note saying "read this article" or "enjoy this." Every time I travel I make it a point to send her a postcard from whatever city I'm visiting.

It's really just about making that connection. I've made my mom a few of those beautiful digital photo books with pictures of our family through the years. I made her one this past year that I titled "It's a Wonderful Life." The album began with the newspaper announcement of when my mom and dad were married, and was filled with photos and holiday cards that told our family story. The best part of making that album was seeing how the photos jogged my mom's memory. As she flipped through pages of black and white images of herself as a young woman being courted by my dad, I saw a glimmer in her eye that I rarely see these days. I was thrilled by how it reconnected her to her life — it was the best gift I could have ever given her. It was so simple, cost so little, but meant so much. You could achieve the same thing with a scrapbook — I'm just not artsy enough to make one. No matter how you create your book of memories, the bottom line is about helping your loved ones make the connection to their families so they feel as though they still belong.

I feel very fortunate to have had the opportunity to connect with many families and experts for this book and for my television show on caregiving called *Taking Care with Joan Lunden* (on RLTV). I have also heard from many of you on my website, www.joanlunden.com, as well as Facebook and @JoanLunden on Twitter, and I have learned so much from your caregiving stories.

I never cease to be amazed at how many people contact me to tell me how overwhelmed they are as caregivers. They tell me how their lives were absolutely turned upside down when they took on the caregiver role. They talk about its emotional and financial burden, and how they sometimes feel that it squeezes every ounce of strength from them. Now, they say, there is simply no time left over for themselves. They are emotionally, physically and often financially drained. This drives my passion to help families find solutions and resolve.

In fact, studies have shown that there is a real toll taken on the health of a caregiver — that many caregivers may actually die at a younger age because of that toll. It's thought that the constant stress of providing care can take as many as 10 years off a person's life due to greater risks of depression and other health problems. The average caregiver in America today is a 46-year-old woman who has children at home and is working full time. That's a lot for anybody. Many of today's caregivers are part of the Sandwich Generation, like me; they are simultaneously raising children and also caring for parents. People often report that their caregiver role has resulted in less time for family and friends, and a substantial number report giving up vacations, hobbies and social activities as a result of their caregiving responsibilities.

Not surprisingly, studies by the American Academy of Family Physicians show that depression is the most common health problem among family caregivers. One study revealed that anxiety was present in about 20 percent of caregivers, and those who provide more than 36 hours of care each week are more likely than non-caregivers to experience symptoms of depression. For spouses, the rate is six times higher; for those caring for a parent, the rate is twice as high. And for those caring for a person with dementia, the rates of depression can be as high as 43-46 percent, nearly three times what is found in the general population.

Caregiving can devastate families and marriages and it also has a major impact in the workplace. Many of today's caregivers work either full or part time while providing care. More than half of those working caregivers say they have to go into work late, leave early or take time off during the day in order to provide the care. Some report having to take a leave of absence, shift from full time to part time, quit work entirely, lose their job benefits, turn down promotions, or choose early retirement.

American businesses are reported to lose between $11 billion and $29 billion a year in reduced productivity costs related to caregiving responsibilities. That includes workplace disruptions, scheduled and unscheduled absences, leaves of absence, reducing full-time work to part-time, taking early retirements, and leaving work entirely to care for a loved one.

Any way you slice it, caregiving is a difficult role, no matter how much you love your mom, your dad, or whoever you're caring for. When a surviving parent or spouse cannot live alone, we must take charge of finding a solution for their care, sell their home and their cars, and get their business affairs in order. Of course if they don't have a will, when that day comes you won't know how they wish to be buried, or how they wish to distribute their belongings. Without an "Advanced Health Care Directive" you won't know their wishes if faced with tough decisions when their life is in the balance. Without a Durable Power of Attorney, you cannot conduct business for them. If you do not have permission to ask questions of their physicians, doctors cannot give you vital medical information.

It will never be easy emotionally; however it doesn't have to be such a financial and legal struggle. You just need to take steps in order to be prepared. Don't wait! We never know what life has in store, or when a major event will occur.

People are simply living longer. Today there are more elderly citizens than ever before. Since 1960 the number has doubled from 17 million to 35 million. In the next 20 years, the number of people 65 years old and older is expected to shoot to 70 million, which means more parents will be in need of care and that means that the need for caregivers is going to skyrocket! As baby boomers and their parents get older, so does the demand for better health care. In many cases, the kids or the spouses will be doing the caring. It has been projected that boomers will spend more time taking care of their parents than they did raising their children. Wow! That's a big chunk of time.

The Baby Boom generation is approaching retirement age like an avalanche in terms of volume of people each year, causing what's described as a "silver tsunami." Millions of Americans are now reaching that particular stage in life and will require both medical and non-medical care going forward. Meanwhile, a comparative trickle of physicians and other health care professionals have geriatric training and experience, and shortages of many caregiver types have long been a problem.

According to recent surveys, at least 66 percent of the U.S. population—or more than 138 million Americans—believe they will need to provide care to someone in the future. At the same time, the majority of Americans say they have not taken adequate steps to prepare for the possibility that they will need to be cared for themselves in the future. When asked what steps they have taken, only 4 in 10 adults have set aside funds to cover expenses or signed a living will or healthcare power of attorney. Only a third of all adults say they have purchased disability income insurance or looked into independent or assisted living arrangements, or purchased long-term care insurance. Only 34 percent of Americans say they have talked with a family member or friend about providing care to them in the future.

Family caregiving is most certainly the next big health crisis to face our country. If it's not already going on in your home, it's probably right at your doorstep. We all need to begin the discussion so that we can be ready, and that is why I am so excited about this Chicken Soup for the Soul book. Storytelling has always been a highly effective way to pass on wisdom, and the 101 stories and interviews in this book will open your eyes to the caregiving experiences of other people, and give you some tips about what you can do yourself. You'll also feel comforted when you see how many other people are going through the same ups and downs as you may be experiencing in your role as caregivers, or as the recipient of that care. I hope that this book will expose you to some new ideas, encourage you, entertain you, and above all, help you put your experiences in perspective and make you feel part of that big community of caregivers out there.

~Joan Lunden

Chapter 1

Family Caregivers

Lessons Learned

The only real mistake is the one from which we learn nothing.

~John Powell

The Caregiving Labyrinth

A Note from Joan

I'm often asked which interviews have been my favorites over the years, and one might assume that I would point to presidents, world leaders or celebrities. However I have always been fascinated by those who study the human condition; medical experts who help us understand how our bodies work and cultural observers who help us understand what makes us tick.

I have always enjoyed interviewing Gail Sheehy, bestselling author of 15 books, and world-renowned for her revolutionary *Passages*, which was reprinted in 28 languages and named by the Library of Congress as one of the 10 most influential books of our time. Gail literally changed the way millions of people look at their lives. In her history-making books, she has examined how men and women move through the stages of adult life from adolescence into their seasoned years.

I had an opportunity to sit down with Gail Sheehy to talk about her latest book, *Passages in Caregiving*, in which she is helping a generation to navigate caring for loved ones. With so many people living longer than ever before, Gail revisits the stages of adult life to map out this new frontier. In this book she is not only a cultural observer, she has been a caregiver herself for years.

Joan: Gail, you became the caregiver to your husband Clay Felker when you were both in the prime of your careers and he was diagnosed with cancer. Tell me about the day you learned he had cancer.

Gail: Well, one day I got the call. Cancer? My husband has cancer? We don't expect it. No one is prepared for it. We don't know how long it's going to take. I had nine months to prepare for the birth of my child. I had about nine hours to prepare for the dependence of my husband. They told me I had a new role: caregiver. Again? We're all going to have this role—this is the big passage for boomers today.

All of a sudden you get a call that changes your life, diverting all your hope and energy to an entirely different priority. It's a call about a fall, or a stroke or a cardiac arrest. Or maybe it's about your dad who ran a red light and hit somebody but doesn't quite remember what happened. This call throws most of us into shock and denial and a frenzy of learning how to take charge. We don't know the medical lingo, we have no idea how to navigate our way through the patchwork of care alternatives, insurance regulations, Medicare rules, or the conflicting advice of traditional doctors versus holistic practitioners. And we have no concept of how long it will take, how much it will cost, or how we will pay for it.

No one really expects it, but just about everyone has been—or will be—expected to provide unpaid care, for a sustained period, to someone close to them. We need help in learning how to take charge, create a circle of care, outwit our fractured health care system, and give a loved one a safe and stimulating life without sacrificing our own.

Joan: You were a caregiver to Clay for 17 years. What did you learn from your experience that you want to share with others now?

Gail: I think caregivers desperately need someone to pull them together and understand how vital and how honorable and generous a role we perform. The biggest hurdle is most people who do this don't identify themselves as caregivers. Women especially say, "Well you know that's just what you do. I'm a daughter, you know, it's just what I'm expected to do. It's what I want to do." But in fact today it's become a professional-level job.

Joan: This is a crisis facing millions of Americans today. What should people be doing to try to prevent being sideswiped by this?

Gail: The best thing that you can do is to have a family meeting before there's a crisis. Have the meeting with your brothers and sisters primarily. You want to get the conversation started before the tension of "We've got to get hospitalization for Mom and Dad or we've got to figure out what treatment"—it'll be so much better because when you're under tension and somebody's got to make a decision, you're likely to go back to squabbling like five-year-olds.

Joan: It can be very difficult to get your parents engaged in this conversation because they don't want to think about their mortality. And yet it seems critical that you get this information, so that you become the owner, so to speak, of the information, and have it when the time comes that you need it.

Gail: I think the way to persuade parents is to say, "We want you to be independent as long as you possibly can. And the key to that is to know exactly what you want done and what you don't want done. What kind of hospital you'd like to go to, and who you want as your doctor." So make it an active kind of discovery for how to get your health caregiving situation in place and get all your paperwork in place for when your loved one might need a little bit more help.

Joan: There are so many important documents that you will need like advanced health care directives and powers of attorney; it's complicated and it's intimidating. You talk about a growing community of senior advocates who can help you through this maze; how so?

Gail: I think the greatest help, if you could possibly afford it, is a care manager, a professional geriatric care manager, particularly at the beginning of an emergency. If you have, or husband has, in my case, a cancer diagnosis and you've got three different doctors giving you conflicting opinions, you don't know how to decide on the treatment. Everything has to be decided in a hurry. You are entering into a new world. And if you have a care manager, even for the first few days or week, to help you figure out this new language and new world you're in, it may be the best money you've ever spent.

Joan: You call this new world of caregiving, the labyrinth. What do you mean by that?

Gail: My original book, *Passages*, was about the stages of the adult life—they are linear. There's a stage and then there's a passage when we need to change again and there's another stage. We kind of wrap up the tasks at the end of each stage and move on. It's all very nice and neat.

Caregiving is more circular. You go around and around the circle and you come back to the same place again and again. A labyrinth is one path that takes you around the circle and you go through quick twists and turns that you didn't expect, just like caregiving. But it gets you to the center and the center is when you finally acknowledge and accept that your loved one is not going to return to the same independent person he or she once was. And that begins your coming back. And it's in coming back that the caregiver has to begin to find his or her own transportation to joy, your own way of living a new kind of life after this passage is over.

Joan: Tell me about the stages you go through in this labyrinth of caregiving.

Gail: The first stage is **Shock and Mobilization**. You get a call that your mom's fallen, your dad's had an accident or your spouse has a frightening diagnosis. Who to call? Where to start? It's a roller coaster—you may be up and down for weeks or even months.

Then there is **The New Normal**. You realize, perhaps for the first time, you have a new role—family caregiver. This isn't a sprint. It's going to be a marathon. You are living with a new uncertainty and you're not going back to the old normal.

The next stage is **The Boomerang**. Everything has settled down into a new normal routine. It's been months, maybe a year or more. You're handling it all and thinking "Okay, I can do this," when BOOMERANG! A new crisis erupts. You need to call a family meeting. Who else can help? You need to start thinking about how to take care of the caregiver—that's you!

There is the **Playing God** stage. You've become very good at caregiving by now. You're the only one your loved one trusts. You believe you're the only one who truly understands what he or she needs. You're seen as heroic. You're playing God. But you know what? We ain't God. We can't control disease or aging. And if we keep trying we'll be overcome by stress and fatigue and come to a dead end.

And that is the **I Can't Do This Anymore** stage! So you were convinced you could do it differently. But a few years into it you break down in tears and total fatigue. You've given up so much. You absolutely must come up for air or you'll go down in despair. Call for help! Start taking at least one hour every day to do something that will give you pleasure and refreshment. Your loved one also needs some time with other people who offer stimulation of a different kind.

And that leads to the **Circle of Care**. You need to create a circle of people who will assume some responsibility for aspects of care. Let members of your family and friends who have not been involved know that you have reached the end of your rope. They may assume you're handling it all. Even long distance, they can definitely be helpful. And don't be shy about asking for assistance from neighbors, coworkers and your community. A professional care manager can save your life.

This is when you enter the **Coming Back** stage. At the seventh turning, you begin coming back. It is clear now that your loved one is not going to get well and will become more and more needy and dependent. You are approaching the center of the labyrinth. This is where you must begin the process of separation. It is a slow and painful process, but the other way is to lose yourself and go down with the person you're caring for. That would be a double tragedy.

There is life after caregiving. What were your lifelines before caregiving? You must have some transports to joy? Pick them up again. They will lead you out of the labyrinth.

And then you are at **The Long Goodbye**. This is the last turning. Inevitably, there will be times that you will likely feel: Why can't you die? Enough already! Then, of course, you'll feel guilty for thinking such a thing. But it is entirely human and predictable.

No one can answer your most burning question: How long? It's important at this turning to have end-of-life conversations. Encourage your loved one to talk about his fears and wishes and goals. What kind of activities might give him or her pleasure? And what kind of medical interventions does she want—or want stopped? Hard as it may be, follow your loved one's wishes. This is his or her death, not yours. You are on a different journey.

Afterlife of the Caregiver. And then, suddenly, it's over. Your loved one has passed on. You have completed the labyrinth of caregiving. Now what? Maybe you've forgotten who you were before. You've been consumed for so long by caring for someone you love. You have given of yourself and done a beautiful thing. After the first months of mourning, grief will come out of nowhere when you least expect it. Don't sit around and wait for depression to set in. Pick up your passion—whatever you do where time passes and you don't even notice—and follow it. It will lead you on a new path. Look at it as an adventure! And God bless you.

Lessons in the Aisles

Most grandmas have a touch of the scallywag.
~Helen Thomson

As I ride out of the grocery store on a motorized scooter cart, I get funny looks from the other shoppers. People don't know what to make of a 30-something, able-bodied woman riding a device clearly designed for the elderly or disabled. My fellow shoppers also look perplexed to see me ride the empty cart out of the store. Their expressions say, "Where could you possibly be going on that thing?"

The motorized cart isn't for me. I am just the delivery service for my 92-year-old grandmother, who waits in the car until I bring her the scooter, and we head into the supermarket together for our regular grocery shopping adventure. Amazingly, my grandma never gets funny looks when she rides it. I drive the thing in a fairly safe and controlled manner. My grandma is another story. My kids also give me looks when it comes to the cart, but theirs say, "If you are going to drag us to the store to do Grandma's shopping, can't we at least ride the scooter?"

"Do you have my list?" Grandma asks as we head into the store.

"Yes, and first we want to stop at the oranges." Citrus fruits sit by the front door, so we always load up on oranges and grapefruit. And we always have the same conversation. Always.

"Don't they have anything bigger? These look awfully small. Over by my house, there were the best fruit stands...." Eighteen months ago, Grandma moved from her home of 50-plus years, and the differences in available produce seem to be one of the hardest adjustments for her.

The hardest adjustment for me is the fact that my grandma always seems to want to get away from me, especially while we are shopping. Perhaps she is embarrassed by me, even though I always brush my hair and put on clean clothes for the trip, and am sometimes the only one in our party to do so. Maybe she just wants a little freedom. Whatever the reason, the moment I turn my back, Stevie McQueen races away in her motorized cart, headed for parts unknown.

"Dear, can you get me an avocado?"

"Sure," I say. "I'll be right back, so don't go anywhere."

The scooters have two speeds: 1) slow as a snail and 2) escape mode. There is no in-between. I leave her looking at bananas, but in the 30 seconds it takes me to grab an avocado, she kicks her machine into high gear. When I realize she is gone, I search the produce section for her short frame between the towering racks of fruits and vegetables, grabbing items I know she wants while I look for her.

When I finally spot her at the deli counter, I am reminded of another adjustment that has been hard for me—seeing my grandmother's regard for people change. From across the room I witness her using the cart to bully her way in front of other shoppers waiting in line at the counter.

In the deli, our rehearsed routine shifts from the size of the produce to the price, and probably sounds something like the old radio comedy shows she listened to as a child.

"I want a quarter-pound of sliced chicken. You know the kind I like," she says to me.

"I know what you like, but it is eight dollars a pound. Are you sure you really want that?"

"How much?"

"Eight dollars."

"Did you say seven dollars?"

"No, I said eight. Turkey is on sale for four dollars a pound. Can you have turkey this week?"

"Did you say five dollars?"

"No, I said four. Can you have turkey?"

"I don't know. What else do they have?"

The deli man smiles and watches us with more patience than I can muster as we discuss the price of every item in the cooler before finally settling on the four-dollar turkey, as always. Annoyance begins to rear its ugly head inside my heart.

While I wait for the meat to be wrapped, Grandma escapes again. I send my kids to scout her out. They come running back in a panic. "Grandma just hit the muffin table, and a bunch of stuff fell on the floor!"

The kind deli man simply nods and hands me the turkey as I run off to survey the damage. Curious shoppers flock to see the bakery boxes on the floor, and Grandma looks bewildered by the fact that she can't move forward or backward without running over pastries. Thankfully, I see the tightly packaged baked goods are clean and unharmed as I restock the table. The baker glares at me with an expression that says, "Can't you teach her to control that scooter?" My return look says, "Can't you put more space between the tables?" We visually agree to disagree as I lead Grandma toward the canned foods.

"We can't forget the orange juice," Grandma tells me, with no mention of the events in the bakery. I find it disconcerting that knocking things to the ground has become so common that it doesn't even warrant a comment from her, but she is only concerned with her juice. "Make sure we don't forget." We never forget the orange juice because, not only is it on the list, but she will remind me at least three more times.

As we work our way through the list, we negotiate what to spend money on and what can wait. I remind her to be polite to the other shoppers, and send my kids to find her when she scooters off. It is not the best time in the world, but it is time.

I love having time with my grandmother. Despite the frustrations, the repetition, and the funny looks, I wouldn't trade a minute of it. Amidst the mundane conversations about greeting cards and which brand of soup is best, she works in tidbits about her opinions on politics and social issues, and what it was like growing up in Colorado in the 1920s and '30s. She raised two daughters, as I do now, and while the details of childrearing have changed with the generations, the essentials remain the same, and she encourages me with her wisdom.

And while we navigate the aisles of the store, I remember the aisles of life she has walked me through as well. Whenever I went to the movies as a child, I went with my grandmother because she knew it was important to go out and have fun together. I learned how to cook from her, and she taught me that the love you put into things made from scratch makes them taste better than those from a box. I learned how to garden and how to can fruit so you always have something to share with your family and friends. Fun. Love. Generosity.

Now that she is older, she teaches me different, but equally important lessons. Patience. Tolerance. Humility. And I am blessed to learn these lessons as we journey together through the aisles.

~Dianne Daniels

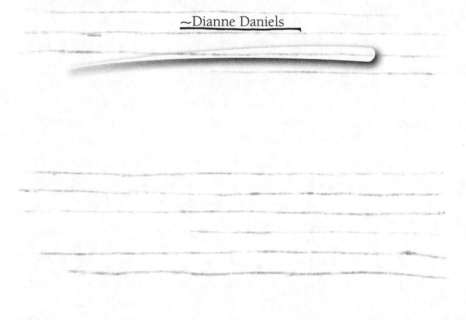

Love Unconditionally with No Guarantees

He who has gone, so we but cherish his memory, abides with us,
more potent, nay, more present than the living man.
~Antoine de Saint-Exupery

Life is very precious. With every breath and every cell in my body, I know that now. My teachers and role models were my husband, Stephen, and daughter, Maddison. From them I learned what being courageous really means, and I learned to love unconditionally, with no guarantees.

I find it ironic that I am considered their caregivers. Truth be told, I took so much more than I ever gave. I attained valuable life lessons that changed the way I think and act, and now the way I love.

The truth is, we are all interdependent and need each other. We will not survive our time on this earth on our own. It is why we are truly here on this planet — to care, connect, and love. In our caregiving role, we get to experience all three.

This is my story as a caregiver. May my lessons and insight guide you, lessen your load, and provide comfort on your journey.

I was a soldier in the Canadian Armed Forces, stationed in our nation's capital city, Ottawa, when I first met my husband-to-be, Stephen. He was a civilian working at a large downtown company. It was love at first sight for me.

We had been dating a few months when he started to occasionally slur his words and stumble for no apparent reason. We thought maybe he was working too hard. Just in case, Stephen made a doctor's appointment.

The doctor ran a few tests and had us back for a consult the following week. Never believing anything was really wrong, we were unprepared for the shocking and devastating news. Stephen was diagnosed with ALS—Lou Gehrig's disease. We were told the typical life span was two to five years after diagnosis.

Our world, as we knew it, changed in that minute. Our plans for a wonderful carefree life were gone. Everything seemed uncertain.

Stephen's first reaction was to end our relationship. This was what the doctors suggested. I had to convince him to let me journey with him through his illness. I wanted to support and love him, working side-by-side with him as he manoeuvred through this difficult time. He was hesitant at first, then finally relented. We would get through this together.

We didn't know how we were going to deal with this challenge. Our first response was fearful, frustrated, and uncertain about our future. We were always questioning. Would this be our last birthday or Christmas together? We learned over time that this was not the best way to live our lives, uncertain and afraid. We had to have hope for our future; we had to learn to live life fully, even with all the uncertainties. We adopted the philosophy that he was not dying of ALS; he was living with ALS. We decided to marry and bravely start a family. Our beautiful daughter Maddie was born, and four years later a son, Derek.

Over the years, Stephen lost the use of his arms and was confined to a wheelchair. Every time he lost one ability, he seemed to refine another. Although he could not carry the baby in his arms, he could carry her in a snuggly as he rolled along in his motorized wheelchair. Later, he used it as the engine of a "train," pulling his children and their friends in a wagon to the park. Even when I was anxious, I allowed him to fully participate in the lives of his children.

He was limited only in his physical ability; his intellect, wisdom, and courage inspired and guided us.

Life was pretty hectic as his main caregiver. There were many hats to wear—wife, mother, soldier, provider, caregiver, advocate—and balancing them all was difficult. I had no role model, no mentor to show me what was right or wrong. I now know there is no right or wrong way. You just do the best you can.

I continued serving in the military the first eight years of Stephen's illness, then took early retirement when he needed full-time care. The only other option was to have him admitted to a long-term care facility. For us, this was not an option; I was afraid he would lose hope and give up.

I admired Stephen; he was heroic in his fight. He held on as long as humanly possible. He lived nine years, not the two to five he was first given. I believe much of that drive came from the fact that he had meaningful roles to fill—as father to Maddie and Derek, as husband to me.

Six years after Stephen died, my beautiful daughter was diagnosed with cancer. My world collapsed again. I didn't believe I had it in me to go through something so tragic again. I was overwhelmed and unsure if my heart could take it. I would have sold my soul to save my daughter from the pain she was about to go through.

I remembered the lessons I learned while caring for my husband: to love unconditionally, to live each day fully expecting no guarantees. I decided to commit one hundred percent to Maddie, to put my life on hold as I cared for her.

We bonded in a way much more powerful than we had ever experienced. I held her as she underwent three years of chemotherapy, multiple radiation treatments, and numerous surgeries. I held her as we laughed and cried together. I held her as she took her last breath. The same arms that carried her in birth cradled her as she passed away at the tender age of 15.

Thirteen years after the death of my husband and four years after Maddie's passing, I can now speak from a place of wisdom and peace. I did not understand many of the lessons I learned until much later, after I processed the grief. I am now choosing to live with the loving memories. When I reflect on my journey with both of them, I cherish the experience of caring for them.

If you are a family caregiver, remember to love and care for yourself, not judging your performance, but knowing you are doing your best. Allow things to unfold, accepting that you sometimes have no control. Real stress is not caused by the situation—it is caused by our reaction to the situation. Respond to each challenge in a loving, gentle way.

I look back at those caregiving years and realize they changed my life. I learned it was an honour to be chosen (yes, we are chosen), to have journeyed with two of the most extraordinary human beings—my husband, Stephen, and my daughter, Maddie. Both courageous loved ones taught me and gave me much more than I was ever able to give them.

Be fearless, love unconditionally, and cherish every minute.

~Sharon Babineau

The Girl with the Golden Curls

Just like the butterfly, I too will awaken in my own time.
~Deborah Chaskin

"But I don't want to take care of Grandma!" I said. I was 17, and it was the first day of summer vacation. I was looking forward to the best summer I'd ever have. In September, I'd start my senior year, and after graduation I'd have to get a job. This was the last summer I'd ever be completely free, and now my mother was trying to steal my last summer by forcing me to take care of my grandmother. My grandmother lived two hundred miles away. If I went to stay with her, I'd be cut off from all my friends.

My grandmother was 80 years old and had diabetes. She was in bad condition, and it was only a matter of time before her foot would be amputated. She also needed an insulin shot every morning. I would have to learn to give her a shot, cook all her meals, do all the housework and laundry, and take her to her weekly doctor appointment. It wasn't fair!

Although we had a large family, no one else could or would take care of Grandma. I was told that if I didn't take care of her, she'd have to go to a nursing home. A heavy burden of guilt was heaped on my shoulders. If I didn't agree to take care of her, I was a selfish, terrible, spoiled teenager who only cared about myself.

I'd spent very little time with Grandma while I was growing up, and I barely knew her. This was going to be the worst summer of my life.

I practiced giving injections on an orange, but the first time I had to give her an insulin shot, I nearly got sick. Her diet was very strict, and her food had to be measured and cooked a certain way. She blamed me for what she considered "tasteless" meals.

I missed my friends and knew they were having fun going to the mall and on dates. I wasn't going to have a single date all summer. My life was over.

The only things in her house to read were *National Geographic* magazines from the 1970s. I asked her if there was anything else to read, and she said she thought there was a dictionary in the desk. I had the feeling that before the summer was over, I'd be reading the dictionary and be glad I had it.

Twice a day, I had to change the bandages on her right foot. Two of her toes were black. It was only a matter of time until they fell off in the bandage or had to be amputated. Every time I changed the bandage, I prayed when I removed the gauze that her toes would still be attached to her foot.

She was confined to a wheelchair, and one day I pushed her out into the yard under a shade tree and sat on a lawn chair next to her. A butterfly fluttered past us, and she smiled for the first time since I'd arrived.

"When I was a little girl, I loved butterflies. I would chase them, but I never caught them, because if you catch them, they die," she said.

I tried to imagine Grandma as a young girl who liked butterflies, but I couldn't. She was just a sick, old woman, and I was stuck with her.

"When I was a young girl, I had beautiful, long, golden curls that hung past my waist. In fact, when I sat down, I had to pull them aside or I'd sit on my hair. Everyone was jealous of my long curls. My mother would wrap my hair around her fingers at night and tie little strips of rags around my hair to make curls," she said. "My mother died when I was 11. I had to take care of my two younger sisters and my three younger brothers. From then on, I did all the cooking and cleaning. My father was a quiet man; he hardly ever talked. I had to stop going to school in the fourth grade. I cried because I couldn't go to school anymore."

I realized I'd never known anything about my grandmother.

"My father said he'd lost our farm, and we had to move from Kentucky to Kansas. I hated leaving the green hills of Kentucky for the flat, dry plains of Kansas. I had friends in Kentucky. I never got to make friends in Kansas because I was too busy taking care of my father and my five brothers and sisters. When I was 16, a neighbor boy asked me to marry him, and I said yes. We'd never even had a date or kissed, but I was so tired of cooking and cleaning and taking care of five kids that I wanted to get away. He had pretty blue eyes, and so I married him. My two sisters were old enough to take over the cooking and cleaning," she said as her eyes looked far into the past.

Every afternoon after lunch, I'd push her wheelchair into the yard, and she'd tell me more stories about her life. I don't think anyone had ever heard the stories before.

She'd always lived on a farm, and it had barely provided enough food for the family. When she was still in her teens, she had two daughters who were stillborn. She had nine more children.

I'd been upset about not going to the mall and having dates. When she was my age, she'd lost her mother, left school, helped raise five siblings, gotten married, and had two stillborn babies.

Every day, we sat in the yard and drank iced tea while she told me about her life. The days flew past. It was hard to believe that I'd ever dreaded spending time with her.

By the middle of July, her diabetes had become so bad that her foot had to be amputated, and the family decided to put her into a nursing home. She needed more care than I could give her, and I'd have to leave and return to school soon.

I went home. I still had half of a summer ahead of me, but I wasn't the same person I'd been when I left six weeks earlier.

I never saw Grandma again.

The summer I'd thought was going to be my worst turned out to be one of my most memorable. I was always grateful for the opportunity to know and love my grandmother.

When I think of her, I don't think of the white-haired, old woman in a wheelchair. I think of her as a beautiful, young girl with long, golden curls who loved butterflies.

~April Knight

A Young Person
Living in an Old World

A Note from Joan

I first met Dr. Alexis Abramson on the set of *Taking Care with Joan Lunden*, a show that I host on RLTV about family caregiving. Dr. Abramson is a gerontologist (an aging expert) and the author of two highly acclaimed books: *The Caregiver's Survival Handbook: How to Care for Your Aging Parents Without Losing Yourself*, which is a guide to help caregivers balance the responsibilities of caring for others and for themselves, and *Home Safety for Seniors*, a room-by-room reference and idea-book for making independent senior, and homebound, living easier.

I immediately connected with Alexis, since both of us shared a passion for helping others through the caregiving maze. Alexis writes and speaks around the country, not only as an expert in her field, but as someone who became a caregiver herself at a very young age. I want to share with you her personal story and her insightful expertise.

Joan: Alexis, when you were only in your twenties you became the caregiver for your grandmother. How did that come about?

Alexis: I was extremely close with all of my grandparents and when it came time for someone to take care of my paternal grandmother, Mimi Esther as we affectionately referred to her, I stepped up and took the job.

At the youthful age of 22 I was thrust into the role of primary care-giver, yet I was certainly not "primed" to handle all of the responsibilities that I was about to encounter. My father was extremely busy in his thriving practice as a physician, my mother was getting her Ph.D. and my grandfather had already passed away.

So who was there to pick up the pieces? ME—the aspiring gerontologist. Unfortunately that "aspiration" would have to be put on hold for the moment.

I flew out to see my grandmother and quickly realized that she needed a full-time advocate who could help her deal with the complex maze of the medical system. She was in her late seventies and the mixture of emotions and illness was just too overwhelming to allow her the strength she needed to meander through the labyrinth of Medicare, doctor's appointments, long-term care, physical therapy and so on.

I put the pursuit of my master's on hold and instead pursued a "real life" gerontology degree—as a full-time caregiver. As her primary support system, I shopped for her groceries, helped balance her checkbook, coordinated her doctor's appointments, prepared her meals, and made sure she took her medications on time. I was essentially her lifeline to the outside world.

We laughed and we cried together for many years as we progressed on our caregiving journey and eventually it was time for my grandmother to move into a nursing home. Although there were still many details to be taken care of, my responsibilities lessened considerably and I was able to pursue my master's and doctorate in gerontology.

It was my grandmother who demanded I make my education my number one priority—and needless to say she was ecstatic that my degree of choice was the field of aging. For several more years I remained Mimi Esther's primary support system—but this time I was one of the seven million long-distance caregivers in the United States as I was living across the country in California.

The transition was quite difficult for both of us. I remember feeling a great deal of guilt as though I was abandoning her and she faced the daunting realization that this was probably going to be her last move. But we stayed close and I visited often to make sure she was as comfortable as possible.

The day my grandmother passed away my parents were on a ship in the middle of the Mediterranean—this was pre-cell phone days and I actually had to deliver the news via fax. It was not completely unexpected and we had discussed in advance that if she died while they were away I would proceed with the funeral, clean out her condominium and settle her affairs. And that's exactly what I did!

I must admit, although it should have felt incredibly overwhelming it actually almost felt natural... like being her caregiver was supposed to be my role all along. It was as though I was put in that position so that when I became an expert in caregiving I could speak from a place of real-life experience, not just academic education.

I'll never forget the day I received all the boxes of her things that I had wanted to save and had therefore sent to myself—it was such a cathartic moment for me. I recall that it was the first time that I understood that chronological age is simply just a number—one only truly ages as they become wiser and log meaningful experiences that make them more mature. Although in chronological years I was only in my twenties... my life experience had been that of a 50-year-old.

While I was Mimi Esther's primary caregiver I developed a deep respect and regard for the journey of caregiving, but most of all I loved and cherished the time we spent together. I learned from her how to be a strong, independent woman who could stand on my own two feet regardless of the circumstances.

I have continued to learn from both of my grandmothers' legacies—how to age gracefully and with dignity, how to remain strong and maintain a sense of humor during difficult times, and how to unconditionally love and care for another human being.

Joan: What are some of the common challenges that caregivers face?

Alexis: There's a reason why family caregivers often refer to their role as the most "thankless" job out there! Thankless, yes, but a job many of us share. By current estimates, 44 million American adults—or approximately 19 percent of us—care for an aging friend or family member, usually a parent.

As the last of the baby boomers turn 50, and their parents reach their seventies and eighties, that number stands to grow, and along with it, the emotional and financial cost to caregivers and society.

In addition to the emotional price we pay, caring for our aging parents can have a steep financial toll. For the average worker, that cost equates to more than half a million dollars in lost wages, due to either cutting back on work hours or leaving a job completely to handle caregiving responsibilities. For businesses, the cost is reduced productivity by employees who must come in late, leave early, or spend time on the phone tending to caregiving duties. Clearly, caregivers need more paid leave, flextime, and on-site elder care: It's good for employees and employers!

Care recipients need businesses to be more attuned to their needs as well. Sensitivity to the needs of elders is desperately lacking in this country. The *reality* is that insensitivity toward both the elderly and caregivers is a virtual epidemic. Caregivers, who give so much to others, are nevertheless often devalued and made to feel invisible. "It's as if," one caregiver told me, "we don't even exist."

Joan: So many caregivers are overwhelmed by the responsibilities required of them that it takes a toll on their own health and happiness. How can people make sure that they are taking care of themselves while they are taking care of everyone else?

Alexis: While caring for a mature adult may come naturally to some, it can still take a toll and may eventually lead to caregiver burnout. Caregiver burnout is a state of physical, emotional and mental exhaustion that can be accompanied by a change in attitude—from positive and caring to negative and unconcerned.

Burnout usually occurs when caregivers don't get the help they need, or when they attempt to do more than they are able—either emotionally, physically or financially. Caregivers who are "burned out" may experience fatigue, stress, anxiety and depression. Many caregivers also feel guilty if they spend time on themselves rather than on their ill or elderly loved ones.

Perhaps, the most effective means of preventing caregiver burnout is by taking *care of the caregiver*. Below are a few tips to help prevent caregiver burnout:

- Establish priorities
- Reach out to others for support
- Maintain your friendships
- Take time to exercise
- Share the caregiving role with family and friends
- Keep your medical appointments
- Maintain a healthy diet
- Talk to a professional
- Take a break from caregiving—respite time is crucial
- Stay involved in hobbies

- Be proactive and plan ahead

Joan: Is there a "best way" to ask other family members to get involved and share some of the caregiving responsibilities?

Alexis: In a recent survey, 76 percent of family caregivers—most of them women—said they don't receive help from other family members. As exhausting as caregiving can be under any circumstances, it is even more tiring and frustrating if you're surrounded by family members who don't seem to want to help. In fact, many people say that dealing with unhelpful siblings is one of the most stressful aspects of caregiving.

Fortunately, being a caregiver doesn't have to be a one-person job, even in a family full of seemingly self-centered or reluctant individuals. It will take effort and ingenuity, but in most cases, you can gain the cooperation of siblings and other family members and get the help you need. Here are some specific strategies to help ensure you won't have to go it alone:

- **Let them know you need them.** Often caregivers become overwhelmed because they are victims of their own success. When family members see how well you handle the job, they may assume you don't need their help—so they simply don't offer. You must learn to assign tasks—to work smarter, not harder, as they say in business.

- **Hold a family meeting.** Think of everyone who is, or who should be, involved in caregiving and caregiving decisions and begin to consider arrangements for a time and meeting place. Ideally, you should meet with your family face to face. If that's not possible, a telephone conference call or even a private Web chat should suffice. And, by the way, never end a meeting, call or chat without scheduling your next meeting time.

- **Consider caring styles.** Instead of seeing one of your family members as more caring than the others—which can lead to competition, anger and resentment—make the most of your caring styles. Ideally, all of us should be the recipients of our loved ones' touch, time, gifts, affirming words and acts of services. But it's not necessary that we get them all from the same person.

- **Don't discount men.** Do you constantly turn to your sister-in-law for help without considering that your brother might be willing and able to help with your parent? Do you bypass your husband, brothers-in-law, sons and nephews when it comes to caregiving requests? If so, you may have a wealth of untapped resources right at your fingertips.

- **Consider finances.** If a sibling has more money than time to offer your parent, ask her to pay for some of the services that you would otherwise have to do yourself.

- **Hold your criticism.** If you're trying to gain the cooperation of siblings who either don't do enough or don't do things your way, you'll have a lot better luck with praise and thanks (honey) for steps in the right direction than by criticism (vinegar) of what you don't like.

- **Consider talents and interests.** Your sister is an accountant, your brother is a chef, your sister-in-law is a great organizer and your nephew loves nothing better than to drive his new car. Why not ask them to do what they do best? When you help match caregiving tasks to interests and abilities, you're more likely to get cooperation from all involved.

- **Look beyond siblings.** If you need help with caregiving or simply aren't able to be a caregiver yourself, feel free to look beyond your own siblings and "blood" relatives. Your parent's neighbors, longtime friends or members of a place of worship are all good prospects. People don't have to be related by blood to have deep feelings of affection and responsibility toward one another.

- **Show them the money.** Though it may sound mercenary, it may take cold, hard cash to get some family members to help out with your parent. Your parent never needs to know that your siblings are being paid for their services.

- **Consider their circumstances.** If your sibling's failure to help with a parent's care is uncharacteristic behavior, instead of scolding him or her, try having a heart-to-heart about any problems he or she is facing. It just might start a healing process for both of you.

Joan: Alexis, what's the most important advice you would give someone who is just starting to take over the care of a parent or spouse?

Alexis: The daily stress a caregiver endures can be devastating, especially if you're considered to be the primary caregiver in the family and have limited time due to your job and/or other family responsibilities. The most common feeling "primary" family caregivers have toward aging loved ones is guilt.

Guilt can be destructive, making one feel tired, weak and immobile. No matter how much you already do, there are most likely times when you tell yourself that you could do better. Accept these feelings of guilt. Without recognition, guilt can be a destructive force. Know where these feelings come from and be aware that you are not alone in having such thoughts.

Joan: Guilt is such a big issue. You experienced it, and I know that I experience it in caring for my mom. You have some great tips to help us say goodbye to caregiver guilt. What are they?

Alexis:

- **Acknowledge your feelings.** Negative feelings can make us feel uneasy and guilty, but it's important to understand that feelings of guilt, anger and resentment are natural and common. Unless these feelings control us, and our behavior toward our parents, they are not bad.

- **Think quality, not quantity.** If you're feeling guilty that you aren't spending enough time with your aging loved ones, think of how you can improve the quality of your time together. Spending time reminiscing with your mother or playing a game of checkers with your father, for example, may mean more than cleaning their kitchen or delivering a pot roast.

- **Establish priorities.** While no one has the time or energy to do everything for everybody, you must find time (and energy) to do the things that are most important to you. By establishing priorities—and allowing some flexibility for the unexpected—you can help ensure that the most important needs are met and the most important tasks get done.

- **Set limits.** If your loved ones' constant demands are running you ragged, decide and clearly acknowledge what you are able and willing to do for them. By setting limits and standing behind them, you can help reduce the guilt trips that come when you can't meet their every demand.

- **Redefine your concept of caring.** If you find it difficult to provide loving, "hands-on" care for your parent, don't feel guilty—simply think of other tangible ways you can help provide for their care.

- **Act from love, not from a sense of debt.** If you think of caring for an aging loved one as repayment for all she's done for you, you'll always end up in the red. Instead, think of caregiving as one person helping another out of love.

- **Forgive and seek forgiveness.** If your parent was abusive or uncaring when you were a child, now is the time to forgive—even if you truly feel he doesn't deserve it. Holding grudges will not only affect your ability to care for your parent, but it will also hurt you.

- **Foster their independence.** Don't feel guilty for not doing things for your loved one that they could be doing for themselves. Instead, look for ways to help them do what they can. Something as simple as a $1.29 pill dispenser can help your parent become more independent—and can free up precious time for you.

- **Face the facts.** Despite how much you want to help, sometimes your aging relative needs round-the-clock care and constant supervision that you can't provide. When that happens, acknowledge that someone (or some place) may be better equipped to provide the majority of your parent's care than you are.

- **Don't succumb to peer pressure.** Acknowledge, but don't be unduly influenced by, the advice you get from friends and co-workers. Do what your heart tells you is best and what your circumstances permit.

The Beauty of Asking for Help

We cannot live only for ourselves.
A thousand fibers connect us with our fellow men.
~Herman Melville

In my book, people who asked for help were weaklings and wimps. I prided myself on my self-sufficiency. I had put myself through college and graduate school. I had gotten scholarships and job opportunities and all sorts of accolades, all from the very American idea that if you want to succeed in life, work as if everything depended on you. People who asked for help were just too lazy to do it on their own.

Boy, was I an idiot.

Doing everything on your own works great for things like pole vaulting or golf, but not so much for living life. Even lone wolves need their pack. This is the lesson I learned when I became my mom's primary caregiver.

My mom's hip replacement surgery originally appeared to be a success. She was determined to stay the minimum period in the rehabilitation hospital. Both of us had it in our heads that she would recuperate best in her own home. In our arrogance, we thought we were above staying in the hospital longer than necessary. We even talked the director into releasing her early. With my mom being a former nurse, we had this down. That was mistake number one.

In reality, my mom still needed a lot of round-the-clock care. I didn't anticipate the fact that I was going to have to check on her non-stop, bathe her, change her, dress her, help prepare meals for her, set up her medicines—everything. I became a zombie as the weeks dragged on, and she still wasn't fully able to care for herself.

Even when I wasn't with her, I still felt the burden of her care. A gray cloud weighed heavily on me; I was constantly worried. Would she remember to be careful if she got up in the middle of the night? Would she remember the proper way to get in and out of bed, chairs, and the bath? To compound the stress of caring for my mother, my husband and son felt neglected. They complained that I was never home.

This infuriated me as I was doing my best to care for my mom—a full-time job—while still trying to manage my family and all the other usual things I had been doing. I kept pretending I could do all of this and still maintain my life as usual. Didn't my family see how hard I was working? Why wouldn't they support me instead of whining that I didn't do enough? I didn't want to admit I couldn't be all things to everyone. That was mistake number two.

It should have been a huge warning flag that my mom's recovery was taking a lot longer than expected. Because my mom had come home early, she did not heal properly. Soon, she started experiencing problems. First, it was simple things, like searing pain. Then her hip began dislocating on its own if she moved improperly. These bouts prompted calls to 911 and hospital visits to reposition the hip back into place. After the third hip dislocation, we learned she would have to repeat the surgery, rehabilitation process, and recovery again. We had to start over.

I was devastated. My mom was ready to quit. I didn't know if she could physically endure a repeat of the entire process. I didn't know if I could handle everything that would be required to do it all over again. Still, we pressed on.

Looming on the horizon was a planned family vacation to the North Carolina mountains. It was our family's annual tradition. My husband kept reminding me of the upcoming dates. I knew my family was counting on this as an opportunity to reconnect and renew after a long, hard season. I was unsure—could I go away on vacation and leave my mom in the midst of all of this? As the most important advocate for my mom's care, how could I go?

Still, the thought of asking for help never occurred to me. I had hunkered down and done everything by myself so far. Could I still continue as the lone wolf?

I remember having a complete meltdown when my mom's surgery was only days away. It was a beautiful summer day, and what struck me was the irony of it all. Here was the most gorgeous day of summer—my son swam in the pool with a jubilant face, begging me to watch him do flips. All I could do was cry. I was exhausted. I was missing my family and the joys of summer. I couldn't do it alone anymore.

I realized I didn't know all there was to know about being a good caregiver. If I was completely spent as a person, I knew I could not make good decisions for my mom's care. Quite possibly, by doing all of this myself, I may have been doing more harm than good. I needed help.

I started an e-mail and phone campaign to every single friend, neighbor, relative, church member, and girlfriend I knew. I simply said four little words: "Could you help me?" I asked them if they could help in whatever way was easiest for them—through phone calls, prayers, a note, visits, cookies, donating old magazines or whatever they could think of. I didn't ask for help because I suddenly became enlightened; I asked for help because I had reached my personal limit.

What amazed me is that people loved the opportunity to help. They stopped by, wrote cards, called and brought their kids for a visit. Wisely, I did end up going on my planned family vacation for a much-needed rest—leaving my mom's care in the capable hands of the rehabilitation caregivers. Each time I called home from my vacation, my mom happily told me who surprised her that day with a visit or a kindness. It was like Christmas for her as people cared for her in ways she never imagined.

By stepping out of the way and inviting others to share in the care of my mom, I received a beautiful gift. I learned how much better her recovery could be as we both were boosted by the love of friends. Not only did I build a huge support network, but I also built an ongoing system of caring for my mom. Everyone in my circle of friends became invested in my mother's wellbeing and recovery.

The greatest lesson I learned didn't just apply to being a good caregiver, but for life. When you share the journey of life's ups and downs with people who adore you, it makes for a blessed path.

~Cara McLauchlan

What Would I Be Without You?

For fast-acting relief, try slowing down.
~Lily Tomlin

"Wat would I do without you?" my 85-year-old mother-in-law exclaimed, fanning her knobby fingers to admire her fresh manicure. It was our Saturday morning "usual"—washing her hair in the kitchen sink, setting it, then filing and repainting her fingernails. I'd done this for years, after realizing how difficult her arthritis made this simple beauty regimen.

What would I do without you? I knew the answer: plenty. Except she wouldn't be able to do it. Already we were realizing that the memory loss we had observed was the beginning of something serious. Her son (my husband) paid all her bills. I figured her income tax. We took away her car keys, promising we'd always make sure she got to the grocery store and church. When shopping became too confusing and exhausting for her, I just added her list to mine. Finally, I was providing every meal and doing her laundry and housework.

In those hazy days between her "growing old" and facing death, I was pulled into a role I never expected as a daughter-in-law. Thankfully, in a wise move two decades earlier, we had moved her and her ailing husband from their rural mobile home to a small house next door to us. Living just steps away, we walked together through her widowhood, cancer, heart attack, and the slow erosion of Alzheimer's disease.

Progressively came incontinence, wandering, and confinement to a wheelchair and the need to be fed. Finally, when I hurt myself lifting her, we had to place her in a care home. She died 11 months later at 89.

But as I thought back to better times when we could still carry on a conversation, and her losses frustrated her, I remembered my own frustrations. I'd put aside "my" life to serve her—and why?

Then I realized the answer came on ordinary days, like one when I took her to buy a new lipstick. Hers was several years old and down to the bottom of the tube.

"Mauve Rose! Very Berry!" As we stood in the cosmetics aisle, I almost shouted the lipstick names because her hearing loss muffled my normal voice. She reacted in shock at the prices, as her memory of what a lipstick cost was locked into what she paid decades earlier.

"I can't make up my mind," she said. "You choose."

So I did, and then offered my arm to help her walk to the cashier. I paid from her coin purse, knowing how counting money confused her. Then I tucked her hand in my elbow and walked her out to the car. That simple errand was her big, exhausting task of the day.

From that came one of many lessons of caregiving: one thing at a time. For me, who prized the ability to multitask while raising a family and working from home, it was a difficult lesson. As her losses increased, my learning curve steepened.

One lesson was to slow down. I equated "going for a walk" with pushing myself at an aerobic pace for a mile or more. But she was breathless as soon as I led her off the porch. Hanging onto me or her wheeled walker, she went one tiny step at a time. The walk up and down the block meant numerous stops to look at a neighbor's neatly landscaped yard and name the flowers. We'd comment on the sky. I'd point out quail strutting across the street. I learned there is value in noticing simple things.

Another was to major on the majors. When she started losing things on a regular basis, I realized how impatient I was in helping her find a lost bill, hearing aid, or specially purchased birthday card. It wasn't her; it was the disease that was robbing her of her true self. She needed help, not censure.

She taught me to accept help when we need it. I was juggling the roles of caregiver, mom, and wife fairly well when I slipped on ice and broke several bones in my ankle. Suddenly, somebody else had to make her meals, clean her home, wash her clothes, take her to the doctor, and do her hair and nails. And over at my house, I learned the grace of letting others do the same types of chores for me.

We learned together to find the good in the not so good. While setting her hair, I noticed a suspicious reddish patch growing near her ear. Her doctor confirmed it was a type of skin cancer that needed to be cut out. Her incision itched unbearably afterward. I tried to encourage her by saying, "He almost gave you a face lift on one side. You'll look 10 years younger."

She spent most of her last year in a care home with other memory-impaired seniors. Some could still walk, and said and did bizarre things. Others, like her, were helpless and said little. But her eyes still spoke, as they did with me one day a few years earlier, before her losses became so profound.

"I'm just not good for anything anymore," she complained, discouragement in her chocolate eyes.

"Oh, yes, you are," I countered. "See those photos of all your grandchildren and great-grandchildren? They need you to pray for them!" I hugged her and added, "Besides, you still have a really sweet spirit."

To the end, deep inside a cloyed body and mind, we could sense that sweet spirit. And that was the final, lasting lesson of my caregiving years: uphold each person's value. For even when she was just a shadow of her former self, she was teaching me to be patient and affirming, and to realize that life isn't always about accomplishing something.

After she'd taken her last breath, and I closed her unseeing brown eyes, I knew caregiving had deepened me. The original question she posed after each week's manicure was changed. Now, it was this: What would I have become without her? This, for certain: I would have missed lessons in becoming gentler and wiser.

~Jeanne Zornes

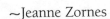

8

My Role Matured as I Did

We don't see things as they are; we see them as we are.
~Anaïs Nin

Even at the age of four, I somehow knew that phone call was the beginning of a significant change in our family. When my shocked grandmother, unable to speak, nodded to Mom to take the phone, I knew that our family would never be the same. On May 26, 1972, I became the daughter of a father with permanent physical restrictions who would need his family in a different way than ever before.

My role as a caregiver—or caring role as I like to think of it—matured and grew as I did. Initially, as a four-year-old, my role was to make sure that Dad was okay and make him smile. Our family temporarily moved to Halifax, Nova Scotia—a big city to us at the time—to make daily visits with Dad during his five months of hospitalisation.

Dad was strapped into a Stryker bed, which was flipped every three hours so that his paralysed body would heal. My role was to entertain Dad, which often involved homemade gifts like painted paper plates with macaroni carefully placed to say "I love you, Dad." As he had limited use of his arms, I would crawl under the Stryker bed that was holding him in place while he was facing down. Replacing his usual view of a hospital floor, I would show him his gift, hoping to make him smile. He always did.

When Dad was released from the hospital—confined to a wheelchair—we returned to our small farm in rural Prince Edward Island. My role grew. I became the helper, the door opener, and the spirit builder. I accompanied Dad regularly to a rehabilitation center for physiotherapy as doors can be challenging when you can't open them yourself.

In my role as door opener, I reaped many benefits. I can vividly remember stopping at Stedman's Department Store. Probably exhausted from physiotherapy and overwhelmed by the idea of climbing the stairs, Dad handed me some change and told me to buy something for my sister and myself. I recall looking at two small toys in one of my little five-year-old hands and the change in the other, wondering if I had enough money. I could see my dad watching me from the car, but I couldn't exit the store with the toys or read the price. I decided to take a chance. Luckily for me, the cashier smiled and nodded as I held out both hands with the toys and the change, asking if I had enough money. I often wonder if she supplemented my purchase after I left.

As Dad progressed from a wheelchair to a walker to crutches, he had to find ways to feel satisfied about how he was achieving and contributing to the family and community. Carrying out the previously "normal" tasks when you need your hands to keep you from falling became challenging, if not impossible. My role as facilitator began. It included carrying whatever needed to be carried, feeding the cattle, seeking assistance when needed, and watching patiently, ready to jump in when my dad's raw determination was not enough.

As a child, it did not seem bizarre that a man without the ability to walk could run a small farm until I heard a comment on a hot summer day in a hayfield. One of Dad's friends dropped by with another man. Dad was on the tractor. My older sister, Raeona, and I were tossing bales of hay onto the wagon where Mom was building the load. I noticed the stranger staring in disbelief as I heard him say to Dad, "How do you get your family all out here working together? I can hardly get mine to have a conversation." At that moment, I realized that we made sacrifices. Interestingly, I hadn't considered that not helping out was an option.

We did miss out on some "normal" events. Dad could not come to school concerts, basketball games, and other events when my friends had a strong family presence. I didn't have the chance to run in the park and be carried on Dad's shoulders when I was tired.

But as an adult, I realize what I did gain growing up by watching my dad heal his body, spirit and life with the determination that only a temporarily broken man could demonstrate. I learned that it is okay to crawl when it is too icy to get from the house to the barn or when your crutches fall out of reach. I learned that shame and respect are closely related; it is up to us to decide whether we will be ashamed or accept ourselves and others as complete with fully functioning and broken pieces. Mom still has a family portrait I painted in second grade showing my father with two silver sticks as extensions of his arms. That was my family as I knew it—crutches and all.

Most of all, caregivers learn to care. They see the need to open the door for the next person, even if it may be inconvenient for a few seconds. They learn to see the needs of others even when it hurts. They learn to protect more than be protected. I am shocked over and over when people do not hold the door for others, do not think to offer their bus seat to an elderly or struggling person, or show genuine indifference to the wellbeing of another. Caregivers understand the need to smile and appreciate that everyone needs to contribute and have a sense of community.

In a discussion about a challenging situation, a friend once said to me, "It's like you're an old soul. Where did that come from?" Without hesitation, and admittedly to my own surprise, I responded, "I grew up with a father who is disabled. Early in life, I would decide when it was time to be a child or time to be a problem solver. I guess it affects your perspective." My own words reminded me of the sacrifices and benefits of being a caregiver.

Recently, a participant in a seminar that I facilitated commented that I had "comforting eyes." Although I may have missed out on having my father applaud or cheer at concerts and sporting events, on enjoying a ride on my father's shoulders in the local park or the chance to watch my parents dance at my sister's wedding, I had the opportunity to develop comforting eyes and everything that goes with that. I watch with delight and a little bit of sadness as my nine-year-old niece and 20-year-old nephew develop and grow into their comforting eyes; they enjoy the company of their loving grandfather, who needs them in a unique way.

So when you notice "comforting eyes" in caregivers that you encounter, know that they will be there for you if you need help—because that is what they do.

~Debbie Matters

In Her Hands

Every problem has a gift for you in its hands.
~Richard Bach

Many of the common struggles of aging can be accelerated by Parkinson's disease. In a much shorter time than normal, a loved one can decline drastically in physical and mental capacities, so drastically that it's hard for family members to keep up with the practical and psychological adjustments demanded by the progression.

For my mother, it seemed that she was healthy and active one day and, in no time at all, debilitated to the point of needing someone with her at all times. The disease left her vulnerable to falls, and the trauma and injuries from two serious falls compounded the challenges of her overall weakened condition. This was a major change for a woman who grew up on a farm, worked most of her adult life in an automobile factory, maintained an immaculate home, and counted her sick days on one hand. It was a major change as well for my father, my siblings, and me because we only knew her as the strong hub of our family.

More than anything else, I remember resisting the role reversal that was imposed on me. I would have done anything to help my mother, but it was as if I was hardwired to be the child and allow her to be the parent. After all, that's who we had been to each other all of my life. When I helped her get dressed, monitored her use of the bathroom, and checked that her food was cut into small enough bites, these were precious opportunities to help meet her needs. At the same time, they were such foreign tasks, running totally contrary to our relationship.

I wasn't the only one who struggled with the role reversal; my mother seemed to resist it as well. Sometimes she looked at me with heart-wrenching regret and whispered, "I'm sorry." It was hard enough for her to be incapable of performing basic daily activities, but it must have been harder still to need help from someone she was accustomed to helping. We made the best of the situation, teasing and joking whenever possible, but both of us felt how unwelcome the circumstances were.

Even though I tried to be the epitome of a pleasant, positive presence in my parents' home each weekend when I visited, in my heart I wanted everything to go back to "normal." I wanted to reverse time, only a few months, back to the point that my mother was only slowing down rather than overtaken by a disease. With every phase of her decline, I had to muster more and more willingness to watch her be redefined by Parkinson's.

Then, one Saturday morning, there was a turning point. I had driven from Missouri to Kansas after I got off work the night before in order to spend the weekend with my parents, as had become my custom. My mother had just finished eating breakfast, and I was settling her into a favorite chair in the family room for a morning of visiting. I couldn't keep from doing what I did every weekend—notice, as if for the first time, the many ways that the disease had changed her. She was just a fraction of her previous size and strength, her face was drawn, and her whole body trembled. I looked at her hair, which still needed to be combed, and the cotton robe that was the only attire my father could manage. That's when I saw my mother's hands.

What caught my attention was that I had overlooked a small spill of oatmeal on one of them. I would have to return to the kitchen for a washcloth. But suddenly I was overwhelmed with the recognition of those hands. They hadn't changed, not really, not from age or from disease. Sure, there were some wrinkles and tremors, but they were so clearly the same hands that had cared for me my entire life.

I saw in those hands the person who had scooped out my meal portions, the person who had tucked me into bed, the person who had checked my temperature and bandaged my cuts and scrapes, the person who had examined how my clothes and shoes fit, the person who had studied my homework and admired my report cards, the person who had handed me birthday presents, and the person who had asked to see the first ring that a boy gave me. I realized that it was still my mother inside that aged, diseased body because those were her hands.

So many things had changed, but the important things were unchangeable. In my mother's hands, I recognized the person who had cared for me more than anyone else in the whole world. That was the person I wanted to care for in return, not some redefined or lessened identity, but my mother, the mother I saw in those hands. That's who she was, still, regardless of frailties or needs.

From that moment until my caregiving ended with my mother's passing, neither she nor I felt any more awkwardness over role reversals or unwelcome tasks. I can honestly say that there wasn't even the slightest sense of drudgery either, not ever. Somehow, in her hands, I caught a change in focus, from the challenging time that would be her last years to the whole that made up her entire life. For other caregivers, it might be a look in the eye, an expression in the face, or a tone in the voice that conveys so clearly, if only for an instant, the person we recognize. Yes, he or she is still there, and that's who we honor with our care.

~Judy Brown

Bernie's Last Thanks

The aim of art is to represent not the outward appearance of things,
but their inward significance.
~Aristotle

I didn't feel old when I retired from teaching that May. I had been a mother, a spouse, a teacher, and a volunteer for decades. Now I would have time to pull out my tucked-away dream to become a writer and artist. That was until I received an early morning phone call, one that placed an immoveable barrier in front of my plans.

It seemed my mother-in-law, Bernie, had fallen in her bathroom. She had no broken bones, but the trauma, and possibly a mini-stroke, made her completely disoriented. Her slight dementia had become severe, making it impossible for her to live alone, even in her well-monitored retirement community.

"You'll have to be the one who cares for her," Bill said realistically, since his medical practice required 12-hour days. My husband Bill, an only child, and I had always known the time would come for Bernie to move in with us.

Reluctantly, I relinquished my dream and went through the motions of being a good caretaker. Throughout those first weeks, as I sat with Bernie in the hospital, I observed how many trained nurses and attendants it took to care for Bernie's basic needs. When Bernie was moved into a rehabilitation unit for her physical and speech therapy, I was again overwhelmed.

"Bill, it takes two, sometimes three people to lift her out of bed and into her wheelchair," I said.

"Don't worry. I'll take care of the heavy work."

"Don't worry? How can I not worry? What if I do something wrong?" Now I was being the realistic one, convinced my English/art background hadn't prepared me for the science of geriatric care. I could mess up with words or paint, but now I would have his mother's life in my hands. There were no delete keys or paint-overs with someone's life.

"You'll do fine," Bill said.

So while Bernie processed through her rehab, I hoped for another solution to somehow turn up. All the while, my fear mounted each time I heard testimonies from caregivers whose lives had been altered for the worse.

"Don't even try it," one woman instructed firmly. "My brother-in-law had to move in with us over 10 years ago, and our lives will never be the same."

Too many stories poured in, infused with guilt, bitterness, and sorrow. In turn, I related each one to Bill, hoping he'd realize our lives could easily slip into theirs. He could choose not to come home, confident that I would care for her. I envisioned how I would become haggard and embittered, and our reduced lives would end our marriage.

"This will change me," I confessed. The loving spirit I possessed was paralyzed by fear of the unknown.

Yet, I questioned if I even had a choice. For each day when I delivered Bernie's milkshake, her face beamed like a child for this simple gift. How was this dear woman, now dying before me, to finish out her life? Intelligent, well-spoken and reserved, Bernie now babbled incomprehensible phrases, interspersed with sobbing. Dante failed to mention this circle of hell.

So what could I do? Since Bernie's life was no longer in her hands, I owed it to her to make my hands capable. And somehow, with the Lord's help, I did. By choosing to look at what I could do for Bernie instead of all that I couldn't, I changed the climate of our house — to a place filled with life instead of fear and death.

"Okay, Bill," I said, unwavering this time, "we're going to rewrite the end of our story. We're going to have a good ending, or at least a better ending to tell than those other people."

I suppose it was blind trust. Bill and I worked out his part as he planned breaks during the day to run home and help me with the weighty tasks. I sought to care for more than just her basic needs. I let the Golden Rule become my dictate: "Do unto others as you would have them do unto you."

Bill and I showed Bernie our love and gratitude for her many sacrifices. I thanked her for being the mother of my husband, for her years preparing hot meals, keeping a clean home and making sure Bill minded his manners. Sometimes I sang, and her eyes would light up.

"People still talk about your coconut cream pies," I'd say. "And I'll never be able to make Thanksgiving dressing as good as yours."

When I showed her photographs of her deceased husband, her eyes studied his face, and I talked about heaven filled with her loved ones.

On those difficult days when I ached for her shriveling body, which was wracked with pain, I kept uplifting music or television programs going. Mostly for me, I suppose. The time came, though, when I needed to call in more troops. That's when I discovered our area's hospice home health group. These trained men and women — a band of angels in disguise — offered comfort and expertise for Bernie's last months.

They provided a support group, and Bernie and I both benefited from their competent care. The nurses monitored her changes, the bath attendants pampered her, and a volunteer even sat with her so I could run errands for a few hours one day a week. All were tender and compassionate, releasing warm scents of vanilla and cinnamon through our home.

Somehow throughout this time of caring for Bernie, I did change. I learned about dying, but most of all, I learned about living. I quit making excuses not to paint and write. While the hospice nurse or attendant cared for Bernie, I painted or wrote instead of doing laundry or dishes, even if it was just for an hour. I also experienced my relationship with Bill deepening to a new level as we worked together to care for his mother.

One early spring afternoon while I was feeding Bernie, she grabbed my hand and clutched it to her chest, an unusual gesture. Caught by surprise, I tried to interpret her need. I focused on her piercing blue eyes, now tender, and she offered the sweetest smile, an expression of robust gratitude. That was Bernie's last thanks, and I'm still struck by its power.

"You're more than welcome, Bernie. Thank *you*."

~Ann Robertson

Best in Show

A Note from Joan

I met Dr. Sam Schwartz about 20 years ago and have gone to him for nutrition advice and chiropractic help ever since. Sam is the kind of doctor who takes a very holistic approach to treating his patients. He is a gentle, soft-spoken, compassionate individual who treats your body, your mind and your soul. When Sam's wife, Diane, was diagnosed with lung cancer and given less than a year to live, Sam's alternative treatments kept her alive far longer than the doctors ever imagined.

Recently I asked Sam what he found most difficult about being a family caregiver and what advice he would give to others. He said that even though he is a profoundly optimistic person, he found there was a tendency to "be depressed or even physically sick" because you feel guilty acting vibrant, perky and happy around the person for whom you are caring. When I heard Sam's observation I knew immediately that this was probably something many other caregivers experienced. Becoming aware of why this happens is the first step to protecting your own wellness.

When you look at caregivers overall, studies show that the stress of family caregiving can impact a person's immune system for up to three years after their caregiving ends, thus increasing their chances of developing a chronic illness themselves.

Seventy-two percent of family caregivers report not going to the doctor as often as they should and 55 percent say they skip doctor's appointments for themselves. Sixty-three percent of caregivers report having poorer eating habits than non-caregivers and 58 percent indicate worse exercise habits than before caregiving responsibilities.

Many caregivers report symptoms of depression. More than 1 in 10 (11 percent) of family caregivers report that caregiving has caused their physical health to deteriorate. Family caregivers experiencing extreme stress have been shown to age prematurely. This level of stress can take as many as 10 years off a family caregiver's life.

In light of these statistics, I asked Dr. Sam Schwartz to share his caregiving journey with you.

My life really began in the spring of 1967 when I was 22 years old. I met 18-year-old Diane Christine Spano in May and for the next 41 years, each day was filled with joy.

It was love at first sight. We met in Ann Arbor, Michigan, both working at St. Joseph Mercy Hospital - University of Michigan Medical Center. Diane was a desk clerk on the neurosurgery floor, noticeably cute and perky in her gold smock and dark blue skirt. I was a respiratory therapist dressed in a starched white jacket and tie, looking professional and "geeky" with my large solid-rimmed thick glasses.

We met in the cafeteria on one of the Saints Days. The normally busy cafeteria was silent; the nurses and workers chose to go to the chapel or the garden to pray. I saw this pretty gal sitting all alone, looking like Sophia Loren, and I said, "You are the only one who is not in the chapel. Why?" Then I quickly said, "I'm Jewish. What's your excuse?" She loved my line. It made her laugh and she lit up the world with her smile. I could not get that smile out of my mind the rest of the day. We went out that night and were never apart after that. By the fourth day of our courtship, her mom and dad joined us on a date. We became double-date buddies and we often included her younger sister and brother too; we became an instant family.

We had a whirlwind three months of courtship from meeting till marriage, and we heard plenty of warnings about how it wouldn't last. How could a marriage last between a Midwestern Polish Geek and a Saucy Italian Dish from Bensonhurst, Brooklyn? I guess we found the secret ingredient was not Italian food, but unconditional love and commitment to family values. Now, let's not be mistaken—the Italian food did play a vital role. I remember toasting the family at our wedding and saying that it was not just love at first sight, but love at first bite.

Our early years were spent putting each other through college, often taking classes together and sharing our strengths. Diane was the ultimate reader and interpreter of the written word, and I never read a book in my life. But I loved going to classes and I had a great memory for the spoken word. So, she did the reading and I did the class attending, and after every test we always ranked #1 and # 2 in every class. She was #1 a lot more than I, my smart little devil. Diane became an RN and gave Florence Nightingale a run for her money. She later continued her education to become a psychotherapist and psychoanalyst, giving Freud and Jung a run for theirs. I went on to advanced degrees, eventually building my life as a chiropractor. Without her encouragement and support I would not have gone the distance.

Diane and I were the couple that Walt Disney created. I remember us watching the movie *Pretty Woman*, and when we heard Julia Roberts utter the famous line, "I want the fairy tale," Diane looked at me and said, "Sammy, I got the fairy tale."

In the fall of 1980, Robyn came along after 13 long years of trying to conceive. Life was great. Then came December 24, 1996, the day before Diane's 48th birthday. Diane's doctor called and told us to "come over now." In the office we heard some of the worst words imaginable: "Diane, you have lung cancer." The doctor walked down the hall with me as Diane was dressing and advised I "count her time in weeks and months, not years."

Diane beat those odds into the ground. She was not only a survivor—she went beyond surviving. She held up through chemo and radiation like no other. She lived 12 years, not weeks and months. As time went on, I often found myself feeling bad, especially when everything was "good." I often became sad when the day called for "happy." I felt guilty for feeling healthy and for not having to watch what I ate or drank or wore. I felt guilty when I washed and brushed my hair, for Diane had no hair to fuss over. I morphed into a pretender for I did not want Diane to know how I felt.

Deep inside, I felt she was pretending too. We morphed from being ourselves to being pretenders.

Diane and I had always taken pride in our appearance. Not only to look good for each other, but also for our clients. As her illness progressed and she no longer had "the look," I too lost interest. I gained a lot of weight, stopped exercising, and my grooming was not what it used to be. I felt guilty looking good when she could not anymore. I felt that I shouldn't exercise because she couldn't, and besides I should be with her every free moment. It's hard to worry about a treadmill when your soul mate is throwing up in the bathroom. I felt undeserving of good health, exercise, good grooming, or fun, for my Diane could no longer enjoy these things. Guilt and pretense—hardly chicken soup for the soul.

I cared for Diane with love and support 24/7. Being a Doctor of Chiropractic, of course, I am good with the laying on of hands for comfort and healing. Each day, I worked on her muscles and joints to make her comfortable. Sunday mornings were our favorite sessions. From 10 a.m. until noon, I did a long session of deep massage from head to toe, followed by gentle manipulation of each joint.

While doing so, we listened to this radio program called _The Italian House Party_. This show was full of folklore, ethnic music and commercials for local Italian merchants. Diane would really "get into it" and sing along with each song and add her own stories and memories about growing up in her Italian neighborhood in Brooklyn.

I loved her singing and stories and I could sense the healing as I massaged her and she revisited the time when her life was good and safe.

After her passing, I was able to make sense of some of the lessons I learned. The most important is that guilt is not required as an expression of a caregiver's love. Unhappiness is not required as an expression of caregiver love. Caregiving is the ultimate expression of love.

In the final days, I knew Diane was onto me. She became my caregiver down the stretch; she had given me permission with her eyes to not feel guilty. Words were not required. She looked into my soul. She gave me her approval with her eyes.

When boarding a plane and preparing for takeoff, we all hear these words: "If the cabin pressure drops suddenly, an oxygen mask will drop down. It is important that you put your mask on first before helping others in your party." Well, this says it all: take care of yourself or you will not be able to help those you love. This became my Mantra and Vision once I caught on and once Diane let me know that it was okay to take care of myself.

Diane's last two months were in the hospital and Robyn or I was with her every precious minute. On our last evening together, we talked about the day ahead, Valentine's Day. Robyn had all kinds of plans, presents and all. I still have the lovely card that I never got to give Diane. Even in her last hours, she was laughing away. Little did we know that when we were watching the Westminster Dog Show that it would be our last TV show. Not knowing this, we were being silly—barking and growling and pawing at each other. I remember my words to her as she fell asleep for the last time: "My love, *you* are best in show."

~Dr. Sam Schwartz

Mom's Spa Day

Forgive all who have offended you, not for them, but for yourself.
~Harriet Nelson

Saturdays were our day together. After her lunch, Mom and I would rendezvous at her apartment in an independent-living community. While awaiting her call, I frequently stopped at our local county library for an hour or so.

One Saturday after Thanksgiving, as I walked through the library lobby, I noticed a sign inviting folks to a free meditation class that day at 11:00 AM. Although it was already 11:10, I ventured up to the room to have a look. This became a weekly endeavor—meditation class every Saturday on the way to visit Mom.

Mom was in her mid-nineties and fairly independent in spite of her macular degeneration. She'd have me thread needles for her most weeks, and I wondered how she managed to sew—mostly minor repairs—with such poor vision.

Even watching TV was a challenge. Mom had me mark her remote control so she could see and feel the correct buttons. I started watching some of her favorite shows, like *American Idol* and *Dancing with the Stars*. Discussing her favorite programs gave our conversations a positive focus.

Mom had an impeccable memory, but she had a disagreeable tendency to remember countless flaws of family and friends. "Do you know what she did to me? Well, I can't tell you how many times she..." and Mom was off and running.

When I'd respond with a question like, "When did that happen, Mom?" she would go back some 50 or 60 years until I managed to find her soft spot during one of our afternoon visits.

Mom loved having her feet gently massaged, but my strong hands were sometimes too rough for her tender, arthritic feet. Since she was no longer able to cut her own toenails, I became her pedicurist as well as her manicurist. For years, I had always cut her hair, so Saturday turned into Mom's Spa Day.

Since the leader of our meditation class suggested we soak our feet in salt water once a week while meditating, I added that procedure to Mom's schedule. Gradually, I began to guide Mom in meditation and prayer while her feet soaked. She loved the foot soaking so much that she had the basin and salt ready every Saturday when I arrived, just waiting for me to add the warm water.

The focus of one of our library meditation sessions was forgiveness. Since Mom had a challenge forgetting and forgiving events from yesteryear, I began incorporating a customized adaptation of this forgiveness exercise into her spa schedule as well. I would say slowly, "I forgive everyone who has ever done anything to me at any time. I am sorry for everything that I have ever done to anyone at any time, and I am forgiven."

Mom would repeat each phrase after me.

Mom's Saturday spa sessions continued every week for more than two years until, at the age of 95, she grew very weak. She fell at least a dozen times, but never broke a bone. Finally, six months later at 96, it was time for her to go home to the Lord. As I look back, the time we spent together on Spa Day helped both of us prepare for Mom's final journey.

~Tom Lagana

Being Strong for Mom

We acquire the strength we have overcome.
~Ralph Waldo Emerson

"We need to call the doctor," I told my mother.

"No! I'm fine," my mother shouted at me.

"He was very clear. We should call if anything changes."

"I said no," Mom declared. She turned to the visiting nurse. "Can you believe this? She has OCD, you know. She had a nervous breakdown."

It was the worst, most hateful thing she could say. I told myself it was the illness talking, even while I hated her right back. But I realized it was time for me to be the parent. Shaking, I dialed the doctor's number.

My mother had always been the strong one. A scientist at a time when most women didn't even work, she was the life force of our family, the one we all relied on. Once when I was very young, Mom came home from a night class, exhausted, to find that my brother Jeff had gashed his head on a radiator. The babysitter who'd instigated the wild romp that led to the injury? My dad. Why hadn't he brought Jeff to get stitches? He couldn't leave my sister and me. Exasperated, Mom snatched up all three of us and dashed off to the emergency room, my hapless dad in tow.

It seemed like Mom had imparted little of her vigor to me. At five, I screamed and cried the five blocks from our apartment to the doctor's office in anticipation of a vaccination. "That wasn't so bad,"

I admitted in shocked amazement after the tiny jab. That insight didn't stop me from repeating the same behavior. A few years later, Mom had to carry me screaming into the dentist's office to have an abscessed tooth removed.

At 21, my anxieties combined forces with an undiagnosed obsessive-compulsive disorder. Overwhelmed by psychic pain, I found myself poised on an overpass at my parents' beachside community, staring down at foamy waves crashing against sharp rocks. My life had come to a screeching halt. As the result of the obsessive-compulsive disorder, I saw visions: flocks of birds exploding in mid-air, faces rotting, flesh dropping from skulls and eyes rolling out of their sockets. I felt as though I had died inside. I came to the bridge to see if I had the courage to die for real.

Then Mom pounded down the road to me. Sobbing and screaming, she pulled me away from the railing. "Don't ever, ever do that again. Don't frighten me like that. You're going to get better. I'll make you better."

And she did. She found the right therapist, who gradually convinced me that the visions grew out of fears inside me. They lost their power over me, and eventually faded away.

I returned to school, married, and had children. I made my own decisions, but still liked to talk through problems with Mom. I especially valued her scientific insights when it came to illnesses. When my son had recurring strep infections, it was Mom, not the pediatrician, who told me that I needed to change his toothbrush after he started on the antibiotic.

But when Mom reached her seventies, I began to question her judgment, at least as applied to her own health. As we walked up the steep driveway of her house one day, I noticed that she had to stop several times to catch her breath.

"What's wrong?" I asked, alarmed.

"Nothing," she replied. "Well, maybe my heart valve. They say I need surgery, but I'm positive my vegan diet is helping. I'll beat this yet."

"Uh, okay," I replied, uncertainly. My father had been a vegan for over 20 years, and had recently persuaded my mother to give up meat and dairy as well. She told me she had chosen veganism as a healthy lifestyle choice. I hadn't realized she expected the diet to reverse her heart valve disease. And since this was my brilliant, scientist mom, I almost believed her. Unfortunately, she kept getting sicker.

Finally, we sat across from her cardiologist, Dr. W. At this point, Mom could barely cross a room without needing to rest. We'd reached consensus that she needed the surgery; the question was, who would perform it? Mom was holding out for the surgeon who'd performed Bill Clinton's bypass. A good friend said she knew him professionally and could arrange it. Having a celebrated surgeon would go a long way toward allaying Mom's fear of the eight-hour ordeal. The only problem was Dr. W. hadn't been able to reach him yet.

Although Mom wasn't in danger, we needed to move quickly. A different doctor, the head of cardiac surgery at a prestigious hospital, could be scheduled immediately. My father offered no opinion—at 80, he hadn't become any more practical than the day Jeff cut his head on the radiator. The decision would have to be made by my mother and me.

"I don't know," Mom said finally. "I feel like I'm not making good decisions anymore." She turned to me, a panicked look on her face. "What do you think I should do?"

My panic matched hers. Over the years, I'd learned to manage my anxieties and obsessive tendencies. I loved my life—my husband, children, and job. But in some ways, I was continually surprised at my achievements. I focused on my occasional bad decisions, blaming them on the anxiety and OCD. I worried now about telling Mom what to do. I took a deep breath and tried to summon wisdom, or at least common sense. "What would you do?" I asked Dr. W. "Would you want this man to operate on you?"

"Absolutely," Dr. W. said, and in that moment both Mom and I believed him completely. Our decision was made.

The surgery was every bit as hard as we'd feared, but by the end of her hospital stay Mom had more strength than when she was admitted. At her discharge, the doctor commanded me to memorize the pattern of redness at the suture. "It should only be getting smaller and fainter. If you see more redness, you must call us."

Over the weekend, I thought I saw a little spread of the red, like a tiny foot creeping out from the base of the zipper-like scar. It looked new to me. I was going to get my mom to the doctor, even if she cried all the way.

I realized it was tough being the strong one. Mom had been there for all of us, and now I was grateful I could be there for her. And after dragging her into a cab, Mom finally agreed with me. "You were right. I'm just so tired. I didn't mean it."

"I know," I said, hugging her back. The doctor agreed with me and put Mom on an antibiotic. If I hadn't acted when I did, the wound could have become infected, leading to serious complications. As we snuggled together in the cab, I realized that Mom really had given me some of her strength.

~Nancy Hoffstein

14

True Healers

In the sick room, ten cents' worth of human understanding equals
ten dollars' worth of medical science.
~Martin H. Fischer

I had always hated hospitals. I didn't care how colorfully they painted their walls or how cheery their therapy dogs make the patients feel. All I could see was tragedy hidden in every room. Doctors rushing from patient to patient, making their rounds, with clipboards and charts, scribbling away, and then disappearing for the day.

Then my husband suffered a traumatic brain injury from a car accident. He couldn't find the correct words, could not understand humor or nuance, and lost his sense of taste and smell. He also lost his social filter, and told my neighbor that if her son sped up their driveway one more time, he'd slash his tires. I often had to explain that his remarks were part of his illness. And there was the pain—the constant sensation of burning at the top of his head.

There wasn't a thing the neurologists could do for him in the hospitals on Long Island where we were living. Friends suggested we contact the brain injury outcome unit at Johns Hopkins, so we did.

We took the train from Stony Brook to Penn Station, and then on to Baltimore. Traveling with a man who has a brain injury brings certain challenges. He dressed like a schoolboy—sneakers and socks pulled almost up to his knees, khaki shorts that were too short, and an untucked polo shirt. His condition left him with the capacity of a seven-year-old boy, which was probably why he was dressing like a seven-year-old boy. "How much longer till we get to 'John Hoskin'?" he asked repeatedly.

When we arrived at Johns Hopkins, it reminded me of a modern-day Lourdes. People from all over the country, even the world, made their way in wheelchairs, limping, using crutches and braces, bandaged and patched. Each seeking advice from gifted doctors. Each praying for a miracle. Each carrying reports and X-rays and test results. Each with the hope that there was some hope.

Making our way to the sixth floor of one of the nine thousand buildings in the sprawling complex, I saw bodies so broken there were times I selfishly had to look away. Clutching my husband's medical reports, I had my own fear, my own tragedy, and my own hope for some hope.

In the waiting room, doctors came out from their examination rooms to apologize to patients for any delay. "I can see you in 15 minutes. I am sorry, but I have a patient who requires a bit more of my time." They crouched down to talk to patients, people, who were sitting in chairs. The doctors looked straight into the faces of their broken bodies. Eye to eye.

"Dr. Dan" came into the waiting area and welcomed us with a warm smile. "Come with me." I expected the standard 15 minutes usually allotted to patients. Dr. Dan talked with us for an hour before he examined my husband. He spent another hour going through neurological tests and reviewing the records we presented to him. He comforted me so that I could comfort my husband. He covered everything from disability insurance to good places to find the best crab cakes and steaks in Baltimore. "I'm not your cardiologist. Enjoy the steak." He spent three hours tending to our needs, and then walked us to the person who would schedule a follow-up appointment. He gave us his personal cell number. "Call anytime with any questions."

With the treatment program prescribed for my husband, he was able to make a full recovery. It took a year, but Dr. Dan was with us through every step, adjusting plans as progress was made.

I look at the medical profession differently now. There are doctors, and there are healers. Gifted human beings who touch and look directly into the stricken, fear-filled faces of the wounded. These exceptional professionals go beyond practicing medicine. They care. And I am convinced their love comforts and heals the sick and injured.

Paint the entire hospital bright yellow. Fill it with beeping machines, wires, and tubes. None of it matters without true human empathy. It is the love of healing, and the ability to recognize the dignity of the whole person, that makes the difference. I believe these special human beings have a divine gift.

We enjoyed the best crab and steak dinner in Baltimore that night. Everything tastes better served with a dash of hope and a bit of love.

~Barbara Joan

Chapter 2

Family Caregivers

All You Need Is Love

Love is, above all, the gift of oneself.

~Jean Anouilh

An Experienced Caregiver Talks from Experience

A Note from Joan

I want to introduce you to a very important person in my life, James Ashley, the man who is in charge of the daily care of my 93-year-old mom, Gladyce. To truly understand the level of James' compassion and understanding of the elderly, I must first tell you a little about the man himself.

When James was born in Santa Monica, California, it was a bitter-sweet moment for his mom Betty. Betty was married, but it was while her husband, a soldier, was overseas during the war that Betty had become pregnant by another man. Betty was ashamed and devastated by her situation. She was also let go from her job because of the pregnancy and ended up living in the back seat of her car.

When her obstetrician heard of her bleak dilemma—that she had nowhere to live—he invited her to come and live with him and his wife and spend the remaining months of her pregnancy with them. The doctor's wife was also expecting to deliver about the same time. When little James was delivered, Betty left the hospital and gave the baby up and the doctor and his wife agreed to take little James home with them to raise him along with their own newborn son. However it was a bit more than the couple had bargained for, raising two young boys at once, so when good friends of theirs from their church expressed the desire to have a child, the doctor arranged for little James to make his new home with Dr. and Mrs. Robert Ashley who lived in Napa, California.

James had a wonderful life with the Ashleys, who also ran nursing homes and were very much of the missionary spirit. James worked in the nursing homes caring for the elderly alongside his father. After college and four years in the Air Force, James was working in contracting, which took him abroad, where he met and married his wife Rowena in the Philippines.

James had been told at age seven that he was adopted and he had always wondered what happened to his birth mother. He very much wanted to meet her. When James was 44, with the help of an adoptive search group, he finally found his mom Betty in Los Angeles. Betty had never had any other children and her husband had left her, so she was alone in the world. The two met, and over the years they established a warm relationship. As Betty grew old and frail and could no longer live on her own and had no one to care for her, James moved her into his home. She was 87 when she came to live with him and his wife Rowena. Today James takes care of all of Betty's needs and she is thriving at 92.

Years before, James and Rowena had already taken his elderly adoptive mom into their home and cared for her in her final five years. And then they had also brought Rowena's elderly parents from the Philippines to live with them. Clearly James's desire to care for others—especially the elderly, who he believes are all too often deprived of compassionate care—has been a dominant force in his life. Five years ago James decided to make this passion his life mission. He bought a house near his own home and established a senior care facility that would house six residents.

James says he loves caring for the elderly, although he is quick to point out that it is certainly one of the most difficult jobs, one that requires constant attention and personal dedication. He says, "You can't fake being a good caregiver." James feels he is blessed with a gift—the gift of truly enjoying interacting with the elderly. He says he doesn't really have to work at it.

I always marvel at how lovingly and respectfully he interacts with each resident. His face lights up when he sees them and his effervescent smile is absolutely contagious. He talks with them about their life's accomplishments and what they did "back in the day." He may have heard the stories a hundred times, but he is just as interested at each telling. And the residents revel in sharing their life memories. James points out that this is not always so easy for many people, since they may have had difficult relationships with their loved ones. These situations make it much harder to be a loving compassionate caregiver.

I feel James has a unique perspective, since he deals with the elderly and their adult children on a daily basis and he sees how they interact. I asked him what advice he would have for others who are providing care for loved ones, and here is what he shares:

Joan: James, how do you help the elderly find some happiness in each day? What makes a person happy at that elderly stage of life?

James: The most important thing for the happiness and contentment of the elderly is for them to be able to feel like they are not alone—they don't want to feel like they are just a number—they need to feel like they belong. You can accomplish this by treating them like they are special and by telling them each time you see them how nice they look. Tell them that they are looking very healthy—sometimes that can make them feel better. Then I talk to them about things that THEY want to talk about, NOT the things that I want to talk about. Let them know you care! It doesn't always matter who gives them caring attention; it's just really important that they are getting the loving care and attention.

As dementia increases in the elderly, they are not connected to the world in the same way as the rest of us, and they are not comfortable being made to relate to our reality. For instance, with your mom, Gladyce, I don't talk to her about things going on in politics today since she doesn't connect with that, but we have great conversations about things that happened 10 or 20 years ago. I can always get a happy and lively talk going with her if I talk to her about life with your dad, and about you and your brother growing up. Your mother has never been able to accept the death of your brother Jeff, so I usually speak of him as though he is alive today. I call it a "therapeutic lie."

You can't argue with dementia. You need to connect with the elderly in their reality. You just can't expect them to come and live in your reality. Don't argue with them or keep telling them they are wrong when they are confused and disoriented. People desperately want their loved ones to be a part of their world, but the more dementia sets in the more we must let them live in their world because that is where they are comfortable.

Joan: I notice that some of the adult children who come here to visit their folks will sometimes complain that they feel their parents should read more, exercise more, walk more. It's always something. And I've often wondered what seniors really want to be doing. What do you feel seniors really want to do all day long?

James: Many adult children have an agenda for their parent. For example they will tell me, "My dad should shower and shave every day. He should go out and take walks and be active and he should go to bed early." However Dad or Mom may have their own likes and dislikes and sometimes they just don't have the energy to do what their kids think they should still be doing.

I always try to find out what my residents enjoyed doing when they were younger. If they loved to draw or paint when they were young, I go out and get them art supplies. If I find out that they played a musical instrument, I try to get that instrument for them. It's sometimes amazing how they can pick it right up and play it again. Quite often the elderly will tell you that they are not interested in any of it. However all you have to do is break out the paints and paper, set up the Bingo game or start singing, and before you know it they will join right in and their spirits will be lifted right away. Don't tell them to sing—just start singing and they will join in with a smile.

Joan: I was amazed when you told me that my mom often joined in the singing—my mom was always so shy about singing, I don't think she even sang "Happy Birthday" at my own birthday parties. And she was never really a card player or one who would join in games. So I never would have predicted that she would be your reigning Bingo champ. What advice would you give to adult children like me to make your job easier?

James: In order to provide the best quality care, it takes a team, and we need the family on our team. It's a very difficult job when the family just drops their loved one off and doesn't give you ongoing input. If the family will join the team, that will always bring a better level of care. The family knows the resident's medical history and their interests, and this is incredibly valuable information. With this kind of information I can make their loved one safer and more content.

I think that grown children may not think their visits really matter, however visits from family members can absolutely make the day for their loved ones. Trust me, even when it seems like your loved one isn't connecting or recognizing you, it still makes a huge difference. And when I see that the family cares, it makes me want to try even harder to make their loved one happy.

Joan: When a family checks out respective places for their mom or dad to live, what should they be looking for?

James: Of course it's important to check for cleanliness and to make sure that the facility is organized and keeps good records—they are going to be in charge of your loved one's medications and wellbeing. Meal preparation is also very important. Go into the kitchen and open the refrigerator and look inside. Check to see what kind of food is inside. Do they have fresh fruits and vegetables? Do they cook fresh or are they using frozen prepared foods? Do they bake fresh? Food is so important for the elderly. The elderly often lose interest in food and stop eating as they get older and dementia creeps in. So it's important to keep them interested in eating so that they thrive. In addition to providing a good level of care it is also important that the staff will pay attention to the residents.

If you are hiring a caregiver in your home, make sure that they have references and that you call all of those references. You must also do a background check and fingerprint check to be sure they have no record and won't steal from your loved one. They also need to have a sufficient grasp of the English language so if there is an emergency situation they can talk to emergency care workers. As caregivers, we are part humanitarians, but it is also a business and you must pay attention to the details and the business side.

Joan: So what are the most important suggestions you would give to the caregivers reading this book?

James: #1 Don't wait too long to take action! Don't wait until Mom or Dad isn't able to handle taking medications properly. You don't want them to end up in the hospital because they overdosed themselves. Don't wait till they are eating cold food out of cans because they aren't cooking anymore. Don't wait till their clothes are filthy or smell bad because they aren't showering or doing laundry. Don't wait! Everyone waits till a crisis hits. And more often than not, it was predictable. Talk as a family and plan ahead. When folks age, they often get stubborn and they don't want their kids telling them what to do—this turns kids off and makes them back off, when this is the time when they need to be involved. Every family needs to have a plan in place. Figure out how you are going to do it or better yet, get professional care to help you (or assist you).

#2 Don't try to do it yourself—I advise finding professional help when looking for qualified senior care. Find yourself a senior advocate. Call a reputable senior referral service like A Place for Mom, to help you determine the needs and desires of your loved one and find the right living arrangement for them.

#3 Don't abandon them! Once you find a place for them don't abandon them. Everyone is busy, but visits are so important. If that means sacrificing some time to go see aging parents, just do it, it's that love connection that allows the elderly to thrive. Don't ignore them. Hug them, kiss them, and talk to them. Bring up their past. Show them pictures from their lives. These are the important things that help the elderly experience moments of happiness.

Be Sure to Call

Ritual is necessary for us to know anything.
~Ken Kesey

My relationship with my parents was a warm one, particularly in later years with my mom. She was always concerned about me, especially after my divorce. If I traveled out of town, she'd admonish me, "When you get there, be sure to call." And when I would oblige, she'd sign off with, "When you get home, be sure to call."

Though I often fussed about having to report in to Mom when I was an adult, it was comforting to know at least one person in the world cared where and how I was at every moment of my life. It was her way of showing her love and concern, and the ritual became a part of our lives. When I'd hang up the phone after "reporting in," I'd often feel a smile spread across my face.

Always self-sufficient, Mom became even more independent when Dad died. At age 62, she bought a car and learned to drive for the first time in her life. In the following years, there were many more firsts for her, and she handled them all with the same courage and determination. As she aged, she remained the backbone of the family, always there when someone was ill, available to babysit the grandchildren, and she still played hostess for the constant stream of visiting family. At the same time, she enjoyed an active social life with her own circle of friends.

Then Mom began having what the doctor described as "mini-strokes." With each mini-stroke, Mom's personality changed a little more. At first, it was only minor things like memory lapses. Being the sibling living nearest, I assumed the role of caregiver. My mother, the independent woman, did not accept the reversal of roles easily. As she so succinctly put it one day, "Who do you think you are? My mother?"

My siblings and I hoped for the best, but her condition slowly deteriorated until my daily visits weren't enough. My older sister, also widowed, moved in with Mom. Soon things were going well enough that I accepted an out-of-state invitation to a friend's graduation.

Mom hadn't given her ritual order for me to phone, but when I arrived at my destination I automatically did so. When she answered and I told her I made it safely, her response devastated me.

In a voice devoid of emotion, she said, "Okay," and then hung up.

I held the phone while waves of disbelief flowed through me. When the knowledge crashed over me that Mom wasn't capable of loving me anymore, the grief that followed spawned a torrent of tears. Her physical body was still there, but that one person in the world who cared where I was at any given moment was gone. It was as if my mother had died, and I had already lost her.

In the following months, additional strokes weakened her even more. Until then, we'd been able to include Mom in decisions about her care. Now she was incapable of participating. When my sister could no longer handle Mom's physical needs, we hired additional help. Then Mom fell and broke her hip. When she left the hospital, it was to go to a nursing home where the family stayed with her in shifts until she was able to leave.

After her hip healed, we found a family care home with loving people dedicated to their residents. After a few months, Mom became non-ambulatory, and the family care home's rules wouldn't allow them to keep her.

Horror stories about nursing homes haunted me as we searched for a decent facility. The one we finally decided on wasn't perfect, but it wasn't a bad place either. It was short-staffed, as all such facilities seem to be, but the people who worked there appeared to care.

My job allowed me the freedom to drop by every day. I staggered my visits, often getting there as early as 6:30 in the morning. I guess I thought if the staff didn't know when to expect me, Mom would receive better care. And no matter how hard and long my day had been, I made sure to be there every evening so I could sit with Mom until she settled in for the night.

Conversations during those long evening visits were difficult. She often thought I was her sister or asked about people from her childhood as if they were still alive—including her long-deceased parents. I tried to tell her family news, but most of the time she didn't know who I was talking about. My own children had spent a lot of time with her when they were babies, and she was especially close to them. When she couldn't recognize their names or photos, it broke my heart.

As the months went by, in order to get through those visits and attend to Mom's needs, I built a wall around my heart and feelings. I thought if I didn't I'd never get through the long haul ahead. After that, I didn't allow myself to see and love her as my mom, but only as a dear one who needed care.

There were moments when I thought Mom recognized me, but those were rare and short-lived. Then one night, after a particularly difficult time, I prepared to leave and went as usual to her bedside where she was nodding off.

I placed my palm on her folded hands. "I'm going home now. See you tomorrow. I love you." That had become the new ritual—words mouthed to make me feel better because she no longer understood or cared what I said.

She stirred and opened her eyes. For a fleeting moment, I thought I saw recognition there. Her facial expression didn't change, but she spoke in a sleepy soft voice. "Call when you get home." Then she closed her eyes again.

I froze at the realization that my mom was still in there, the one who'd always loved and cared for me. The wall I'd built around my emotions crumbled, and that old feeling of comfort and warmth enveloped my entire being. It humbled me to think that even in the darkness that filled her room of memories, she could still find the remnants of a long-time ritual to show me her love and concern.

I left her that evening with something I had lost when I built that wall around my feelings—hope. Hope for more moments like that night's, and hope that I could again love my mom completely.

Until Mom's death at age 93, our times together were filled with love. Sometimes, we carried on simple conversations where I answered as her beloved, deceased sister. Occasionally, we'd have a moment of laughter. Often, we sat in peaceful silence. And, once in a great while, glimpses came through of my still loving and concerned mom, the one who hadn't abandoned me, but had only stepped into the next room.

~Delois McGrew

The Skateboarder and Schizophrenia

I consider skateboarding an art form, a lifestyle and a sport.
~Tony Hawk

I knew a boy once who traveled by skateboard. He would glide effortlessly through life over rough terrain. He had the ability to hover for seconds at a time over stationary objects before crashing down on them. He always surprised me when he landed on his feet. The wind would blow through his sun-bleached hair and cool off his sweat-soaked neck on most summer days. He lived on macaroni and cheese and swilled Gatorade with his ragtag group of skater boys.

Our local newspaper captured him in a photograph one day. It depicted him in midair, his skateboard a foot below him beside a sign that said "One Way" as he faced the opposite direction. His 15 minutes of fame garnered much criticism from local townsfolk. Comments appeared in the same publication and spoke of the youth who were defacing town property as a result of grinding their skateboards on park benches and curbing. He didn't mean to harm the world around him. His only crime against nature was to be out and enjoying it the only way he knew. He loved to get on his skateboard and ride.

It was amazing to watch him flying high in those youthful, carefree days. He dreamed of slinging a backpack over his shoulder and skating his way across the country like a modern-day Jack Kerouac after high school graduation—not knowing his carefree days would end well before graduation commenced.

Throughout the late summer days of 2002, his skateboard began to spend more time parked in our back hallway. At the age of 17, storm clouds had begun to gather in his mind. Secretly, he harbored increasing doubts about the world as he knew it. Common gathering spots and trusted friends began to present themselves as strangers. The country he had dreamed about exploring for so long became something to fear. His skateboard held no more magic or adventure for him. The faces of his family and friends held no more warmth or familiarity. The school he had attended for well over three years became foreign territory, a new frontier that he could not conquer.

As the months wore on, he became a shadow person—a shell of the boy we used to know. His eyes were too wide and held such fear. His mouth had all but ceased to move except when he pushed down food at another's insistence. As parents, we wished desperately that he would find his words again. His words, thoughts and ideas had been buried under the storm clouds that continued to gather in his mind.

Finally, in the fall, the storm broke. His words gushed forth and forced their way into our lives. They were hard to control and gather up. They swirled around us like autumn leaves pushing and forcing their way into our home every time the door was opened. He would open his mouth, and they would tumble out. They didn't make any sense to us. "If only he would pick up the skateboard again and go flying," I thought.

I wished for him to sail through this turbulent time and sea of emotions. I wanted him so badly to just be himself again—to beat whatever was pressing down on him like a freight train. Why couldn't he outskate this thing? Stay ahead of it? Some engines are just too fast. It was never a fair match to begin with—a freight train versus a boy on a skateboard. Luckily, we caught him just before he gave up. We stopped and really listened to his words. We heard his fears, saw his pain, and let go of our own.

Sweeping away the dead leaves and broken thoughts, we lifted him up off the train tracks. His father and I wept as we entered the facility that would help him sort out his disordered thinking. We left him there, even as he begged us not to, but we had no choice as parents. The dam had broken, and he was being swept away from us. That is what happens to a young man as schizophrenia slowly begins to splinter his reality. There is nothing left that is familiar. There is no safe haven in the mind of someone who is slowly descending into unreality.

His skateboard remained in the back hallway like a soldier standing at attention. It seemed as though it were waiting to be called into service. I never dared to move it for fear it would send my son the message that he would never get back to "normal" again. As the first year blended into the second year, Andrew began to make sense of his illness. His remarkable intelligence afforded him the ability to understand the disorder. He accepted it for what it was and never questioned why this happened to him or felt sorry for himself. He just trusted the people around him who loved him unconditionally to seek out the best possible care. Andrew complied with treatment and endured many drug trials and physical discomfort during those early years.

As he entered the third year of his illness, he noticed the skateboard, covered with a thick coating of dust. It still stood, like a sentinel, guarding the memories of his carefree youth. That day, he ran his hand along the top of it and wiped the dust off on his pants leg. Then, without warning, he hoisted it up and slung it across his shoulder. I winced, knowing that was where the backpack of his dreams should have been.

A man now, he turned to no one in particular and asked, "Hey, do you think I should give this skateboard to Michael? He skateboards, doesn't he?"

"I think so," I heard myself answer.

I watched as he shoved the skateboard into the backseat of our car as if it were of no more importance than a sack of potatoes. I stifled the desire to scream, "Be careful with that!" as if that would change anything. Eventually, we arrived at my sister Susan's house.

She is the grandmother of Andrew's young cousin, Michael. Andrew made no motion to get out of the car. He had done the very hardest part already, I reasoned to myself. It was only fair that someone else finish it for him. I opened the back door and reached in for the skateboard. I repeated to myself over and over, "It's only wood. It's only wood." As I passed the board to my sister, I desperately tried to find the words to tell her what this meant to our family. How could I tell her that I felt as though I were passing on an Olympic torch of sorts from a retired champion? It seemed to me that in the game of life, my son had met his match and held his ground. He didn't crash down on it anymore the way he used to when he came out of a kick flip in the glory days before schizophrenia, but he had achieved firm footing again.

Before I had a chance to say anything, I heard the car door open behind me. My son emerged with a big grin on his face. He gave his aunt a big bear hug and said, "I hope Michael likes this old skateboard. It's still good, and I used to have a lot of fun on that thing." Understanding the significance of the event, Susan squeezed my hand long and hard. Our brimming eyes met finally when she said, "Andrew, Michael will be so happy to have it. Thank you so much for thinking of him."

"No problem, Aunt Sue. I love you. You're my favorite aunt," he stated, unabashedly.

"It's nice to see some things never change, because you are my favorite nephew," she replied.

Andrew's illness has taught our family that nothing can stop love. Illness can make things difficult and messy, but it cannot change the core of a person at the spirit level. Andrew has battled many symptoms of schizophrenia, and it has impacted his quality of life, but it has not taken away the heart of him. His immense capacity to experience love and think outside of himself is amazing. He will forever be our hero, a champion and beloved son.

~Yvette Moreau

Touch

We all yearn to return to those days when we were completely
taken care of—unconditional love, unconditional attention.
~Mitch Albom, Tuesdays with Morrie

It was a gloriously sunny Sunday morning. Even the thick drapes in my bedroom couldn't completely shut out those beautiful golden rays. I lay in bed, reminiscing as I did on most occasions when I had the luxury of a lie-in. On this lazy morning, my mind drifted randomly to a night more than two decades ago.

There were always certain memories from my childhood that resurfaced more often than others. That night in particular would replay itself in my mind quite often. I remember pulling the soft white pillow over my ears and sobbing hysterically as I lay in my bed, wishing that the shouting would stop. It was like that most nights. They would be downstairs in the living room. He would be yelling at her, and she would be crying silently as he did. I couldn't understand why he was so horrid to my mother. She was such a gentle soul.

I remember my bedroom door suddenly being swept open, and my brother barging in. He flipped on the light switch and stormed over to my bed, looking enraged. I had stopped sobbing and was trembling in fear. At 17 years, my brother was just as scary to me as my father was at that point. "Get out of bed," he said in a gruff voice. He grabbed my hand, roughly pulling me out of bed. I started to sob again as he dragged me unwillingly down the stairs and toward the shouting. I remember my father whirling around in mid-sentence as he heard my whimpering sounds coming from behind him. My brother then shoved me in front of my father and yelled, "Look at what you're doing to your daughter!"

I guess as I grew older, I forgot what happened after that. Maybe things got better. Maybe worse. I couldn't remember feeling hatred for my father. Perhaps I stopped hating him after a while. Or perhaps I never did quite hate him. He was, after all, my father. In the past eight years, he suffered two debilitating strokes and was reduced from the alpha male he once was to a meek man with an almost childlike disposition. The roles between us switched. I was now the caregiver. The breadwinner of the family. My father had been emasculated.

I yawned and stretched my arms as I sat up in my bed. I reached over and pulled a book that I had been reading the night before off the nightstand. It was a book by Mitch Albom called *Tuesdays with Morrie* and had been highly recommended by many friends. I opened the book to where my bookmark lay and began to read. A couple of pages later, I stopped and went back a page to re-read what I had just read.

Mitch, the author, was talking to Morrie about how he managed to stay positive in spite of having lost his independence and needing a nurse to bathe him, lift him and wipe his behind. Morrie's response was that, strangely enough, he had begun to enjoy his dependency. He said it was like going back to being a child again. I read that section over and over again as the tears welled up in my eyes.

I couldn't remember the last time I had hugged my father. Truth be told, I didn't enjoy being too close to him. He always smelt like medicine and something that reminded me of a nursing home for the elderly. It made me uncomfortable.

I got out of bed and made my way to the bathroom. As I washed my face and brushed my teeth, I thought about this some more. My father and I had never been that affectionate in the past either. He had been revered and feared before his present condition. What was I to do? Completely shock him with an embrace out of the blue? What would he think? How weird would it feel for me? Did I really even care enough to try it?

I could hear my mother bustling about in the kitchen as I walked toward the living room, where I knew my father would be watching TV. Sure enough, there he was—in his comfy single-seater couch with the clicker in his hand, staring blankly at the moving images on the screen before him. He barely looked up at me as I walked into the room and mumbled good morning. I settled onto the loveseat at the far end of the living room, watching my father's lack of response to the comedic actions of the characters in the sitcom.

Suddenly, I felt a surge of emotion run through my body as I stood up and walked slowly over to my father. He continued to look straight ahead at the TV screen, seemingly oblivious to my movement. I knelt down beside his couch, with my arms resting on the cushioned right arm of the sofa, and softly rested my head on his shoulder, my hair nestled in his neck. What was probably seconds felt like an eternity, but then I lifted my arm and placed it over his other shoulder and held him as tightly as I could. If I had had any doubt in my mind about whether I loved my father, they were obliterated in that moment—when I felt his body trembling under my head as he began to sob uncontrollably.

~N.R.

"Now I Take Care of You"

A Note from Joan

I'd like to introduce you to 91-year-old George Schoengood, a retired college professor. George was happily married for 50 years to Leah. The two of them had moved from New York to Florida when George retired and they were enjoying their golden years with considerable independence until eight years ago when Leah had a stroke.

George and Leah's son, Matt, is married to my good friend and colleague Elise Silvestri. Matt was 46 years old when his mom suffered the stroke and Matt became the primary caregiver for his parents. Like so many others, Matt got thrown into the role of caregiver when crisis struck, and his life forever changed. It was "initiation by fire" and it's been a roller coaster ride ever since for Matt (and Elise). Since Matt is an only child, all of the responsibility falls on him.

After Matt's mom Leah passed away, Matt continued to be responsible for George's care.

I have always wondered how a person feels when all of a sudden he can no longer live on his own or take care of even the simplest tasks. Since George still has a very sharp mind, I asked Elise and Matt if he would tell our readers about it. He seemed like the perfect person to ask.

Here's George's story on receiving care from his son:

Eight years ago my son Matthew became the primary caregiver for my wife and me. In looking back, I didn't realize how this would redefine my life. You see, it didn't all happen at once—actually things always felt "normal" to me. I guess I didn't want to accept the fact that I could no longer take care of myself.

My name is George Schoengood and I'm 91 years old. I spent my life as a college professor and always loved my teaching career. I was married to a wonderful woman for over 50 years.

But everything changed when Leah had her first stroke. My son Matthew had been visiting us in Florida that weekend, a two-day visit that turned into a month-long stay managing her care. Matthew was away from his job and his family.

Even after I lost my beloved Leah, Matthew continued to manage things. I just didn't realize to what extent.

Don't get me wrong; I know he does many things for me but I still always thought "Hey, look at me. I can shower and dress myself. I can eat my food without someone helping me. I'm independent."

What I didn't realize is HOW much Matthew was doing and actually how dependent I really am on him.

One might think it would have dawned on me when Matthew took away my car keys. I have macular degeneration and my eyesight has been failing for years. I wasn't very happy when I was told that I could no longer drive, but even when that happened, I still thought that I was okay.

Another reason I considered myself independent was that even though I had lost a good deal of my sight, I didn't seem to suffer from any dementia. Quite the opposite—doctors and people in my everyday life always comment on how sharp I am, asking me questions about politics and things in the news. I thought, "If I still have my mind, then I'm okay." I guess I was just deluding myself but then again, all my life, other people have been taking care of the daily details of my life… first my mother, then my wife, and now Matthew.

My family and friends often joked, "George lives like a guest in his own home."

Then, I began to realize that there are a number of things that I can no longer do, even if I wanted to. For example, I can't write my own checks, or even read the bank statements. I also can't go grocery shopping or cook my own food. I can't even pour my own cup of coffee. I can't go to the doctor or even get a haircut by myself. The list goes on and on.

In thinking about it, what I have come to realize is that Matthew makes it easy on me to accept his caregiving. He never makes me feel like I'm imposing on him or his family. In many ways, he's allowing me to keep my dignity and self-esteem. For example, even though I haven't taught a class in 25 years, he still calls me Dr. Schoengood. We discuss politics and he asks me my opinion on many things that are in the news. He also asks me advice about his own career.

He focuses on the things that I *can* do and not on the things I *can't* do anymore. Things that I am good at like playing the harmonica. I learned how to play as a young boy and my family still asks me to perform for them. My niece, Jo Ann, often brings her clarinet over and we play duets together.

Recently, I fell and broke my hip. I was in rehab and saw how Matthew was running between his job, his home and visiting me every night. I thanked him and he said, "No problem, Dad. You took care of me and now I take care of you."

It's that simple and I'm grateful.

~George Schoengood

Commitment Doesn't Come with an Escape Parachute

Winners make commitments they always keep.
~Denis Waitley

I took my elderly dad out for a rare father-daughter bonding breakfast one morning while visiting my parents. Over the course of the meal, the conversation turned uncharacteristically serious, and I found myself asking him what he wanted to be remembered for after he was gone. He thought for a moment and then replied, "Sticking around to take care of your mother."

This was a man who had immigrated to America when he was 17. He struggled to get his GED in his adopted language, went on to become a fighter pilot during WWII and flew missions in the South Pacific, where he was shot down behind enemy lines and came home with a metal plate in his chest. He subsequently learned the electrical trade on the G.I. Bill and worked two jobs to put his kids through college. But he didn't want to be remembered as a hero. At least not a war hero.

Growing up, my mom was the one the neighborhood kids went to when they skinned their knees. Not only did she know just what to do, having trained as a registered nurse, but her gentle presence was calm and reassuring. And it was a good thing she had that training because she was always patching up my father. Those were their roles: He'd fix things around the house, and when he hurt himself in the process, she'd fix him up.

When they reached retirement age, all of that changed. In a cruel twist of fate, my mother became a paraplegic, and he became her caregiver.

She had been having trouble walking, and a routine surgical procedure to alleviate pressure on her spine from a malformed blood vessel unexpectedly left her paralyzed from the waist down. It was a major blow to the whole family, but an especially huge adjustment for my parents. My sister and I lived five hours away, so we were unable to help out regularly, and it fell to my ill-prepared father to care for my mother.

Now, I love my dad dearly, but he's not at all the nurturing type. On the rare occasion that he tried, his clumsy attempt to comfort you amounted to a heavy-handed pat on the back that would nearly knock you over.

My father's new vocation had a rocky start. Some of the trial-and-error home healthcare routines were a total disaster (such as the rolling commode chair), some laughable (duct-taped clothing), and the remaining attempts actually became workable practices. My dad would rig up all sorts of contraptions to make life easier for the two of them—from coated electrical wire pull-straps so my mom could raise the legs on her wheelchair, to a series of lights and mirrors that allowed her to catch a glimpse of her nether regions. He was really proud of his homegrown techniques, even declaring that he ought to patent some of them.

"The accident" not only forced my mother to withdraw from her busy life, it also required my dad to curtail his activities. He tried to keep working at the trade he loved, coming home at lunch to check on her, but it was a strain. The added burden of preparing all the meals, doing mountains of laundry, and assisting my mother with countless tasks took its toll. In moments of discouragement, he'd lament the fact that he'd been robbed of his golden years when he had planned to travel—but he never blamed her.

As time went on, he not only became her legs, but he became her proxy—going to parties and funerals he never would have attended otherwise, to "represent the family." She would grill him when he got home on who was there, what was served and discussed, and how everyone looked. He even participated in the local garden club's annual flower show at my mom's insistence—cutting blooms from their garden under her direction, building miniature props for the arrangement, and delivering the finished product to the church hall. For weeks afterward, he boasted about winning first place!

Despite my dad's best efforts, we almost lost her a couple of times. I believe she pulled through solely by the sheer force of his will. When she was in the hospital, he'd go every day to make sure she was getting top-notch treatment. He confided to me in an imperious tone that he had to teach the nurses there how to dress her bedsore and show them how to use the Hoyer Lift to get her in and out of bed. I'd witness him, in his tactless way, bossing them around: this old man with no medical training lecturing the RNs about the correct way to do a certain procedure. He'd sidle up to one of them, poke a stubby finger at what they were working on, and say, "I see you're using Baza [anti-fungal cream] on her. You've got too much there. You know you should just use a little, right? Because if you use too much, it slows down the healing. I only use this much—" (he'd make a tiny "O" with his thumb and forefinger) "and rub it in good. I speak from experience." I cringed at the times he stormed the nurses' station and demanded in a loud voice that my mother be given the Tylenol she rang for half an hour ago. Oddly, though, he was her comfort and the one she'd ask for—more than her daughters, the compassionate nurses, or the kind social worker—despite the fact that he'd change her TV to the station he liked (a boxing or tennis match) and then fall asleep in the guest chair, snoring loudly, while clutching the remote out of her reach.

He's been taking care of her for 23 years now, and his devotion has allowed them to live independently into their late eighties. Ironically, they probably wouldn't still be together if it weren't for her disability. I always marveled at how their marriage—which was never affectionate in good times—withstood this incredible strain and even became stronger because of it. The intervening years haven't softened him any. They still argue all the time. She nags him; he's gruff and unsympathetic. And yet, it works for them.

When people hear that my parents have been together for almost 60 years, they often say, "They must really love each other."

Love?

There are never any terms of endearment uttered between them—no soulful looks, passionate embraces, or tender kisses. Not even a warm smile. But every once in a while, I'll catch a glimpse of something... I'll turn as I'm leaving her hospital room and see them in an unguarded moment. He'll stop on his way out to look down at her and lay a gnarled hand on her shoulder. She'll look back up at him with serious, trusting eyes, and something will pass between them—something I'm not a part of and never will be. It looks to me like commitment.

And maybe even love.

~Susan Yanguas

Spirit of Love

Watching a peaceful death of a human being reminds us of a falling star;
one of a million lights in a vast sky that flares up for a brief moment only to
disappear into the endless night forever.
~Elisabeth Kübler-Ross

The day I met my future mother-in-law, I was exhausted after spending more than two days in airports before arriving in Beirut. Rafiq, my soon-to-be fiancé, paused in the Lebanese sun before we entered the mezzanine-level apartment to ask if I was emotionally ready to witness the effects of his mother's disease. "It's pretty bad, so be sure that you are prepared," he advised.

I was prepared for Madinah's baldness and lethargic movements, but what surprised me was her love. It flowed from her freely and created a glowing aura of warmth that enveloped me and drew me to her. At that point, she was still able to move around with a walker, slow but still capable. The brain cancer had not yet taken hold of her limbs. She was in bed, and so I crouched down to greet her. She hugged me close to her and kissed my cheek, "Daniela!" she exclaimed, tears running down her cheeks.

Neither one of us had known whether this day would actually arrive after my trip months earlier had been postponed due to the bombing campaign that Israel had launched on Lebanon only days before my intended arrival date. The cancer had progressed to the point where it had been unclear whether she would live long enough and whether the country would stabilize enough so that I could come. We were blessed to spend the time that she had left building a relationship that would give me a lifetime's worth of memories.

Over the final two months of her life, I stayed in her home and assisted my future sister-in-law, Isa, and Rafiq in caring for her. Having grown up in the United States, I was familiar with the practice of admitting ailing family members to nursing facilities where they would receive 24-hour care and tending. I had heard of people caring for family members in their homes, but I had never witnessed or participated in the amazing feat of love, patience, and endurance it required.

While caring for Madinah, I took my place in the family, carefully navigating the line between guest, family member, and caregiver. Isa was her primary caregiver, spending every waking moment close to Madinah's side unless work, errands or other responsibilities dragged her away. As her cancer progressed, our roles as caregivers were ever changing and evolving to compensate for her consistent decline in abilities. The hardest to cope with physically was moving her. The sheer weight of a human body when the connection between brain and limbs no longer functions presents a challenge, but the three of us worked together to move her to where she wanted or needed to be.

Our family members all coped with the frustration of watching a human life degrade in different ways. I would seek escape on social networking sites, connecting with my friends and family back in Minnesota. Rafiq would leave the house any chance he could, so as not to have to witness the decline of his mother. Isa, on the other hand, spent every moment that she possibly could at her mother's side. They were exceptionally close, having shared a bed for the majority of Isa's life. This continued clear through to the end. There were times where Isa would hold her mother's large body on top of her petite slender frame, cuddling her from behind, like a mother would support a toddler between her legs; the two of them sleeping peacefully with one of the cats dozing nearby.

There were moments of pure jubilation, too. Somehow, every moment becomes sweeter with the knowledge that few days together may follow. Opportunities for joy become as precious as the first raindrops following a drought, overflowing into puddles as our souls, like the parched ground, could not consume the elation quickly enough to take it all in. Rafiq proposed to me with his family and friends present at a surprise party he planned in our home. Madinah held onto the ring and gave it to him just before he took to his knee. When she was lucid, her memories were sometimes distorted from the tumors and the medications. Her face would light up with her beautiful toothless grin every time her eyes would fall upon my simple gold band. She would kiss my cheeks and my hand and bless us both together, sometimes multiple times a day when her memory was especially faltering.

For several weeks, she would request a Lebanese breakfast food: a sticky sweet covered in syrup with a French toast-like outside stuffed with cheese. Her requests would come multiple times a day, at all hours, morning, afternoon or evening; it was all that would satiate her hunger. Eventually, Rafiq would prepare for her cravings, rising early in the morning and leaving to seek out the vendors of the treat, purchasing up to six a day, as the three of us loved them as well. We would either freeze or refrigerate the others in preparation for her demands. Rafiq would playfully tease her every time she would place her demand—"Knefeh... where are we going to find knefeh at this hour?"—before dutifully warming one of the filling delights for his mother.

In her final weeks, we hired a home healthcare nurse to assist us in her day-to-day care. It had become too much for us to bathe her, and to manage the transfers should she need to go into the hospital. At that point, Madinah was unconscious, fading in and out, and uttering incomprehensible phrases from time to time.

I believe that caring for a loved one is one of the hardest things that a person can do, but it is also the most selfless act of goodness that one can perform during their lifetime. Just as no one questions the importance of caring for babies, so too should we recognize the life-giving quality of caring for those whose every remaining breath is a blessing.

At the end of her life, Madinah was surrounded by family, friends, and neighbors standing watch throughout the evening. We surrounded her with our love and warm conversations, her spirit enveloping us and pulling us closer together even as she lay silently in a coma. We huddled around her bed as she took her last breath, sending her on with our well wishes and love, and mourning the loss of her bright smile with our tears. I knew in my heart that the many days I spent in her presence had left me forever changed. Prior to that experience, it had always seemed as though death was something to be feared, as though being reminded of our own mortality is a threat too frightening to behold. But afterward it was suddenly clear to me that life was a precious gift, and that dying was as much a part of every life as breathing. The love that I witnessed, shared, and received left an imprint on my soul that lasts to this day, as I thank God for every day that I spend living, embracing it wholly and remembering how the cancer could not steal her spirit of love.

~Danielle M. Dryke

Dry Her Tears

Tears are the safety valve of the heart when too much pressure is laid on it.
~Albert Smith

Dani could not dry her own tears as she walked off the airplane trailed by the flight attendant carrying her backpack. I was allowed to go to the gate, which is unusual in this day and age, to pick up my 23-year-old daughter.

There she was, wearing flip-flops, gym pants, and a tank top. Never mind that in Springfield, Illinois, it was winter; she was coming from balmy Florida. These were the clothes her friend found that fit over her two broken arms, heavily encased in casts.

Sometimes small slips have large consequences. In Dani's case, it was literally true. Dani was an event planner. While helping a caterer bring in trays, she slipped on wet pavement and fell backwards. Both of her arms were fractured.

I helped her into the car and covered her with blankets. The ride home, after hours of flying, was excruciating. Looking in my rearview mirror, my mind raced with panicked thoughts of "How are we going to do this?" as I calmly told her how glad we were that she was home and that we would take good care of her.

The "we" in this case was an exceptional word. Thankfully, I was on very amicable terms with Louis, my ex-husband. It meant that we would work as a team.

Once home, I helped her to the couch and really started assessing the situation. Her left arm was cast from above the elbow, hanging straight down the side of her body. The other arm was cast at an angle toward her right shoulder, but she could not reach her mouth.

I thought, "Straws are the first thing on the shopping list." It took about two seconds to realize that Dani was as helpless as a baby. She would not be able to feed, wash, or dress herself.

We found a routine that worked for us, but those first days were filled with adaptations. Solutions had to be found to the challenges we all faced in caring for a handicapped person. Fortunately, Dani was instrumental in being able to help us learn how to help her. What a reminder for me that survival issues do not apply just to the sick and elderly! I salute people who care for those with physical and mental disabilities day in and day out.

It was obvious to her father and me that Dani could not be left alone for any length of time after she awoke in the morning. I sent substitute plans to school for the first few days, while Louis arranged to take vacation time from work. He would come to the house around 10:00 and leave soon after I came home. What a relief it was that he was able to feed her lunch, take her to appointments, and keep her company. We joked that television with Dad was watching the Food Network. Television with Mom was catching up on past seasons of *Grey's Anatomy*.

It was very difficult to dress Dani. The lower body was easy. Her arms, however, were at strange angles. Like a contortionist, Dani moved this way and that so I could get a sleeveless tank top on her. Ponchos that slipped over her head were our clothing salvation.

Soon after arriving home, we braved the cold, snow, and ice to get her to an orthopedist. I took one of my winter jackets and made cuts in the sleeves so she would have something warm to wear. The orthopedist recast one arm into a more comfortable position. She could wiggle her fingers, but not enough to hold a food utensil.

Dani had abdominal muscles made of steel. Hours of ballet had really paid off in developing core strength. She could lift herself up from a seated position without using her arms. What most impressed (and scared) me was that after a bath, when the water flowed down the drain, she would rock back and forth and stand up. Her first bath felt so awkward to me. My daughter accepted that I had to help her, but I was very self-conscious bathing and drying her the first few times. Together, we adjusted to an uninhibited manner of dressing and undressing. At night, instead of getting her ready for bed, I would dress her for the next morning so all she would need was shoes and socks when her dad came. We made arrangements with a hairdresser to have her hair washed every two days.

It was a very difficult time for Dani. She was in physical and mental pain. Thankfully, she could walk, talk, and think, but could do very little for herself physically. She could use her fingertips to dial an oversized speakerphone and to slowly tap out keys on the computer. She tried to be very brave through it all, but it was an ugly day when her boyfriend sent her a computer message breaking off their relationship. I was in the kitchen hearing the tap-tap of the keys and sobbing. My heart ached because I wanted to give her privacy, but I knew even in her misery she could not blow her runny nose.

After that event, she was in such a state of nausea, pain and anxiety that she lay on the bathroom floor and could hardly get up. It was as though a portion of her soul had splintered apart. After what seemed to be a long time (but was actually less than an hour), I took her to the emergency room. Once there, she was given medicine that dulled some of the physical pain, nausea, and anxiety.

It was very late when we got home, and I put my daughter to bed. As I gazed at her face, her eyes spoke volumes of silent communication. I knew I could not leave her room. Dani's raw vulnerability brought out a depth of tenderness and love that had been dormant in me since she was very small. I sat next to her on the bed so I could stroke her hair. I have no words to describe the energetic bond that took place as I held my vigil until she fell asleep.

A month passed, but Dani was not yet physically ready to return to her job as originally anticipated. As time passed, shorter casts were applied to her arms. She wanted to be able to brush her teeth and comb her hair before she returned to Miami. After a few weeks, she had to go back to Florida to coordinate a work project that was due. She could brush her teeth, but not her hair. When she flew back, she was able to stay with very close friends whom we all trusted to see her through the rest of her convalescence.

When people hear stories about the time Dani broke her arms, they ask how we managed it. I say it was difficult, but I think to myself that this experience was one of the most sacred, healing times that we had ever shared as a family.

~Jean Ferratier

The Gift

Gratitude is an art of painting an adversity into a lovely picture.
~Kak Sri

Ours was a love story. Thirty-one years of love, 25 of which I spent as his caregiver. Twenty-five of the hardest years of my life, none of which I would trade for anything. How could I have known during those lonely nights, exhaustion biting at my last nerve, that when this was all over, there would be a big hole in my life that his had so richly filled?

We got married when I was just 23, and he 20 years my senior. The age difference didn't seem to matter because there were so many other ways in which we were kindred spirits. We loved long walks, skiing, dancing, music. There was so much to share. The 20 years between us just melted away, of no consequence. We danced through those first six years together, raising children, having adventures, growing closer.

Then one day, this robust, healthy man came home from work, and I found him writhing on the couch, incomprehensible. He thought he had the flu, but I knew it was worse than that, and bullied him into going to the doctor. He was not strong enough to resist. From there, he was rushed to the ER in kidney and heart failure. The good people there stabilized him, and we began our 25-year odyssey with end-stage kidney disease.

Together, we learned how to perform peritoneal dialysis treatments at home. Later, we weathered a couple of kidney transplants, drug reactions, peritonitis, hemodialysis, a stroke, and so many other challenges. There was no handbook about how to gracefully go from lover to caregiver, how to reverse roles without bruising egos and hurting feelings, how to be terrified and strong all in the same moment because someone you love needs you to be the rock that grounds him. There was no manual that could tell me how to endure the loneliness that comes from being married to someone who often slept most days, tuning out the world, someone who could no longer give anything emotionally to the relationship, so taken up was he with his own survival.

Being his caregiver was like having all my deepest feelings exposed to the elements, the wind and pelting rain, the fiery ice and the lightning. There were no days when I could wake up carefree and excited about what the day might bring. I already knew what the day would hold. Every day took everything I had in me: all my strength, energy, patience, love, tenderness, as well as grit and determination I didn't know I had in me.

Through those years, my husband exhibited courage and fortitude I have rarely seen in another human being. My respect for him grew enormously, as did my love. I went from loving him to cherishing him. We learned to laugh at everything. We had to laugh. What else can you do when everything in your world seems crazy? Laughter saved our sanity I am sure, and to this day I am grateful for it.

I spent those years raising children, working full-time, and rushing back and forth to the hospital, work, and home, sometimes up all night with him and then off to the office in the morning. Occasionally, I actually wished I wouldn't wake up ever again, just so I could finally get some rest. I felt a strange mix of emotions — angry, sad, exhausted, cheated. I felt so inadequate, so scared, so lonely, and oddly, so grateful. I was filled with a profound sense of joy, dancing just beneath the surface, for the love I had been privileged to share, for how powerfully illness can point out to us just what really matters in life. I felt the joy of giving, of how I was filled with happiness every time I came into his room and he smiled, to see how his eyes lit up when he saw my face, heard my voice. It may have been exhausting, overwhelming, gut-wrenching work, but it was also an honor and a privilege to serve as his caregiver.

When he reached his seventies, he really began to decline, and I knew that very soon he would require full-time care. I didn't want to have to put him in a facility. I could not afford to live in the city I had called home for most of my life if I could not work full-time, and I could not afford to hire a caregiver. Besides, I had been there, hand in hand with him all through the years, and I wanted to be there when he took his last breath. I did what I had to do. I left my job, my friends, my home. I sold everything we had, including our car, and I moved 3,000 miles across the country to live with my daughter and her husband.

The move, while difficult, was incredibly cathartic for me. It was a process of reviewing a lifetime of possessions, memories, pieces of my life, and letting them go. Selling or giving away almost everything we had collected together over the years, millions of shards of what had made up our lives. Tears and memories, intertwined with joy and sorrow, placed in the palm of my hand, and blown away like so much dust. It was a time of goodbyes.

My daughter and her husband opened their hearts and their home to us. They were our safe port in the storm, and I will never be able to repay them for that kindness. There, my husband and I began our last chapter together. Caring for him became my full-time job. When I took him to his dialysis treatments at the local hospital, I had several hours to myself, and I often spent them walking in the park by the riverbank, trying to begin the process of separation. My husband's prolonged illness had given us a special closeness that many couples never have. It was like we were joined at the heart. I knew he would be leaving me soon, so I needed to slowly recover pieces of my heart during my solitary walks. This became my healing time. I'm sure I cried enough tears to water a forest during that last stretch of our journey together.

In those last months, he and I talked about our life together, his death, how each of us felt about it. I reassured him that I would be okay after he was gone, and he acknowledged that he was exhausted and would welcome the arms of death. And he did, just seven months after we moved across the country. I was with him, holding his hand, kissing his forehead, wishing him a wonderful afterlife, feeling gratitude for the caregiving journey we had shared. It was a gift, you see, because ours was a love story.

~Ruth Knox

24

Family Business

I think many women would agree that aside from our best friends and family, the other people in our lives that we confide in the most might be our hairdressers, manicurists and our fitness trainers. These are folks that hover over women for an hour at a time, making us feel and look better. And somehow during the process we tend to spill the beans about our lives.

During my workouts with fitness trainer Adam Cass I learned about a wonderful real life love story. It's the story of Adam and his two brothers and how they cared for their mother when she was diagnosed with a rare form of mesothelioma cancer.

Their mom had been a strong, loving and constant presence in their lives. Orrie Cass, affectionately known as "O" to her close friends and family, got married when she was 17 and had her first baby at 18. She was a vivacious woman who loved her family and enjoyed raising her three sons. But O's idyllic life didn't last—upon discovering that her husband was a compulsive gambler and had lost all their money, she went out and got a full-time job and supported her family as a single mom. She reinvented herself and worked hard to provide for herself and her boys. She went to work as a door-to-door insurance salesperson and she not only flourished but went on to become one of the most successful and highest ranking female executives ever at Prudential. She sent one of her sons to law school and helped the others get started on their careers too.

Her sons, Adam, David and Lewis, always had a lot of respect for their mom and how selfless she was to them. So when the brothers learned that their mom was terminally ill with cancer and had only six months to a year to live, they were determined to make that last chapter as wonderful as it could possibly be for her. I was so inspired by their story that I asked them to share it with you. Here is their story:

Joan to Adam: Before your mom got sick, she was at a point in her life, at 62, when she could have kicked back and lived a life of leisure. But instead, she opted to take over the daily care of your young daughters while you and your wife worked. In essence she decided to take the opportunity to be the stay-at-home-mom that she had wanted to be back when you guys were little. She got a do-over; she finally got that chance to be that stay-at-home mom.

Adam: Without us even asking her, she stepped up to the job. She was taking care of my kids. She wanted them every day.

David: From 7 in the morning to 7 at night. Four days a week.

Adam: Even on the weekends, she wanted them to sleep over so my wife and I could go out.

Joan: It's a true mother's love.

Adam: Absolutely. It started when Sophia was eight weeks old. Even if we wanted to get some help, she said there wasn't ever going to be a stranger watching the girls while she was around.

Joan: Things went along great for seven or eight years and everyone was happy. And then when your mom was 70 she got a devastating diagnosis.

David: She had a rare form of cancer, from asbestos. She had had signs but it went undiagnosed for five years. She never complained about anything so we had no reason to suspect anything terrible. My mom smoked so when we took her to the doctor we expected it to be lung cancer. We were surprised when the doctor asked, "Has your mother ever been around asbestos? I think she has mesothelioma."

Adam: She could have had surgery, but the doctor said, "She might only have six months to live. If it were my mother, I would do nothing. Just enjoy the time you have left."

Joan: So when you get that kind of a dire diagnosis, and learn that your mom might only have a few months to live, tell us what you did. Because all three of you jumped into action right away, and David, you seemed to take the lead.

David: We just decided to be ourselves, and do what we did best. I took the lead intellectually. I am a lawyer and I was the one who was most comfortable talking to all of the doctors and handling the managing of her care. I constantly researched her cancer and who were the best experts. I was able to get a better handle on the best way to handle our mom's illness.

Adam: We knew David would be the best one to call all the doctors, and he was incredible. There is such a specific skill to knowing how to deal with appointments, doctors, meds and the follow-through and follow-up, digesting all that information. It was mind boggling. He ran it as a business. David actually left his job and formed his own company so he could have flexibility.

David: I'm the eternal optimist who believes in miracles and I wanted to do everything possible to keep her alive. My brother Lewis was the pragmatist who brought us back to reality, and insisted on planning out every minute of her time remaining. Lewis was a contractor and used to pulling a lot of people together so he assumed the role of "concierge," planning dinner parties and cruises. He would book and plan every detail of the trips, he would take my mother to her favorite restaurants and, if she couldn't go out, he would bring her favorite foods to her. He made every meal a party; he made cakes and bought balloons that said, "Thank you Mom." We were always celebrating. And Adam was the touchy, feely, loving one, just like he had always been—the quiet "favorite" boy who was always by her side, stroking her and telling her how much he loved her. We each had our styles and our strengths.

Adam: I would just jump right into bed with my mother. That's where I would sleep. We always maintained the relationship we had for our whole lives. That's how I dealt with it, just constantly providing love and comfort.

Joan: And the three of you literally mapped out her remaining time on earth, and made it the absolute best you could possibly make it. Tell me about that.

David: We also kept her in her own home, as she wished, and we took shifts to be with her around the clock. We allowed our mom to still be our mom while she still could—we would go over for dinner and she would cook. At the end, we would set up a table in her room and would eat meals with her in her bedroom. Once she got diagnosed, Lewis, our concierge, began booking cruises; we went on a total of seven trips. We said, "Let's celebrate every day."

Adam: It was important that my daughters went on the last cruise. My mom always wanted to take them to Disney and the last cruise we went on was a Nickelodeon cruise. She even put off having surgery so she wouldn't miss that.

David: Fortunately, during that cruise, she was still able to have a good time. She never complained.

Adam: Her whole life, she never complained, once.

Joan to Adam: In fact your mom continued to be the caregiver for your two daughters even after she was diagnosed. How did you come to that decision?

Adam: We wanted to keep our mother on her regular routine so she could live her life and have happy normal moments with her granddaughters as long as possible. We also wanted the girls to be there and see everything they were doing.

Joan: How did you deal with your daughters during your mom's final days?

David: The week before, Ava and Sophia were at the house, lying with my mother in bed...

Adam: And my mom made sure that she looked as good as possible. Her body was shriveling but she still had her full face. Her blanket would cover her, but she was still dolled up.

David: During this time, she would give me specific instructions... "Make sure when the girls get older, if they want that extra dress, I don't care what it costs, make sure they get it and tell them it's from Grandma."

Joan: Did you take notes?

David: Yes we did.

Joan: It's interesting—you guys really did a lot of things, inherently, and you did them right.

David: When Mom died, I moved into her apartment. I don't normally watch TV but she said to "make sure you keep all the televisions so that when the girls come over, they have TVs to watch." So when she died, we bought all new TVs to keep her memory alive.

Joan: You've told me that even in your mom's last breath, she was watching over you guys. How so?

Adam: She hung on and waited for my brother to come home so that the three of us could be there in the bedroom.

Joan: It sounds like she wanted to make it as easy as possible for the three of you.

Adam: That's exactly what she did. We were disagreeing on how much pain medication was right to give to her and she didn't want us to argue about her, so at that moment she let go and took her last breath.

Joan: Having gone through this caregiving journey with your mom, what advice would you give others who are caring for loved ones?

David: There has to be an agreement between the people who are giving the care so you can operate together. Put the egos aside. Appoint one person to lead, who will delegate the roles so everyone is not competing. It works best that way.

Also we met often and went over everything. There is so much to be done it kept us focused. We scheduled meetings with each other and brought in our cousins and friends, to get different opinions. This doesn't mean that everything always went smoothly; there was some tension from time to time because we were scared and nervous, but that's normal.

Stay organized and on top of the care and always show the person being cared for that you are in control—it's scary enough to be in that position, but when you think no one is "handling it" then that is even scarier.

Adam: Let them know how much you love and care for them. There was not a day that went by that I didn't speak to my mother or say, "I love you." Just keep telling them you love them. If you can't be there, send cards or flowers or pictures—just something to let them know they are in your thoughts.

David: We didn't know how long she had. As far as we were concerned, we were in this until the end. She died 12 months after her diagnosis but if she lived another year, we would have been on six more cruises, and would have had many more thank-you celebrations. We understood the sacrifices that she made for us and we so appreciated it. This experience was life-changing for us. It definitely changed me as a person.

Joan: So many people struggle with how to interact with their loved ones when they are caregivers. It seems that you three brothers did a lot of things right in caring for your mom during her illness. You had such a positive uplifting attitude, and in sharing your story you will help so many others.

25

Trading Places

*We can only be said to be alive in those moments when our hearts are
conscious of our treasures.*
~Thornton Wilder

My mother was one of the strongest, most independent women I've ever known. Her mother died the day after her birth, and she survived a horrendous childhood, filled with two or three stepmothers and an abusive father.

Like so many in her generation, she became the single mother of two small children when my dad was drafted into the army during WWII. Only months before he left, they lost their third baby to whooping cough three weeks after his birth.

My mother struggled through the illness and death of my father when they were both only 41. I was married and had a baby girl at the time, so I did not witness firsthand how strong she really was, but I heard about it.

So it was with dismay and sadness that my two siblings and I received the news that, at the age of 88, our indomitable mother was diagnosed with stage III lymphoma. We had recently faced the fact that dementia was progressing quickly, and that the woman we knew and loved was disappearing before our eyes. With the lymphoma, her prognosis was six months to one year.

Since my mother lived in the same town in Southern California as my sister, Mom's care fell to her youngest child. My brother and I both live in Illinois. Our sister kept us informed of Mom's condition, and my brother and I both flew to California to be with her that last spring. When Mom's doctor told us that our mother could fly to Illinois for one last visit, our reaction was combined joy and sadness.

The three weeks my mother spent with my husband and me in our home is a time I will always treasure. There were moments when she called me "Sweetie," and I knew that she did not remember my name, perhaps did not know who I was. Only weeks before that, she had introduced me as her niece, even once asking my sister who I was. That was tough.

Often, as she napped in the rocker, I sat and watched her with tears in my eyes, knowing that it would be the last time she would be in my home. I cooked the foods she liked, ate with her, sat with her, and tucked her into bed every night. She had never liked showers, but one day I asked if she would let me help her bathe.

She thought about it for a moment. "That would be nice," she said. "I've been afraid that I would fall, so it's been a long time since I took a shower."

I don't know how to adequately describe my emotions as I helped my mother undress and get into the large, walk-in shower in our master bathroom. I eased her into a secure shower chair, padded with a thick towel for her comfort. I soaped and washed her back, and she said, "Oh, honey, that feels so good!" I swallowed tears as I gently washed her pale skin, taking the same care I would have for a small child.

During those three weeks, I did everything I knew to keep her comfortable. I reassured her when she could not find her way out of a room, calling "Barbara?" as she had done when I was a child and she could not find me. Her confusion progressed quickly during that fleeting time, and her short-term memory became nearly nonexistent.

I accompanied her back to California, reassuring her every few seconds that our plane tickets were safe. I left her in my sister's capable, loving hands and flew home, knowing that I would not see my mom alive again. Only 12 short weeks later, she passed away.

Three years later, following a hip replacement, I found myself in need of care. Luckily, I had close friends and family members nearby to provide the assistance I needed. My son loves me, but he was not one to provide hands-on care. My daughter, older granddaughter and my grandson's wife did the hard stuff!

But it wasn't until the day that my daughter told me she would help me shower that I realized I had, so to speak, become my mother. I took a deep breath, knowing that the moment could be traumatic for both my daughter and me, before I shed my robe and put myself in my daughter's hands. She had never seen me nude. Gently, she soaped and washed my back, and I closed my eyes, so very grateful for her compassion and willingness to help me.

"Oh, honey, that feels so good!" The words popped out of my mouth without a thought, and I was instantly transported three years back in time. For a moment, it was almost confusing, for I had suddenly become the older woman, dependent upon care from a loving daughter. I didn't let her see the tears that spilled down my face, but I could have blamed them on the shower.

There is no other vulnerability quite like sitting naked, and helpless, while someone else washes the body we have always cared for. Gratitude, however, far outweighed any shame or embarrassment I might have felt. I am still a distance from being the age my mother was when she died, but I'm aware, up close and personal now, how fragile we are, how quickly we can lose our proud independence, how possible it is that we can become like a helpless child again.

What makes it bearable is knowing, hoping, that there will be someone to love us, to care tenderly for us when we can no longer do it ourselves. I'm grateful for my "trading places" moment, for I now know how my mother felt when, for a short time, I was privileged to be her caregiver. I treasure that moment, holding it close to my heart, remembering.

~Barbara Elliott Carpenter

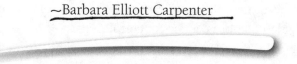

26

It's a Simple "I'm Here"

Life is what we make it, always has been, always will be.
~Grandma Moses

I met my future mother-in-law on a cloudless day 36 years ago as I stood with my wife-to-be outside a small, rural airport terminal and watched her mother's Cherokee Piper taxi down the runway and come to a stop, whereupon she emerged all smiles and shopping bags.

"I'm here," she said, jumping out of the plane and onto the tarmac, ready to hug. "You must be Thom."

When Lisa told me we needed to run to the airport to meet her mother's plane, I pictured Dallas Love Field, not Denton Regional... and perhaps American Airlines, not DillardAir. But here she was, Vaudine Dillard, in command of the skies, in command of herself, ready to embrace the next stage of life—the marriage of her only daughter.

Through the years, we would meet planes flown by Vaudine or her husband, Bill, even loading up our children to fly away with them with no fear or concern. The Dillards may have been the most responsible and stable people I've ever known: college-degreed, business owners, homeowners, strong people of faith, great parents, dedicated community leaders, adventuresome world travelers, dependable neighbors, a perfect couple.

I actually found them a bit terrifying as they brought some predictability into my own life. It took me a long time to really get to know Bill and Vaudine because I found myself peeking around the corners of their personalities, looking for the hidden motivations and manipulations that mar so many people. There were none; they were just who they are. Their lives were models of clarity, poised to descend into fog.

It's hard for children who love their parents to accept changes that are beyond the normal—beyond fading vision and hearing, slight and normal forgetfulness, the steady slowing brought on by aging. Love can cast a softening shadow that hides the early signs of Alzheimer's and dementia. Distance—Lisa's parents were in San Antonio, and we were in Oklahoma—can make it harder to hone in on the slow slipping as it picks up the pace.

When Bill was diagnosed with Alzheimer's, longtime friends of the Dillards commented that they had seen signs of dementia in Vaudine even before Bill. But such is the randomness of mental diseases. His disease moved fast, stripping away his understanding of the day-to-day. Hers chipped away in little bits, enhancing, in a sense, the day-to-day, leaving her content to do things over and over, repeat questions and be satisfied with repeated answers. Bill was ravaged; Vaudine was just reduced.

We sold their home of more than 50 years; moved them to live with us; moved her father to a veterans' facility; moved his body back home, most all outside his awareness. Lisa's pain at her loss is overwhelmed by the continuing need to care for her mother, a complicated process, as her mother seems so unaware of any need for care, something we realize could go on for many years.

At the end, Bill's mind focused on his flying days. Sitting in a chair by the window, watching bulldozers clear the land near ours for the building of a neighbor's home, he said, "I think they're building that runway a little too close." His words were few, his mind perhaps on flights of fancy.

It seems unfair that Lisa had two parents who found their lives drawn backward by the erosive dissolving of dementia. On many days, I—the much-loved, one-and-only son-in-law—feel the weight of unfairness myself, as if I got a little more than I stepped forward for when I said "I do."

But, who doesn't?

Lisa's parents loved me when I needed to be loved and accepted me when I needed to be accepted. They cared not so much that I was a bit different from them; only that I was the one their daughter loves.

So... fairness is not a viable part of the process in caring for loved ones who are diminished despite their best intentions, sweetest dreams, and greatest hopes. They become a little different, but they remain the ones their daughter loves.

On quiet nights, as Vaudine sits in the recliner where her husband spent so many of his final days, she reads letters to herself from a pilot she once knew. Letters from her husband of his days in Japan, full of exciting plans to raise a family, build a business, buy a plane, teach his sweetheart to fly. The fact that he remembered none of it in his final moments makes them nothing less as accomplishments.

We, the caregivers, are sometimes exhausted, scrambling around to meet all the needs of the diminished ones in our care. Get this; find that; repeat it all again. And then, in brilliant returning moments of the clarity we once saw in them, they help us understand.

"Do you need anything?" Lisa will say as her mother turns the pages of her book of letters.

"Only Bill," her mother replies, as she closes the cover and smiles.

If we've learned anything from caring for Lisa's parents, it is that enough love makes all things equal. It is not what you know or how well you retain it. It is not what you can do or what must be done for you. It is not what you give up to give to others. It's just love, plain and simple.

It's a simple, "I'm here."

~Thom Hunter

In Her Footsteps

Just about the time a woman thinks her work is done,
she becomes a grandmother.
~Edward H. Dreschnack

I never wanted to be a caregiver! That role seemed more suited to people like my grandmother. When my father died, Granny came to take care of my siblings and me while our mother worked.

I wanted to be like Mom — a tough women's libber who became the first female executive at a Seattle luxury hotel. Mom was out there. She knew people. She rubbed elbows with presidents and kings.

But Granny? She stayed home to do chores and take care of kids. How boring! And that's how she'd spent her entire life. She began by taking care of her father, a widowed Civil War amputee. For his sake, Granny delayed marrying and having children, though she had plenty of children around her, since she also served as a nanny to the offspring of her six siblings. When Granny finally did marry, her husband died young, leaving her to provide for three kids. She found an abundance of work in private homes, nursing the elderly.

Granny had no interest in status, fashion, or power. She didn't even know how to drive a car. Her only desire was to take care of people. Even when Granny had a chance to sit down, she was boring — preferring to read quietly in her chair. Her face would glow as she pored over the pages of what she called "the good book."

But I was ashamed to be seen with Granny. My friends used to stare at her bent back and her big, gnarly nose. She was embarrassing! I promised myself I'd never be like Granny.

Then, five years into my marriage, a neurologist looked at me with compassion as he said, "Mrs. Bradford, I've just told your husband he has multiple sclerosis."

Suddenly, I felt faint. Had I heard the doctor correctly? Had my chair actually plunged through the floor... or was that my hopes? Had the baby kicking inside of me just become abnormally still?

"Finally, a diagnosis!" my husband said excitedly. "All those weird bouts with numbness and blurred vision weren't just my imagination."

John seemed happy, but I had no idea why until he turned to the doctor and asked, "Okay, Doc, what can we do to fix this?"

John didn't know what I knew. As the granddaughter of a caregiver, I realized that MS has no cure.

Once we got home, my brilliant, young husband began an in-depth study of MS. After the bad news had sunk in, my dynamic, carefree John became a lethargic, angry drunk. He'd already been forced to quit his active job because he couldn't walk without the support of crutches.

I had no patience with John's alcoholic rage. Shortly after his diagnosis, I'd given birth to a healthy baby boy who had me on the run day and night. In addition, I'd taken on John's chores, from lawn mowing to snow shoveling. I had no time to join his pity party. Besides, I felt I was the one who deserved to be pitied.

Exhausted and hopeless, I asked everyone I met how they'd cope with my challenges. Fellow libbers advised, "Aw, leave the bum and take the kid with you!" But that seemed wrong. How could I leave the man I loved—my brilliant, funny sweetheart? He had to be hidden somewhere behind that angry façade. And how could I take my son away from his father when I knew the intense pain of growing up without a dad?

I kept pressing everyone for answers until an angel-faced neighbor said she'd been praying for me and handed me a "good book." I devoured it eagerly in my hunger to glean any tidbit of truth that might reveal why Granny had such a peaceful look whenever she read it. As I pored over chapter after chapter, I came across a totally fresh definition of love. It spoke of a love that's not about self, career, or ego, but dedicated to serving others.

Bolstered by supernatural insight, I began to have compassion for the angry drunk who'd replaced my husband. While I gradually shifted my focus from me to John, I discovered the joy of putting the needs of others ahead of my own.

In time, I sensed I should compliment John daily on his strengths—on all the reasons I'd fallen in love with him. During the months that followed, our relationship began to sprout new life as we both realized what a treasure we had in each other. Amazingly, John even quit drinking. Instead of using alcohol to drown his pain, he got high on being loved, respected, and accepted for the man who remained inside that failing body.

He returned to school to obtain his master's degree in business management, although it took three years and all the strength he could muster. At home, John developed into a stellar father and the one in charge of household business. After graduation, he became an advocate for the disabled, advising them on available services, training programs, jobs, medical help, and equipment. All the while, he kept them smiling, despite the challenges they faced.

One of his fellow MS sufferers told me, "About the time Nick and I start feeling sorry for ourselves, we see a smiling John zipping down the sidewalk in that big electric wheelchair with you, his faithful caregiver, by his side."

Me... a caregiver? What happened to my executive goals?

After all, I could have divorced my drunken, disabled husband and become an ambitious, single, working mom. Yet, I sensed a different perspective reaching out from the pages of Granny's favorite book. It had guided me to embrace, with unbridled love, the brilliant, funny, responsible man I'd married. His works of advocacy and his resource-filled writings ended up making a positive impact on hundreds, maybe thousands of lives during his 30-year struggle with MS.

Yes, my days as a full-time caregiver were often agonizingly long, and my heart broke as I watched John struggle through continual losses in function. Yet, I'm exceedingly glad I made a career of caring for my husband.

Now, when I think of my grandmother, I no longer remember her as a bent-over, boring, old woman. I remember her eyes. They beamed with faith and twinkled with a love she couldn't contain. Now I know why. Granny became wealthy as she gave her all to care for others. It's true that her wealth didn't come in the form of money. Instead, she gained rewards from helping people thrive through her selfless love and care.

Today, I'm exceedingly grateful for my grandmother's example. If I'd never seen her self-sacrificial love in action, I'd never have been inspired to reach out to John and help him rise from the depths of despair. And if I'd never seen Granny's glow as she read her "good book," I'd never have found her source of strength.

As I settle into my own years as a grandmother, I'm honored to be following in Granny's noble footsteps. She left behind a legacy I hope to pass on to my grandchildren—a legacy of unconditional love.

~Laura L. Bradford

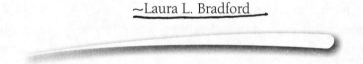

A Wonderful World?

The tree which moves some to tears of joy is in the eyes of others only a green thing which stands in their way.
~William Blake

I do not cry easily. But without warning, tears poured out one morning—the surprising release of emotion, cathartic and intense. I was reading a magazine article that my sister-in-law had passed along to my wife and me about another family's challenges—profound challenges—with two sons who were born with severe developmental disabilities. There was an immense power in the family's story. Their experiences had many similarities to ours. Their fears and worries for the future were much like ours. Their daily lives had to be ordered around their sons' unique and demanding needs, as ours are. Their careers had to be compromised to raise their sons with dignity and love, as ours have, too.

But what caused my emotional eruption was an accounting of the father's own sudden and unexpected shedding of tears at a pub with his buddies, witnessed by his brother who wrote the article, upon hearing the song "What a Wonderful World," the Louis Armstrong classic.

I hear babies cry… I watch them grow.
They'll learn much more… than I'll ever know.
And I think to myself… what a wonderful world.
… Yes I think to myself… what a wonderful world.

It's bittersweet, hearing that song. I could empathize strongly with the emotions of that father. It's a bittersweet life with a child who has disabilities. Our son rarely ever cried when he was little. He didn't… still doesn't… have that emotional ability. He never grew like his brothers. Today, at age 23, he's very short and slight, unusually so. He hasn't learned much more than I'll ever know. In fact, he seems permanently stuck in a two-year-old mental world. He doesn't talk. Still wears diapers. Can't feed himself without creating a huge mess. Can't dress himself. But he can undress, and will, at the most inappropriate times. In fact, he wears a shirt buttoned to the neck and a necktie every day, no matter where he's going or what he's doing. He doesn't know how to undo them, so they enable him to stay dressed. He pulls his mother's hair when he wants her attention. He hits me—because my hair's too short to pull—when he wants mine.

In short, he's a handful. He rarely stops moving, even in his sleep. He throws whatever he can and loves to hear the sound of something shattering on the floor—and our startled reactions to it. If he doesn't get his way, right away, and just as he wants it, he'll bang his head on the living room picture window or the family room glass door. And his head's gone through a few windows that way. He knows that will get a reaction right away. The floors are always sticky because of the things he spills. The walls are streaked with the residue of food he's thrown. All our furniture is banged up, scratched, stained. His loud bellowing interrupts our conversations. His relentless badgering for us to do whatever he wants does not relent.

He is obsessed with the beach. So he packs bathing suits, towels and sunscreen all day long when he's at home—every day of the year. He'll throw himself on the floor of the grocery store if we don't pick up packages of hot dogs or bottles of soda or—for some reason—packs and packs of paper napkins. In church, he claps repeatedly, disrupting the service, and squawks incessantly if he doesn't like the music. He demands attention and knows how to get a reaction—and attention—by the inappropriate and often dangerous and destructive things he does.

Yes, "What a Wonderful World" is a bittersweet song for me. Caring for our son and meeting his needs is a relentless and draining job. There is so little about him that makes our lives easy. There is so little that is uncomplicated with him. We can do very little that is unplanned and not well thought out. Little happens spontaneously. I've had to alter my professional life considerably because of him. It's hard to maintain and sustain many friendships because of the limitations his care imposes. Interests outside of work and home are nearly impossible for us. Life is absolutely harder for us because of him.

But, yes, in spite of all that and every other stressful, challenging day we have with our son, I can declare that it is still a wonderful world. In spite of our son's limitations—those he inherited at birth and those his realities inherently placed on us—there is still so much more that is good.

His eyes, steel blue and vibrant when they actually focus onto mine—so utterly rare for a person with autism—will melt my heart. His smile, with its wildly crooked teeth and food often caked around his mouth, will melt my will and warm my spirit. His laugh, raucous and uninhibited, generously employed and full-throated, will melt any anger at whatever frustration he may have caused moments before. And when he leans in to allow me to hug or kiss him, forget it. That alone will melt into my soul and leave me in complete and utter love.

I know that so much of what he does (and so much of what he cannot and does not do) is out of his control. I know that his developmental disabilities, severe and multiple, bring limitations to him and to us. But those limitations have truly shown me what it means to love unconditionally. To love regardless. To love in spite of. To even love changing adult diapers. And washing layers of fingerprints and mouth prints off the windows several times a week. And saying "I love you," and never hearing it back.

And, yes… it is a wonderful world. I never asked for it. Never would have wished for it. But it is our world, and as hard as it so often is, I still think it to myself all the time.

And that can easily, actually, make me cry… with complete and utter joy.

~Michael D. Gingerich

What's Love Got to Do with It?

If we have no peace, it is because we have forgotten
that we belong to each other.
~Mother Teresa

It was one of those rare fall days when the sun shone brightly, warming everything it touched through the crisp morning breeze. I sat peacefully on my patio as I sipped hot coffee, wrapped in one of my favorite quilts, and savored the cozy contrast of cool fresh air mingled with the warmth of the new day sun. With such a magnificent morning, the promise of a great day seemed certain. Then the phone rang…

I heard my mom's voice. "I'm not feeling very well, and I'm afraid. Would you mind coming over, dear?" she asked ever so sweetly. Well, honestly, it was my day off—and a beautiful one at that. I had a list of things to do, and my list did not include her. You see, I knew my mom as a master manipulator, and she knew it was my day off. I was certain that as soon as I arrived at her house, she would suddenly "feel much better" and want to go out to lunch. However, I sensed genuine fear in her voice, so I agreed to go over.

When I arrived at her house, I found her sitting on the couch, afraid to move or even speak. She was extremely pale, sweating, and clutching her chest. Terror filled her eyes. I will never forget those piercing, pleading eyes. Immediately, I dialed 911. When the paramedics arrived, they suspected she was having a heart attack and rushed her to the nearest hospital. After numerous tests, the doctors confirmed the paramedics' diagnosis—a heart attack, but with serious complications. Then I heard the words, "Your mother probably will not survive."

I was stunned! No one ever expects to hear those words. I felt overwhelmed by the myriad images and emotions that flooded my mind. I needed the world to stop so I could sort things out. But everything around me continued in a frenzied, chaotic turmoil. I turned to my confused, frightened mom to try to comfort her, but neither of us could speak. So much needed to be said, but neither of us knew where to begin. Our thoughts were interrupted by Mom's cardiologist: "Immediate surgery is our only hope of saving her."

The surgery lasted nine and a half hours. The rest, they said, was up to her. Mom fought hard to recover, as though she knew there was unfinished business to be concluded. Miraculously, she was released from the hospital two weeks later. However, her doctors recommended that she no longer live alone.

I considered numerous possibilities for her future care, but ultimately came to the realization that the task was mine. I would be her caregiver for as long as needed. It was the right thing to do. That was how she had raised me—to do what you have to do, whether you want to or not.

Had I known the extent of my commitment, perhaps I would never have made it. Mom lived 10 more years, requiring me to give up my career and devote every waking hour, and countless sleepless nights, tending to her welfare. The physical care was the easy part, but the unspoken emotions between the two of us ran rampant. The make-believe façade of our happy, loving mother/daughter relationship quickly came crashing down upon us with the agonizing weight of a lifetime of secrets, lies and neglect. Our history of pretension was undeniable, but this was the time for healing—for both of us.

The months passed slowly as I cared for Mom, with tormenting memories, long hidden in the shadows of time, surfacing to remind me that she had never really taken care of me when I was a child.

To this day, I cannot recall a single time when she affectionately hugged me or told me that she loved me. I remember asking her once if she loved me, and she replied, "Of course, I'm your mother," but she never said the words that I so desperately longed to hear. Sometimes, I would fake being ill because she would put her lips on my forehead to see if I had a fever, and it felt like a kiss. She never kissed me otherwise. When I was a young girl, I was repeatedly molested by someone close to our family; she chose to look the other way. When my stepfather called me stupid and said the world would be a better place without me, she never came to my defense. When I was raped at the age of 13, she suggested I must have done something to invite it.

At times, the tension between us was palpable. Here I was—sacrificing my own life to care for her when we both knew she had never cared for me. The irony repeatedly slapped us in the face.

As the months turned into years after her heart attack, we began to talk—long, healing talks about our mangled bond as mother and daughter. With every deepening and heartfelt conversation, each of us was set free, little by little, from the sorrowful chains of brokenness.

Finally, one beautiful fall morning, much like the one where our journey began, my mom died while I held her in my arms. The last words she spoke, as she looked deep into my eyes, were "I love you, baby girl." I knew in the very depths of my heart that those final words were not only meant for that day, but were meant to reach back through a lifetime of neglect and yearning to re-write our history. And I wept. I wept for the loss of the relationship we had finally attained. But, more importantly, I wept for the little girl still hiding in the dark places inside of me, who at last truly felt a mother's love.

I have come to understand that caregiving is more than the job of helping someone get healthy. It is something we do, not because it is "the right thing to do," but because it is the purest expression of love. And when it is done from the heart, we receive far more than we give.

When I offered to care for my mom, I never dreamed the outcome would be my own healing. I will be forever grateful for the privilege of caring for my mom in her last years. Because of this very special time we shared together, she was released to die in peace, and I was released… to live in peace.

~Sandy Adams

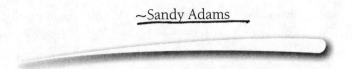

The One Who Was Chosen to Go

The heart that breaks open can contain the whole universe.
~Joanna Macy

This is the story of a mother. Her name was Tiep Du Huynh. She grew up in Vietnam during the war with four sisters and a brother. After the war, her brother, who had been in the navy, was asked to help a group of people escape by boat. His payment was that he could bring one family member along. They had to choose one sister and choose fast. Tiep was the youngest. She would go. She placed her life in her brother's hands and said goodbye to her family and her home.

After a harrowing journey, which is a story in itself, she found a home in Portland, Oregon. Tiep married and had one child—a son, Dan.

As Dan grew up, it was clear that something was different about him. He had autism. Tiep did the best she could, but it was hard. She became isolated in her community because of the stigma of having a disabled child. Her limited English prevented her from connecting with other support for herself, and from getting needed services for Dan. But life got harder still. Her husband developed severe diabetes and became an invalid. So she cared for both of them.

I used to see Tiep standing on the sidewalk waiting for Dan after school. I waited, too. My son, James, is also autistic. He and Dan were in the same special education class in middle school. Tiep stood away from others, looking small and sad. We never spoke.

Then, one Friday after school, the teacher brought the kids out and came over to me. Her eyes were big, and her hands fluttered. She blurted out that a terrible thing was happening to another student. Dan's father had died. But that wasn't all. His mother, Tiep, had just been diagnosed with terminal liver cancer. What would happen to Dan? There was no family to take him. Social Services was now involved, but there was no foster family qualified to care for him because of his disability.

I felt the ground shift under my feet. Somehow, I knew this story was meant for me. I tried not to listen. In my mind, I covered my ears with my hands and started singing, "La la la, I can't hear you!" But I did hear.

I thought and prayed all weekend. And then, on Monday morning, I did one of the craziest things I have ever done. I called the teacher and said I would take Dan. A few days later, I sat down across the table from Tiep. She was bone-thin. Her skin and the whites of her eyes were yellow. Her eyes were full of fear.

We had an interpreter, but I didn't need an interpreter to understand Tiep. I understood her better than I understood most people who shared my language and culture. I knew that every time she looked at her son, her heart filled up with love beyond measure and broke into a million pieces with grief and worry. I knew that she couldn't sleep at night, terrified about what would happen to her son when she was gone, picturing him all alone in the world with no one to love him or care for him. I knew Tiep like I knew myself. She was living my worst nightmare.

I looked into her desperate eyes and promised I would take care of her son. She cried. I cried, too. She had to trust a stranger with what she loved more than anything in the world.

We thought we had a few months to help Dan prepare to transition. The social worker helped us make a plan to begin with some short visits and gradually move to longer and overnight visits. But less than two weeks later, I got a call to pick Dan up from school because Tiep had been taken to the hospital for her final hours. So my first experience with Dan was to take him to a dimly lit hospital room and stand by his side as he said goodbye to his mother. And then I brought him home. He was 14 years old and had just lost his whole world.

That first night was chaos. I was not yet prepared for his arrival. I had no bed for him, not even a toothbrush. I didn't know what he would eat. His language skills were very limited, and he couldn't communicate his wants or needs. He became frantic and kept trying to tell me something I couldn't understand until he suddenly stood still, and I saw the dark spot on the front of his pants and the urine pooling around his feet.

The social worker came over that evening and certified me as a foster parent on an emergency basis. I made a bed for Dan on the floor of James's room. I sat with him and sang lullabies until he fell asleep.

I bought bunk beds the next day for him and James, and went by his house to get his clothes and things. I called the highest-up person I knew in the special ed department and listed the services I needed for Dan.

A few days later, I took Dan to his mother's memorial service. He said his final goodbyes. And life settled down into the new normal. Because of their autism, Dan and James were not really friends, but they became brothers. And we became a family. We honored Tiep on special days with prayers and offerings of incense.

So now I was a single mother with two autistic sons. What had happened to Tiep could happen to me, so I began to plan for their future. I wanted them to have a full and rich adult life that was not dependent solely on me, so that when the day came that I was gone, their lives would not be totally destroyed. After years of searching, I found a wonderful organization—Edwards Center—that provides lifelong care with various levels and categories of services to meet each person's individual needs.

Dan and James are now adult men. They share an apartment supervised by Edwards Center. They work at an Edwards Center work site. They take tae kwon do lessons and art lessons. James loves to go to the library and the zoo. Dan loves to cook and make origami.

They have such busy lives that they are sometimes too busy for me to see them on the weekends. I was taking them home once after a family dinner, and as I turned onto their street, James looked at me and said, "This is the treasurest place on earth." When I asked him what he meant, he thought for a second, and then said, "I have everything I want." I think Dan would agree.

Dan was able to go to Vietnam last fall. He met his aging grandmother and other relatives for the first time. And he completed a quest he had waited years for. He took his mother's ashes back to the country of her birth so she could take her place with the ancestors.

I hope that Tiep rests in peace now, peace she never knew in life. I hope I have honored and continue to honor my promise to her to care for her son. And I hope that when it is Dan's turn to take his place with the ancestors, she will be there to welcome him back into her loving embrace.

~Galen Pearl

Family Caregivers

Finding Joy

One joy scatters a hundred griefs.

~Chinese Proverb

Remembrance

He who sings scares away his woes.
~Cervantes

After my father's death, I lived with my mother for three months. Afternoons could be challenging for both of us. In the early middle stages of Alzheimer's disease, her memory and ability to cope could cause her to become confused and agitated by mid-afternoon.

One afternoon, I sat down at the piano. As a child, I had loved playing it. However, that was many years before. Now I found myself staring at black notes on sheet music—once familiar to me but now unreadable. Hesitantly, my fingers attempted a scale and clumsily felt their way up and back down the eight notes. Twice. The impromptu recital ended.

Two days later, I again leafed through the sheet music. I hoped to recognize something—anything—that I might be able to play. My right hand laboriously stumbled over "Bali Hai" from *South Pacific*. My left hand became the designated page-turner. I attempted "Younger than Springtime," my favourite song from *South Pacific*—a song played so repetitively many years before that I thought my fingers touched the notes before my eyes read the music.

My mother approached and stood silently, tapping her foot in time with the uneven tempo of my faltering right hand's solo interpretation of "I'm Gonna Wash That Man Right Outa My Hair." She began to hum and then very softly sing the lyrics.

"You still play well," she said, and sat down beside me.

"And I like your singing, Mum," I replied.

That was the beginning of our afternoon recitals.

Each afternoon, my mother's voice — at times, sweetly beautiful, and at other times raspy in its attempt to keep pitch — rose in volume. My hesitant fingers lumbered over black and white keys, my head bobbing up and down as I tried to match the notes on the sheet music to the piano keys.

On those afternoons as we accompanied each other, the apartment filled with — well, let us just say, sound.

After a few days, it became obvious that it was not just my uneasy playing or my mother's voice that was out of harmony, but the piano itself. It desperately needed tuning.

I said all of this to the piano tuner on the phone. We made the appointment. He arrived at the agreed-upon time.

He approached the piano with a quick step, took a cursory look at it, and made a quick comment on the general look of the instrument itself. "Apartment size, not known for a lot of sound quality."

He played a few individual notes and then a quick tune. He cleared his throat. His facial expression visibly changed, and I knew our talk would be about the last rites of the soon-to-be-departed piano. Tuning forks and turning pegs to resuscitate the soul of this musical instrument would do no good; its time had passed.

The piano tuner looked in my direction and delivered the diagnosis. "The soundboard is cracked; it's shifted forward, perhaps a result of the last move." His voice sounded almost annoyed that the expectation was for him to do CPR on a piano with rigor mortis. "The pegs are dry. The piano wires are so old that they will probably snap if tightened. It isn't going to hold any tuning for very long."

I told him I just needed the piano to stop sounding like a cross between a howling dog and a retching cow.

Silently, he began his work.

In the den, I turned up the TV volume to cover the yowl of the piano strings as they were coaxed to adopt a new and unnatural position. The TV volume went up and down several times over the next 45 minutes. Finally from the living room came the sound of a piano being played—not the pure sound and tone of a finely tuned instrument, but it was a definite reprieve from the disharmony that had echoed in the apartment an hour earlier. I smiled. The operation was a success. The piano tuner looked at me. He did not smile. He felt otherwise.

"You have to promise me you will never tell another person I am the one who tuned this piano. It is," he continued, "the worst job of tuning I have ever done. I don't think it will hold for more than a week."

Gathering his tools, he walked to the door. He apologised again and hesitated to take his fee. He offered to come back—for free—to wrap the pins and re-tune the piano if it didn't hold.

The piano tuner was wrong. For the next six weeks, the piano gave my mother and me its soul—it became a Steinway and served us well.

Over those six weeks, I began to read and anticipate the notes. My fingers became more agile with daily practice. And my mother, seated beside me, would sing—her voice strong, her memory sure. Sometimes, we sang together; sometimes, we chose songs from my father's sheet music. Other times, it was tunes from Broadway shows. We laughed a lot over who was the worse singer. But mostly I played, and my mother sang.

For my mother, those afternoons spent at the piano were singular events, each time new, enjoyed and then forgotten. There was no memory thread of previous times.

As I played, my mind at times would revisit those distant evenings when my mother and I held recitals in the living room, and my father, our attentive audience, listened to "his girls" as he looked over his evening paper, his gentle foot tap our metronome. On occasion, he sang a phrase or two with us.

For me, those six weeks were a shared time that blended into a peaceful, happy, and singular memory of time with my mother. During those afternoon sessions, I had my mother as I knew her to be.

The certainty of her future, which we would face together, was temporarily banished as the piano music and her sweetly beautiful voice filled not just the apartment, but also our minds, hearts and souls. It was a shared point in time that ultimately would not exist except in my memory.

I think it was the piano tuner's finest work.

~Wendy Poole

Those Sparkling Irish Eyes

A Note from Joan

One of my best childhood friends from my hometown of Sacramento, California is Michele Dillingham. We were in each other's weddings and were there for each other when our children were born.

Tragedy hit Michele's life when her husband died suddenly of a heart attack at only 50 years of age. Her two children were very young at the time, and since then she has raised them as a single parent.

Years later, when her children were grown and off at college, Michele took on the role of caregiver to her mother and father as their health declined. Her mother suffered from Alzheimer's, which of course made the job of caregiving even more challenging. Michele lost both her mom and dad about 12 years ago, but her role as a loving caregiver has continued.

With me living so far away, Michele has made it a point to visit my mom at least once a week back in our hometown. Michele showers my elderly mom with love and compassion. It has been such a blessing for me to know that Michele is there on the other side of the country, keeping a watchful eye on my mom and exchanging wonderful memories with her. It has also been a blessing for Michele, who once again has an opportunity to make a real difference in the life of another through caregiving.

So often, providing care and emotional support is looked at as a burden. However, those providing the care reap many rewards as well. The smile on my mom's face when Michele goes to see her really says it all. At 93 years old, my mom is dealing with dementia and no longer lives in her home. So she gets great emotional comfort from seeing a familiar face from the past come into the care home; it makes her feel like she is still connected to her life. There are no words that could ever express my gratitude for the time, attention, and compassionate care that Michele gives to my mom. I want to share with all of you, my friend Michele, a model caregiver.

My mother was a real Irish beauty and always quick to laugh. She was actually half Irish and half Italian but she favored the Irish side in looks, with her dark hair, fair skin and those sparkling eyes. My beautiful mother was also a dignified and private person. She loved being with people and she loved to laugh, but all with an incredible dignity about her.

St. Patrick's Day was of course always celebrated in our home, but perhaps the luckiest St. Patrick's Day was the one when Mom fractured her hip. I know that seems odd and even a little cruel, but you see my beautiful mother also had Alzheimer's.

Dealing with a parent who has Alzheimer's or even dementia involves many different steps as the disease progresses. It is very difficult for family members to watch a loved one go through that, and ultimately the child becomes the parent.

My sister and I were like most others coping with the disease. There was frustration, anger, despair, and sometimes even laughter. My son still remembers the time we were all sitting in Mom's living room and suddenly she said, "Where are my lights?" We all stared at her and she went on "These aren't my lights—where are *my* lights?"

Any family dealing with Alzheimer's knows that these moments happen.

Imagine what it must be like for the person *with* the disease… to not know where they are or even who they are. It's a scary thought. It becomes even more difficult when those you love have to be watched carefully so they don't wander off, knowing that they would not be able to find their way home or even let someone know who they are.

Mom, however, didn't want to leave home unless she was with either my sister or myself, and even then, the outgoing mother we had always known became more and more reclusive. On a few occasions she was hospitalized for one thing or another but she would become so agitated that they didn't keep her long.

Looking back on that fateful St. Patrick's Day, I remember how Mom fell. It wasn't unusual for her to fall, but it was unusual for her to be hurt. As we used to say, she had bones of rubber! But this time she fractured her hip, and it immobilized her with pain too great for her to move.

From the hospital she was sent to skilled nursing and it was there that they quickly recognized that she had Alzheimer's. Fortunately they had a wonderful wing that specialized in caring for those with memory problems. Mom wound up being there for the last six months of her life, where she was not only well cared for, but lovingly cared for.

Moving a parent to a facility or care home can be difficult for the parent because they are leaving the security of their own home. Mom would have been terrified if we had just moved her there, but because of her injury it was different, because the pain was so distracting and the people there were helping to ease her pain.

Mom remained bedridden because after the fall she never regained the strength she needed to walk. She had a lovely room, and in her mind she was in her own bedroom in her own home, which made her happy and was a great comfort to her. This not only comforted her but comforted my sister and myself as well. My lovely dignified mother was being impeccably groomed by other people, which in her case was far better than if we had been doing those very personal tasks for her.

Her memory may have been gone but the sweetness and humor remained with Mom, as did the sparkle in her beautiful eyes. Mother "held court" as everyone was eager to help her. For the last six months of my mother's life, my sister and I were free to simply enjoy her, and she was comfortable and happy. Seeing her eyes light up when one of us or her beloved grandchildren entered the room still brings such joy to me. It was such a special time and a time that brought my sister and me to a new closeness we had never enjoyed before—a surprising legacy my mom would so have loved.

A fractured hip in most cases would never be considered "lucky," but for my beautiful Irish mother that fall did make for a lucky St. Patrick's Day, as it gave the last six months of her life the dignity and happiness she so deserved.

~Michele Dillingham

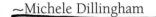

Thank You,
Mr. Carny Man

All God's angels come to us disguised.
~James Russell Lowell

Each year for some 30 years, I took my daughter Laura to a huge county fair. As long as it was physically possible for her to enjoy the fair, we went. Touted as one of the biggest in our county, this fair had acres of farm animals and dozens of buildings the size of aircraft hangars exploding with exhibits. Plus, there were miles of food booths, enough to keep us both stuffed with dreadfully wonderful "fair" foods.

Why do I say "physically possible?" Well, sadly, my daughter had a progressive form of cerebral palsy. In early years, with my help, we walked together after a fashion. Years passed, and too soon the time had arrived to accept that a wheelchair was required for our annual fair trip and eventually for all of Laura's activities. Our family—Mom and Dad and a brother—were blessed to have Laura in our home for 35 years. Laura gave a radiant smile, love, and joy to everyone who met her. More importantly, she opened doors in the hearts of people that brought forth acts of goodwill and kindness. Laura was a gift, and her stories are never about our time and efforts, but of countless sublime moments of spontaneous human warmth and charity.

County Fair Day was a special day for Laura and me. We visited every animal, every exhibit, and then, finally, the Midway, where we rode screaming, raging, swirling rides together. These wild rides give handicapped people such joyous freedom and escape, and Laura was fearless. They were gravity-defying, looping, twisting, spinning machines, often assembled in the dead of night by road-weary crews possessing unknown mechanical abilities, but Laura and I rode every one.

Then, when I had reassembled my essential body parts, we moved on to the carnival booths to try our luck. One particular year, Barney was at the pinnacle of his popularity. Sure enough, there was a carnival booth with monstrous Barneys lined up across the top of the tent.

Laura's eyes were fixed on the purple dinosaur. I looked at the difficulty of the "Win the Barney" contest. One needed to throw a ball, striking a complex of standing objects so precisely as to cascade them into specific numbered holes. If you somehow did this, bells went off, and you won—an extremely small, hand-sized stuffed animal, of indeterminate species. I read the posted rules. You had to accomplish this miracle of physics and eye-hand coordination 20 successive times, each time trading up for a larger stuffed toy, and only then did you win the giant purple Barney!

Laura's eyes were gleaming, her face determined, her confidence overflowing—as always, greatly exceeding her abilities. Laura had always loved the "throw the dart at the balloon" games. Over the years, her limited coordination had resulted in the puncture of several carnival workers, some unwary bystanders, plus one surprised and thoroughly innocent passing dog. Laura had not one possibility in a zillion at this complicated game of "chance" to win the Barney.

I looked at the "carny," the desperado in the booth running this game. The stereotypical carny seldom reminds one of a teacher or a preacher. It is a wandering, itinerant profession, a calling folks associate more with sinners than saints. This carny's appearance fulfilled all my worst fears. A novelist might describe his face as "weather-beaten" and miss the mark widely. This man was life-beaten. He was at least 30 years of age, and yet could have been 60. His countenance was a vast continent of worn-down crags and deep canyons, rivers of veins running in diverse directions. His eyes, bleary and semi-focused, resembled the tangled red spiderweb road maps of any great city. His motley clothes clung to a defeated frame, a frame not that of a man of substance, but that of a man who regularly consumed substances, legal and possibly illegal.

His voice, raspy and whining, insistently intoned, "Win Barney! Win the beautiful giant Barney! Give your kids the thrill of a lifetime. One quarter a throw. Step right up! One small quarter. Win the Barney."

Laura said to me, "Dad, I am going to win Barney. Take me over there!"

So I did, and then I stepped up to the derelict carny man and put down my quarter. "For my daughter," I said.

I helped her out of her wheelchair and propped her up against the counter. The grizzled ruin of a man growled out the rules of the game and handed the ball to Laura. She wound up and let the spheroid fly! It landed somewhere. All the standing objects miraculously fell, and moreover, fell into the correct places. "A winner!" cried the carny. "Wudja like ta try for a bigger prize, young lady?" he asked.

"Sure, mister," Laura said. "I'm going to win Barney!"

She threw again. Once more, the complicated set of objects fell exactly as they had to. The carny shouted, "The young lady wins again!" Laura traded up for the bigger stuffed animal. This discarded relic of a hard life handed the ball to Laura. Another mighty flailing heave ensued, and to the amazement of a growing crowd, again the cascade of objects found their mark. Laura grinned in triumph. Another bigger prize!

This went on for several more wins. The raspy voice pouring out from that battered face seemed to get stronger and mellower, gaining depth and character as he announced each step in the victorious march to Barney. A crowd gathered. Laura had not had much of a crowd cheering her on in life. But they were there now. And somehow, the carny made each throw seem a stunning act of athletic prowess by Laura, an achievement by her and her alone. He remained impassive and professional in his duties. How he was involved in Laura's success, I have no clue. But—he made it clear—it was Laura and her skills and her accomplishment all along.

Finally, he said, "One more perfect throw, and this young lady will win Barney!" Laura was easily several wins shy of the required number. But she made the throw. All the bells rang, horns blew, and lights flashed. The crowd went wild. Laura shone like an angel as the carny placed the six-foot purple Barney in her arms.

As I shook the carny's hand, saying "Thank you, thank you, thank you so much," a transformation flashed before me. For an instant, I looked upon a beautiful face, and into the deepest, clearest, and kindest eyes I have beheld. In a warm, soft voice, he replied, "You're welcome."

Folks are entitled to make sense of that as they wish. I believe I had the great fortune to be holding the hands of an angel. Looking back, I would guess maybe Laura knew that, too. Thoughtfully, I pushed the wheelchair away while Laura hugged Barney. Good chance I was standing between two angels. We never seem to get it exactly right—what an angel should look or act like. Thanks again, Mr. Carny Man—wherever you are.

~William Halderson

34

An Unexpected Bond

Our grandchildren accept us for ourselves, without rebuke or effort to
change us, as no one in our entire lives has ever done...
~Ruth Goode

"Not as fine as frogs' tails, my pickle-nosed sweet," said my elderly father when I called to ask how he was. At least he still had his sense of humor. But I could hear deep weariness in his voice, and I knew it was time for a change. Dad had been doing his best to take care of Mom for the past decade, ever since she first showed signs of Alzheimer's.

When I discussed the situation with my husband that evening, he said, "I think your mother should move in with us."

"I agree. It's the right thing to do. Dad needs a break," I said, but not without some apprehension.

That night I couldn't sleep, thinking about Mom and the changes ahead for our family. I was especially concerned about our 18-month-old son, Kegan. How would he respond to her? Would he be jealous of the time and attention I would need to give her? Would he be uneasy around her or afraid of her? How sad that he had never known his fun-loving grandmother the way she used to be. She would have read to him and played with him and made him feel special. I wished the two of them could have had a chance to bond. If only her mind hadn't been destroyed by this awful disease.

My mother arrived with only two suitcases, so it was easy to find room for her belongings. But afterward, things got more difficult.

Feeding her took a great deal of time and patience. I had to stroke her lips to try to get her to open her mouth so I could give her a spoonful of food. Once the food was in her mouth, she chewed, but seemed to forget that she needed to swallow. After I brushed her teeth at night, she would hold the toothpaste in her mouth and not understand that she needed to spit it out. One morning, I found that she had used her bedroom wastebasket for a toilet. Since I didn't want to put her in diapers, I began a regimen of getting up every two hours during the night to take her to the bathroom.

Mom, who had raised five children of her own, seemed to think she needed to watch over my children. Kegan was a blue-eyed, towheaded boy, as my older brother had been, and maybe Mom thought Kegan was her son. Kegan didn't mind—he was used to being supervised—but our 13-year-old daughter found Mom's constant shadowing annoying. Mom would follow her and poke at her with her finger. I suspected that Mom was trying to understand who my daughter was. When Mom wasn't trailing one of the children, she followed me everywhere, particularly hovering over me when I worked in the kitchen.

I realized that my formerly hardworking mother needed things to do. Soon, she and Kegan became a team. I gave them unbreakable plates and cups so they could set the table together, which kept them occupied arranging and rearranging items in random ways. When I did laundry, they sat at the kitchen table together folding the clothes. I had to refold everything later, but that was okay. Mom also kept herself busy tucking Kegan's toys in odd little places here and there. I don't know what was going on in her brain, but perhaps she thought she was cleaning up the house.

"Look!" Kegan might say, wiggling with excitement and pointing. And there would be his missing rubber ducky hidden amongst the leaves of a houseplant or his set of plastic keys dangling from a lampshade. To him, this was a fun game he and Grandma were playing.

One day, the two of them disappeared into the living room and were unusually quiet. I peeked in to see Kegan cuddled up next to her on the couch. She was reading a book out loud to him. Most of her words were unintelligible, but that didn't seem to bother my son. He sat with his thumb in his mouth, looking radiantly happy and content. Never mind that my mother was holding the book upside down.

In her pre-Alzheimer's days, Mom had been an elementary school teacher and had always loved children. Even with her disease, she retained that interest in children. Mom spent hours playing happily with Kegan. Once, I heard her call one of his toys "cheese."

"No, Grandma," he said patiently, but with animation, "it's not cheese. It's a school bus."

She didn't understand, but that seemed to be all right with him. He truly accepted her just the way she was.

One night after I had gotten Kegan and Mom ready for bed, I said to him, "Can you help Grandma find her way to her bedroom?"

Kegan took Grandma by the hand and led her down the hall, she in her long nightgown and slippers, and he in his diapers and plastic pants. On Kegan's face glowed such an expression of joy. He was helping Grandma. He was doing an important job.

At that moment, I had the sweetest realization: Mom was doing all the things with my son she would have done had she not been struck by this terrible disease, but in a completely different way. In her own unique way, she read to him and played with him, and here she was, making him feel very special.

Though I hadn't expected it, my son and my mother had bonded after all.

~Ann McArthur

35

The Garden

There can be no other occupation like gardening in which, if you were to creep up behind someone at their work, you would find them smiling.
~Mirabel Osler

Although he doesn't remember it — and Oscar Bailey seldom forgets anything — Theodore "Teddy" Roosevelt was still the President of the United States. Two months later, William Howard Taft would begin his term in the White House. The year was 1909, the same year Oscar, my grandfather, was born.

Over the following decades, the Delawarean from the small mill town of Milford would live a simple but fulfilling life that would intersect with the lives of hundreds. He would become a devoted husband, a father of one son and one daughter, a grandfather and a great-grandfather. Professionally, he would serve the people of the First State as their Head Forester, a job he finally had to be crow-barred away from in the 1970s at the age of 72. Even the Governor of Delaware at the time, Pete du Pont, commented about Oscar's commitment to quality and his loyalty to his job.

On a more personal level, Oscar enjoyed fishing, hunting and beekeeping, but he excelled at repairing watches and antique clocks. He was particularly proficient with German cuckoo clocks, and since many of his ancestors were from the Old Country, it seemed appropriate that these skills were in his bloodline. For many years, he enjoyed a good pipe in the evening, too, puffs of cherry-scented tobacco filling his den.

But the thing Oscar will be best remembered for when he finally departs this earth will be his gardens. He credits eating fresh produce from the earth, grown by his wife Mildred and himself for nearly eight decades, as the life-sustaining tonic that provided longevity of life and health for more than a century.

Every year, Oscar would lay out a garden that would rival Eden. Each row was perfectly aligned, hoed and plowed, fertilized and watered, weeded with care and pampered. Seeds would cultivate, sprout and produce tasty, colorful vegetables and fruits. He grew everything: strawberries, blueberries, blackberries, lettuces, tomatoes, sweet corn, cucumbers and squash, sweet potatoes, carrots, radishes, peppers, and eggplant.

One year, after retirement, Oscar was featured on the front page of the local newspaper for growing perhaps the tallest tomato plant in the entire state! A black-and-white photograph was published of him standing on the top of a six-foot, A-frame ladder, stretching his hands to the sky in an effort to touch the top of the fertile plant.

And then one day Oscar's wife died. He was old, frail, and failing. And sad. But also stubborn. After Mildred was gone, there was some foolish talk about Oscar moving to an assisted-living community for senior citizens, but he quickly nipped that in the bud. Fiercely independent, he insisted on living and dying in his home in the countryside.

Always a regular visitor, his daughter, my mother Phyllis, began to go there with greater frequency, often daily. She assisted in many ways, along with a part-time caregiver, who was also a nearby neighbor. My mother cooked, cleaned and handled laundry chores for Oscar as he sat there and read the paper. She ensured he took his medications in the proper dosages. She grocery shopped for Oscar and ran him to the doctor when scheduled. Mostly, they talked and reminisced. My brother, Michael, helped with the outdoor chores, grass cutting, stacking wood during the cold winter months, and feeding the birds — Oscar's "neighbors." And somehow every spring, Oscar managed a garden.

In his late nineties, Oscar's health had deteriorated to the point that he simply could not work in the garden anymore. Everyone thought that finally the garden had been permanently retired, the soil turned over for the final time. It made sense. After all, it was a lot of work in the humid, dusty days of June, July, and August. And Delaware was more and more prone to droughts, adding to the misery of keeping a garden alive.

When the signs of spring finally arrived one April day, with birds building nests while tweeting joyful tunes, my mother could tell there was something wrong with her father. He was especially quiet, reflective.

"What's wrong, Dad?" she asked.

"Oh, nothing…" he replied with an empty tone, his voice trailing off.

"Are you feeling okay? Are you sick today?"

He stared outside in the direction of the unplanted garden. She followed his aged, foggy eyes behind his horn-rimmed glasses. And then it hit her.

"You're thinking about the garden, aren't you?" she presumed with a smile. "Do you want us to plant your garden for you this year, Dad?" And then he smiled like a child surprised with an unexpected gift.

The past few years, Oscar has had his garden—fresh vegetables and juicy fruits to consume and give away to family, neighbors, and friends. His role, as a high-level subject-matter expert, is to sit in a lawn chair or his wheelchair on days when it's not too hot outside, and supervise, offering direction to his daughter and grandson. They are his laborers. He's the foreman. Together, thanks to family, it all works out.

When Oscar does depart this world one day, he has asked my mother to handle his affairs, which includes cremation of his thin, bony body. One of his final requests is that his ashes will be spread in the woods behind his house, on a small hilltop… near his garden.

~David Michael Smith

Soul Caregiver

Attitude is a little thing that makes a big difference.
~Winston Churchill

"Would you be available to take care of Dale for a week in August?" my mother asked. "You could bring the kids and stay up here in Lake Isabella or we can bring him to you. We're going to Hawaii, and Nanny is going to go, too."

Dale is my mother's brother and Nanny is their mother, and of course, my grandmother. Nanny was Dale's primary caregiver, with my mother assisting when needed. When they both were away, I was often next in line. I had cared for Dale during other vacations and while my grandmother recovered from breast cancer.

"Sure, Mom, no problem." I saw it as an opportunity to spend some time with Dale and my two kids, and earn a little extra money. Besides, spending time with Dale always seemed to correct my often-myopic perspective on life.

Dale had joined the U.S. Navy right out of high school. He has told me many times of his high school years—his love of music, muscle cars, and girls. He entered the Navy a healthy, strong, 18-year-old with his whole life in front of him. He came out of the Navy a 19-year-old paraplegic with a brain injury that would change the course of his life and the life of his family. And yet, I have never heard Dale complain about his situation or say a disparaging thing about the Navy.

The kids and I made the drive from the coastal communities of Orange County to the high desert in California where temperatures rose to over 100 degrees by the end of summer. Lake Isabella is a small community with limited things to do, but we were determined to make it a memorable week for Dale.

Dale's injury resulted in paralysis on the left side of his body, some memory issues, and a stutter. It did not result in a loss of good nature or humor! He is always up for a good time.

Sometimes we take Dale to Knott's Berry Farm, an amusement park in Southern California. I will never forget the time we took him on the river raft ride with the help of my husband and a park attendant who were able to lift him out of his wheelchair and into the raft. There we sat, enclosed in a circle of rubber gently bobbing along in the water ride and Dale's face lit up when we hit the occasional fast spots or he got sprayed with water. I will never forget the look on Dale's face when what seemed like 100 gallons of water poured over him from a waterfall that he didn't see coming because his back was to it. After the shock, he laughed with delight. Park admission — $30. The expression on Dale's face — priceless! We all wondered how we would explain to Nanny why Dale's wheelchair seat was soaking wet!

And good times for Dale are made even better by good food. Each year, my mother takes him to the Orange County Fair. Sure, there are nice things to look at, but what about the food? Dale is as good-natured and easy-going about food as he is about life. Fried avocados? You bet he's eaten them!

So we were going to do our best to make our time with Dale memorable that August week. We played indoor board games. We played shuffleboard outside. We sketched. We took photographs. We tried to stay cool. And we included a couple of field trips to town.

One day, we decided to go into town to watch a movie — something Dale doesn't get to do very often. It was my idea to get an ice cream cone while we waited for the movie theater to open. There we were, the four of us, in my grandmother's car. Chocolate-dipped cones sounded good — after all, this was vacation! Live it up! It was also August in Lake Isabella, and it was blazing hot. Our cones were melting faster than we could eat them. And because Dale only had the use of one hand—the one that was holding his cone—his only method of defense against the run of ice cream was his mouth! But even that couldn't move fast enough to keep him from getting covered with ice cream. Since it was my idea, I felt terrible! But in Dale's usual fashion, he took it all in stride. And after we got ourselves cleaned up, we had a good laugh.

As the years have passed, and many have gone by, we still look back at that week in Lake Isabella and smile fondly. I know it isn't easy to be a caregiver for someone who needs you to make it through the day. I watched my grandmother, and now my mother, dutifully care for Dale. I see the challenge of renewing one's patience and strength each day to meet the needs of someone else. And so I imagine it must be hard for a regular caregiver to see the blessings the way I do, as a relief caregiver.

Every once in a while when I complain about my day, I think of Dale, who doesn't complain. When I become impatient about how long it takes me to get ready in the morning, I remember the hours it takes to get Dale ready to start his day. When I wish that I had one more hand to get one more thing done, I remember Dale, whose one hand held the ice cream cone as it melted on his shirt. Perspective. Attitude. Choices. Yes, there have been times during my life when I have been a physical caregiver for my uncle, a paraplegic Navy veteran. Yes, he is reliant on others for his care. But I have come to see Dale's positive attitude as "soul care" for others.

~Lynne Leite

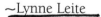

37

Saturdays with Dad

It is astonishing how little one feels alone when one loves.
~John Bulwer

"Hello, Twinkle Toes."

"Hello, Dad." I smile as he engulfs me in a huge bear hug.

"What's the plan of the day?" he asks as we walk into the kitchen.

After my mother died, the family had some hard decisions to make. Dad was in the early stages of Alzheimer's, and Mom had been his sole caregiver. We decided to honor his pleas to stay at home rather than live in an Alzheimer's care facility.

My cousin moved in and, with my sister, cares for Dad during the week. I am the part-time caregiver. I work full-time and stop by most days after work.

On Saturdays, I visit Dad and take him shopping. Luckily, my children are grown, and I am blessed with a husband who understands the importance of family, why dinner is always late, and why I disappear on Saturdays.

My life feels as if it's turned upside down; sometimes I feel I have no life. I dream about going on a long vacation or sleeping late.

Yet when I pull into the driveway, and he greets me with a hug and calls me by my childhood name, my heart melts. My resentment fades.

Before answering Dad's question, I glance at the calendar kept on the front of the refrigerator. All of his doctor's appointments, expected visitors, places he has to go, and calls that have to be made are marked on the calendar. His medicine schedule is also posted there. You could say the refrigerator is our command center, and it dominates his life and mine.

We sit down, have a cup of coffee, and he hands me the list. The list is very important. As a military family, money was tight. Dad only got paid once a month. When we wanted something, he would tell us to put it on the list. On payday, we would sit around the kitchen table and talk about what things were needed most. Shoes always won over a new skateboard.

In the beginning of his disease, he would make out the list himself. Now that he has lost the ability to handle written words, we write it for him.

"I need to buy a new pair of eyeglasses. It's on the list," he assures me.

We have this conversation every week. Dad always wants to buy eyeglasses. We had his eyes checked, but the prescription was correct. Yet he feels that if he only had the right glasses, then words would make sense again.

While I barely have time to balance my own checkbook, I handle all his finances. It took me months to get everything straightened out. I had to call people, cancel magazines, return unwanted merchandise, and convince my dad that you do not have to pay for address stickers that are sent in the mail. I finally had to take him to the post office and let them verify that I was right.

"Verify" is his favorite word and one I've come to loathe. Nothing is accepted until it is presented over and over. If you say a storm is coming, he has to watch all the weather channels to verify that he can't stay outdoors. If a doctor's appointment is changed, we have to call and let the nurse verify the new time. The constant verifying can be mind-numbing. I try to be patient and not let my frustration show.

I pray for patience every night. For some reason, if I tell Dad he has to do something, he will listen. Maybe it's because I am the oldest child. Once my sister was taking him to the dentist, and he wouldn't get in the car until she assured him that I said he had to. Of course, they had to call me at work so I could verify it.

After checking the list, Dad and I go to Dollar Tree. We had to stop shopping at the major department stores. He wanted to buy everything he saw. I was taking things out of the shopping cart and putting them back on the shelves. He would constantly complain it was his money and tell everyone within earshot that he needed that $200 electronic nail clipper. I got angry looks from other customers and ended up feeling like a villain.

My life became much easier when I realized he could buy anything he wants at Dollar Tree. I still cringe when he puts another pair of reading glasses in the cart. I have to bite my tongue not to remind him that he has more than a dozen pairs at home.

Flashlights are another item that captures his attention. At one time, I counted 23 flashlights around the house. He will explain that it's best to be prepared to anyone who comments, then offer them a flashlight.

I found the simpler I make things, the less stress we have to endure. A stress-free day is a good day for both of us. After shopping, it's on to lunch.

Lunch is the highlight of Dad's week. I skip the sit-down restaurants with their written menus and instead go to a small neighborhood Chinese buffet. Here he can walk up and down and look at the food.

The staff knows him. The head waitress calls him Papa and gives him a hug when we enter and when we leave. He flirts with her, and she smiles back. She tells me I am a good daughter and that it is a good thing to honor our fathers.

After lunch we return, unpack the car, and put the items away. Now it's time to sit and visit.

He's happiest telling tales about his childhood and life in the Navy, and I'm content to listen. I learn about the boy he was and what made him the man he became before Alzheimer's stole him away.

I often make a peach cobbler like Momma used to bake before she died. We pour cream over it and talk about her. For a few minutes, I can pretend everything is normal. Then he asks where Momma is and when she's coming home. Reality sets in. I tell him she's gone shopping and will be back soon.

He never wants me to leave and can't understand why I don't stay. I explain I have my own family to care for now, but I'll be back. We mark it on the calendar in bright red letters so it can be verified.

"I don't know what I'd do without you girls." Even when he's having a bad day and names are beyond his grasp, he always thanks me for coming by.

I don't know what I'd do without my dad.

~Jeri McBryde

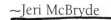

38

Anam Cara

The one you love, your anam cara, your soul friend,
is the truest mirror to reflect your soul.
~John O'Donohue

The day I first met my soon-to-be stepdaughter, Tiffany, she ran across the room shouting "Mary!" and flung herself into my arms as if I were a long-lost relative back from the dead. The Celts would call this a greeting of *anam cara* or soul friends. Indeed, as soon as that short, compact, 11-year-old body made contact with mine, I knew we were kin.

Tiffany was one of those "miracle babies" who had a one-in-a-million chance of living after she was born with one non-functioning kidney and one operating at only 10 percent. An early CAT scan revealed the likelihood of mental disabilities too. When I first met Tiffany, more than 18 years ago, her partially functioning kidney was starting to give out, her life energy declining. Although an inherently joyful child, she had dark circles under her eyes and little desire to eat. Right after her father, Richard, and I were married, she went on dialysis and was placed on a transplant list.

About two years later, I was on a business trip when Richard called with the good news. Tiffany was getting a new kidney! He and Tiffany's mom, Connie, were anxiously awaiting the outcome of the operation in the hospital's surgical waiting room. The kidney had come from "a large man in Alaska."

I wondered if Tiff would exhibit any of her donor's attributes, like other transplant patients have experienced. Would she develop a passion for fishing, for instance, or riding snowmobiles? The juxtaposition of this large, and in my mind, burly man with this fragile 15-year-old girl seemed comical, and yet something about the match seemed right. Time would tell, of course. Meanwhile, she needed to get through the operation.

"Connie and I have been talking here in the waiting room, and I just wanted to warn you about something," Richard told me over the phone. "The doctors are telling us that Tiff will need supervised, around-the-clock care for about three months after her transplant. Neither Connie nor I can afford to leave our jobs for that long. Since you work at home, you'll need to be the primary caregiver. Tiff will come live with us full-time."

"Oh," I said, stunned. "I see."

I simply didn't have the words to express my mix of emotions. On one hand, I felt jubilant about Tiffany's new kidney. On the other hand, I felt terrified by the thought of three months of caregiving. What sacrifices would be required? Could I even do it? I also felt angry with my husband for giving me this daunting task without asking for my consent.

I returned home, and for the next two weeks, while Tiff recovered from surgery in the hospital, Richard and I were in the thick of what we lovingly refer to as a "process." Although he felt compassion for me, Richard's analytical mind saw only one solution to the family dilemma and remained unwavering in his resolve. I saw the same solution and felt trapped in it.

On the eve of Tiffany's arrival, I still felt resentful. This sweet, vulnerable little girl was coming to live in our home, and here I was with a reluctant heart. I desperately wanted to reach inside myself and turn on the light, but I couldn't find the switch. That's when I prayed.

"Please, God, change my heart," I pleaded, "so that I may welcome this child with open arms."

Miraculously, conversion was immediate. By the next morning, my heart not only felt lighter, but I felt excited. As Tiffany crossed our threshold with an armload of pills and a list of operating instructions at least a mile long, I felt nothing but boundless joy.

I don't remember all the details of Tiffany's care that spring into summer, but there was certainly a pill-taking regimen morning, noon, and night. There must have been a regular change of dressing and inspection of her wound. I clearly remember the incessant reminders for her to drink, as the regimen was four liters a day. She recorded each glass of water on a chart with an X. The running question was, "How many Xs do you have?" usually followed by, "It's time to gulp!" because she often lagged behind.

Although her condition demanded a lot of attention, these trappings of care only deepened our intimacy with each other. I was still able to get my work done during the day, and Richard took over most of Tiffany's care at night. In those three amazing months that Tiffany was under my care, I honestly don't recall a difficult, frustrating or anxious moment. It was all good.

Tiffany experienced her own conversion when she came to live with us. Most likely, it was because "Lefty," what she called her new kidney, was cleansing toxins from her body like a good kidney should. I liked to think it also had something to do with the large man from Alaska. For the first time in her life, Tiffany loved to eat. In fact, she didn't just eat—she dined, she relished, she savored, all the while complimenting me for being an "artist of food." You can't begin to imagine the incredible joy I felt, preparing meals for a child who hadn't enjoyed food for years.

One afternoon about a month into her recovery, Tiffany sat at our round, maple table in the kitchen, coloring a mandala in a coloring book, as I stirred relish into that day's tuna salad. We chatted about all the things she was going to do when she got stronger, like swimming with the Special Olympics and horseback riding. We spoke with the ease of friends who had known each other for years.

All of a sudden, she looked up from her coloring, stared pensively at me with those sparkling brown eyes of hers, and said, "You know, Mary, I came here for you."

At that moment, time seemed to stop, and I knew what she said was true. Although it looked like I was the one caring for her, she was also caring for me. She came to add to my life, not deplete it, to return my love a thousandfold. Tiffany took my fear away — the fear of giving myself over to another human being, a community or a cause — and I found myself in the giving.

In the summer of 2008, ten years after she received the gift of a kidney, Tiffany passed away. She lived 25 years longer than her first doctors ever expected, and yet we all wished she could have lived, in health, for at least 25 more. There were many challenging times with Tiffany over the years — hospitalizations, procedures, dialysis and surgeries — but to this day, those three months I spent as Tiffany's caregiver were three of the most joyful months of my life.

~Mary Knight

Mi Casa Es Su Casa

God, with his mercy, gave us this work to do,
so we won't give up.
~2 Corinthians 4:1

Wisdom comes from unexpected places. My housekeeper held me by the elbow and said, "You are a lucky woman, *señora*. You know this?" I nodded in agreement.

She continued, "I see my father rarely. Each time I see him, I memorize his face; I think it is the last time. You have your father living with you. You get to see him every day!"

I looked her in the eye. "You are right, Angeles; I am lucky."

As the vacuum whirred in the next room, I thought how different her reaction to eldercare is from those of my friends who live in comfortable homes like mine. Just the night before at exercise class, one fit friend in her fifties commented, "How do you do it? It must be so confining! I know I'm not cut out for it."

Another joined in. "It would never work for me and my parents. We'd kill each other."

Tolstoy said that all happy families are alike, but all unhappy families are different. In some ways, the situations with elderly parents are different, but in some ways the situation between seniors and their adult children is alike for everyone. The bond between my friends and their folks may have been weaker than mine, or their folks may be needier than Dad. Yet, we all have the same obligation: Do we take care of those who took care of us?

I believe in living in the present. My sister likes to project into the future and ask: "What if this happens or that?"

My brother queries, "Wouldn't Dad prefer a retirement home with people his own age rather than live with you?"

Invariably, I answer, "I take one day at time, and the choice of living arrangements is always Dad's."

I sleep soundly at night. Do I trek out shoe shopping with gal pals often? Can my husband and I run off on a spree to the Caribbean or even to the Carolina shore? Is my lifestyle more cramped than before I launched into eldercare?

To these concerns, I answer myself: Didn't raising me hamper my parents' good times? Didn't they put their kids' needs before their own? Don't I want to treat Dad the way I want to be treated under the same circumstances?

Everything is finite. I won't be someone's child forever. For now, I seize the moment to still be a daughter. I live each day knowing I am appreciated and a contributing member of humanity. I am blessed in that I am able to stay home to care for my father, and that I have the room in my house to do so. And, even more essential, I have a supportive spouse!

Taking care of an aged parent has some of the same deep joys as nurturing an infant. Just as a new mom gets to experience the world with fresh eyes, now a different world reveals itself through the blurred eyes of an older parent—and what you witness amazes you. You see the kindness of strangers, the goodness of warmhearted folks, and the total altruism of people who hold doors, jawbone a minute, listen to an old story, share a smile, and act gracefully toward those impaired by age.

To be a caregiver with no financial reward is an invaluable service. To feel the peace, contentment, and righteousness of giving one's time and energy to the one who nurtured you is a priceless joy. Do I envy my siblings who are not responsible for the daily care of Dad and are free to follow their pursuit of happiness? No. I am the lucky one, as Angeles, with the wise heart, pointed out.

Mi casa es su casa. Perhaps the expression was first formed when an adult daughter said to her parent, "Come live with me!"

~Erika Hoffman

Stepping Out with Gail

Sometimes questions are more important than answers.
~Nancy Willard, quoted in The Meaning of Life,
compiled by Hugh S. Moorhead

My Reeboks awaken from their winter hibernation. It was a long, cold, and snowy New England winter. Although it is not quite spring, the weather has eased a bit so that I can resume my daily walk.

In the room next door, I can hear my sister Gail rummaging through her closet trying to locate her sneakers as well. "Are you ready?" I call out to Gail.

"I'm ready," she answers.

As we step out the door, I notice that Gail's jacket is not zipped closed and the lace on her left sneaker is loose. I quickly remedy this, and we begin our walk.

There is an eight-year difference in our ages. Actually, the age difference is much greater. Gail is developmentally disabled. Although she is 46 years old, she has the enthusiasm and curiosity of a young child and functions at about the level of a six-year-old.

We have a usual route that we take for our walks. Any walk with Gail includes a running barrage of questions.

We pass several people walking their dogs. "What kind of dog is that?" she asks.

"It's a German Shepherd," I say.

"Is it a boy or a girl?" asks Gail.

Granted, I've never seen this animal or its owner before, but Gail needs an answer from her big sister. To Gail, I am a fountain of all knowledge, and I do my best to provide the information—even if I do so with a little white lie.

"It's a girl," I say.

"What's her name?" says Gail.

"Gloria," I say. A few minutes later, we pass another dog, and Gail asks the same three questions. "Pug. Boy. Toby," is my rapid reply.

Babies are another of Gail's interests. Each baby she sees gets a smile. After they pass us, Gail always asks, "How old is that baby?"

I do my best to estimate the age of the baby. "Eight months old."

I could say any number. The actual number is unimportant, as she doesn't have a clear understanding of what various numbers mean. She simply wants answers to her questions.

I don't know when or how Gail and I ended up bonding so tightly. I think our chemistry was a gradual process that began in childhood and blossomed throughout the years. It may have started when she was a toddler and occasionally would have a mild seizure. I was a kid myself and didn't understand what was going on. I just knew Gail was in distress. I would sit by her side and hold her hand until the seizure passed. I guess that's when I started being a family caregiver.

Gail is thankful for even the smallest gesture. Little things like buying a package of her favorite brand of cookies. Hunkering down on the couch on a rainy afternoon and watching a movie together. Spontaneously singing and dancing in the living room when a popular song plays on the radio. No matter what it is, it brings a smile to her face.

I'm not pretending that there aren't challenges to being the caregiver to an adult with special needs. Every day, there are issues that cause me concern. I worry about her safety. I worry that she is healthy. I worry that others will be kind to her. Most of all, I worry that she's happy. I don't have a magic wand that can make everything better for Gail, but I try to make sure she has a good life.

Because of her developmental limitations, there can be some moments of frustration for both of us. Sometimes I can't figure out what's going on in her head, and she can't always express her thoughts clearly, which often leads to some tears. But her feelings are easily soothed.

As we pass a gnarly-looking tree, Gail suggests, "That tree looks like the one in the scary movie with the little girl."

The computer in my brain turns on and starts running through all the scary movies we've watched. "You mean *Poltergeist*?"

"You're right. You're right!" she says, delighted that I filled in the blank for her.

After we've walked about a mile or so, we turn around, and the questions resume. We pass a gray house, and Gail wants to know who lives there. We hear an airplane overhead, and Gail wants to know where it's going.

"There's those little men dogs," says Gail as two Jack Russell Terriers pass by with their owner.

"What's that squirrel doing?" Gail asks.

"He's looking for food," I answer.

"He must be hungry," says Gail. "Does he like spaghetti and meatballs?"

"No," I say. "He likes nuts."

After a walk with Gail, I feel like the smartest kid in the class because I'm able to answer all her questions. And that's all she really wants—just someone to connect with. Isn't that what we all want?

As much as she enjoys our walks, I think I get more from our relationship and time spent together than she does. Gail will never fully understand that going for a walk with her is quite simply the best part of my day.

~Maryanne Curran

The Perfect Solution

The only rock I know that stays steady,
the only institution I know that works is the family.
~Lee Iacocca

"Honey, I miss you and all the children," Mom said, calling from her small apartment in Wisconsin to my home in California.

"I miss you, too, Mom. I'll see if I can get up there soon." She had lots of friends in the senior living complex, but she craved being with family, as all mothers do. And to be honest, I loved those warm hugs Mom so generously doled out. I wished there was a way to combine seeing Mom with seeing all the children and grandchildren at the same time, but Mom's apartment was so tiny that I had to blow up an air mattress to sleep on in the living room.

I went online, found a flight, and clicked the "purchase" button. It jumped to the next screen and up popped an advertisement for a special Internet deal on a hotel suite.

I clicked on the ad. Three nights with two double beds, a separate living room with a sofa, television, and even a round table with four chairs for dining. It had a bathroom and a small refrigerator, microwave, and coffee maker. And to top it off, it came with free breakfast each morning and fresh chocolate chip cookies and milk at night. "You've got to be kidding," I said out loud when I looked at the price. It was affordable. My mind started whirring. Take Mom to a hotel, right there in her own city? But Mom's apartment was a perfectly good place to stay. Why rent a room at a hotel?

Then I thought "Why not?" And at these prices, maybe my brother and his kids and my two sons and their kids could join us.

Flutters of excitement bubbled up as I punched in her number. "Mom, you'll need to pack a weekend bag. I'm taking you on a mini vacation."

"What? Where?"

"Right there near you. We're going to stay three nights in a hotel suite. They even have a pool." I held my breath. At 80, she got around quite well with her walker, but would she want to pack a bag and check into a strange place?

"I can't remember the last time I stayed at a hotel. That sounds like fun. Would it be just the two of us?"

"I was thinking about inviting all the family—your grandchildren, great-grandchildren, and the newest great-grandbaby."

"A regular family reunion! I'll prepare food to bring along."

"This is a vacation for you, Mom. We'll pick up snacks and eat out for meals."

Over the next few weeks, Mom was like a little kid. "When are you going to get here? What time can we go to the hotel?" I loved hearing the excitement in her voice. I flew in late on a Thursday night. We couldn't check in until the next afternoon, but Mom couldn't stop looking at her watch as we picked up a few things at the store the next morning. Finally, it was time.

"Oh, honey!" she exclaimed as we walked into our suite. "This is beautiful. And so big!"

My cell phone rang. "We're at the front desk. What room are you in?" my brother asked. A few minutes later, they bounded down the hall. "We're here!" the grandchildren cried out, the tiny grandbaby in a stroller. Mom doled out kisses and hugs. Soon my two sons arrived with more great-grandchildren in tow. The kids instantly picked up where they left off. "Let's go play video games," one said. After everyone unpacked, we went out for a fish fry, and later, the adults kept an eye on the kids as they splashed in the pool. "Hey, guys," I hollered as I pulled out my digital camera, "get together in the shallow end." Mom beamed as she watched her family, all together again and around her.

The next morning, we met downstairs for breakfast. The kids chose from a variety of cereal, fruity yogurts, chocolate milk, and orange juice. Colton was especially fond of the chocolate-covered donuts. Mom loved the fresh, made-to-order pancakes with maple syrup.

"Can we go in the pool, Daddy?" Amanda said to my brother.

"Sure," he said. "Just let me finish my coffee, and I'll supervise."

Our day started with a frolicking game of foam football, and Mom even took a dip in the hot tub wearing her turquoise-blue bathing suit. I captured the action on my digital camera after the teens helped me figure out how to take video. After joining Mom at a table where she was drying off, I whispered, "Look, there's the new baby taking her first dip in the water." Mom's great-grandchild giggled and splashed in her bright yellow floatie as her grandpa held her tight.

We had remembered to grab Mom's digital picture frame, and granddaughter Kayla loaded it with photos that Mom could watch in a slide show, and even helped me download video from the digital camera to my laptop.

Saturday afternoon we called a truce to the water. "Everyone up to our suite for a movie," I called out. The living room turned into our own personal theater where we spread out on the sofa, chairs, and floor with bags of microwave popcorn, sodas and snacks, and laughed and giggled at the antics on the screen.

Later that evening, the adults reminisced. "Remember when we'd get together for backyard summer barbecues, fall leaf-raking parties, and ham and rolls after church on Sunday?" my brother said. "No one has a place big enough for everyone to get together anymore. The kids have missed being around each other, and I've missed it, too. This vacation has been perfect. And just think—we don't have to rake leaves or do dishes!"

Too soon, it was time for everyone to check out. We all hugged and kissed goodbye in the parking lot to shouts of "Let's do this again," and "What a great weekend." Mom and I walked back to our suite to finish packing and then drove the 10 minutes to Mom's apartment. She unpacked her picture frame and then turned to me. "Thank you, sweetie, for bringing me to a beautiful hotel and for gathering the family together. We've made some wonderful new memories, haven't we?"

I hugged her warmly. "I love you, Mom."

She laid her hands gently against my checks. "I love you, too."

Mom and I had been doubly blessed. We both got more than we could have ever hoped for: togetherness with family in a whole new way. And it warmed my heart to see her so happy.

We had so much fun that the next year we did it again—and the year after that, too. It's shaped up to be an awesome annual tradition.

~B.J. Taylor

Family Caregivers

Acceptance

*Happiness is life served up with a scoop of acceptance,
a topping of tolerance and sprinkles of hope...*

~Robert Brault, robertbrault.com

Make Your Wishes Known

A Note from Joan

I've known Leeza Gibbons for years. Our careers have somewhat paralleled each other as television hosts and working moms. Over the years we have laughed about how the press has always portrayed us as "the ultimate multitaskers who are handling it all" when in reality it's been a lot of hard work and dedication to have an amazing career while also raising our families.

When you are responsible for fronting a major network show you take on a sort of superwoman mentality. You can do it all and nothing can take you down. Well, almost nothing. For Leeza, she found it more and more difficult to put on a happy face as her mother's state of mind began to deteriorate.

Joan: When did you first learn that your mother had Alzheimer's?

Leeza: My mother was actually the one who pushed us out of our dens of denial. She was one of those strong southern women who could see a crumb on the floor two rooms away and whose disapproving look was the harshest punishment I could ever imagine. She ran that household as Chief Goddess In Charge! It was when she had paid the same bill three times that she gathered us together and said, "Something's wrong." Mom had seen her mother succumb to Alzheimer's after over a decade and I think she had that sickening churning in her stomach long before she let on.

Joan: How did you deal with the news when you first heard?

Leeza: Look, I knew what was happening, but I wanted to continue to go to that safe place that allowed me to come up with one excuse after another. "She's drinking too much. She's depressed and tired. She's not getting enough sleep." The pain of seeing my vibrant, beautiful mom disappear memory by memory was overwhelmingly sad. If Mom was in trouble, we were all going to unravel. She was the middle of the seesaw and I've been out of balance ever since we got the news. I tried to be the sweet, but stoic, daughter who was always reassuring and strong. I leapt into action trying everything, anything that might help, that might "fix" her so that we could all wake up from this horrific nightmare. My over-busy frenzy numbed the pain for a while, but when I laid my head on the pillow at night, I sobbed at the futility of it all. Mom was dying in slow motion and we were reduced to witnessing her decline.

Joan: In your book *Take Your Oxygen First* you discuss the depression you faced personally while caring for your mother. Tell me about that.

Leeza: Even if you have great coping skills, even if your family agrees on everything, even if you are without an ounce of dysfunction, this disease will rock your world in ways you can't even imagine. Everyone reacts and responds differently, but many are depressed and depleted. I sure was. As the middle child, I got good at negotiating and bargaining. As a TV producer and host, I got accustomed to controlling the environment and making things happen. None of it worked now, of course, and I felt like such a failure letting my mother down. This enemy spit back at me every time I tried to pull out my sword against it. I wasn't sleeping, I couldn't concentrate at work, I cried at everything and my kids had to deal with their mother pretty much "phoning it in."

I felt guilty that I couldn't make her better. I worried about her constantly. I remembered years before going with her to visit her mother with Alzheimer's disease. She brought flowers, music, pretty nightgowns, but Granny didn't react or respond to anything. I watched it all and agreed quickly when she would tell me, "If this ever happens to me, I don't want you to come see me." She repeated that request often and would ask me to promise her that I wouldn't "waste my time" visiting her. "I won't know you're there, sweetheart," she told me. When she got the news that she, too, had the disease that took her mother's life, she ask me to make the same promise. I couldn't do it and I told her "Mom, maybe you won't know I'm there, but I will know. And even if you don't need me, I will need you and I'll never leave you."

Joan: Is there a specific moment that you remember that resonates with you?

Leeza: My mother was visiting me at my home in Hollywood. She had always loved it there and stayed in the guest suite downstairs. One evening after dinner out, we came back home late and decided to go straight to bed. After taking a shower, I came to say goodnight and found my mother looking bewildered in the hallway. "Is there a room for me here?" she said. I knew from the way she was pinching her bottom lip and shuffling in circles that she was truly lost. "Sure there is Mom... let me take you," I said, to which she replied, "You are so nice. Have you lived here long?" My heart was bleeding at the reality and yet I still tried to tell myself she was just drinking too much and I had to do something.

I was ready to take action and lead my family through an intervention to get help for Mom and what I thought was her alcoholism. A few weeks after the incident of Mom being lost in the hall, I had arranged a phone conference for my siblings and my father where I had planned to coordinate how we would get Mom to rehab. My mother walked into the room to find Daddy on the phone and she was furious. "I know what you're doing. I know you're planning to take me to that Henry Ford Center!" As funny as it was, I only wish we had been able to take her to the Betty Ford Center. They could have helped her... people live through being an alcoholic. She wasn't an alcoholic; she was self-medicating with wine. The mental assault of knowing she was headed to the same place where she had lost her mother was just too much.

Joan: What advice do you have for those who are caring for an older family member?

Leeza: I think we are defined by the way we spend our time and who we love. When someone has Alzheimer's disease, it's unbearably cruel to know that those moments can't be called upon to answer the question, "Who am I?" I can't image what it must be like to live in that fog and to feel uncomfortable in your own skin. Your loved one can't join you in your world; it's important to remember to try to find a way into theirs. And that means leaving some familiar parts of yourself behind... like the parts that want to be appreciated and validated.

When someone is sick or forgetting, they can't give us the validation we need and want when we are caregiving. Caregivers have such a tough job and it's hard to do it without knowing we are making a difference. It's hard to do it when the one we love can't say "thank you." Feeling unappreciated causes resentment. No one's version of Happily Ever After includes being a caregiver. When we can't get the recognition we need, it's important to find ways to self-validate. I think it's important to remind ourselves who the diagnosed person was before the disease and to recall how, in healthier times, he or she would be grateful.

Joan: Has this situation given you an opportunity to have a closer relationship with someone in your family—for example, a sibling? In what ways?

Leeza: We were so blessed to have my mother's "marching orders" guide our actions. We never fought over what was right for Mom… we knew. She made certain of that. I suppose it was because she and her sister fought over what was best for their mom, that she didn't want us to go through that. My aunt had promised Granny that she would "never put her in a home," that she could always stay with her. Well, near the end, she was not able to care for Granny, not able to tend to her needs or even keep her safe. My mom insisted that Granny go to a skilled nursing setting where she would be cared for around the clock, but I know it broke my aunt's heart.

To feel guilt over a broken promise is a horrible thing (even if it is the right thing). So, Mom told us, "When I can no longer call you by name, I don't want to live with any of you. Got that, Leeza? Not with your sister, your brother, not with you. And you have to help Daddy know when it's time to let me go." She was courageous and thoughtful beyond belief.

As a result, our family, while stressed and frustrated during the experience, had a wonderful opportunity to be there for each other. We could accept what each person was able to bring to the table, knowing we each had limitations. We didn't blame and shame each other—we really did work together, cry together, and ultimately make some degree of peace with our reality.

Joan: Was there a bright side in your experience?

Leeza: Mom's disease demanded that I slow down, acknowledge my feelings and be more fully present. When language is taken out of the equation, and when there is no familiar backstory or history you can share with another person, you can't fall into old patterns of avoidance. I learned to focus not so much on what Mom couldn't do, but to celebrate the things she could do.

When she was having a good day, what I called a little "kiss from the angels," I was able to be grateful for that. I learned that we are all responsible for the energy we bring to any situation, so I am now much more aware of what I put out into the world.

I believe that while my mother may not have known WHO I was, she was aware that I represented love and safety, so I learned to make sure I was resonating that when I was with her. I told my kids, "Love transcends everything and a heart never forgets."

We get so uncomfortable with people who are incapacitated or different. We don't know how to act or what to say. I hope I learned some empathy and I realized that just being present in silence with someone is powerful and beautiful. I learned not to be afraid of the "dead-space," but to recognize that bringing my love and intention was enough.

Joan: In looking back, is there anything you would have done differently?

Leeza: I don't live in regret, but I realize that I wasted precious time trying to find an answer. While I was making hundreds of phone calls, doing massive research to find clinical trials, exploring and investigating ANYTHING that I thought would help, my mom was slipping further and further away. During some of the periods of her highest cognitive functioning, I was off chasing windmills. Oh, I was doing it for the right reason. I mean, I really DID think I could find something to make a difference. If I could get back those months, I would have spent them in moments with her that were not focused on the disease. It defined all of us, and we could have left more time for laughter and lightness.

I also wish I had more on-camera memories from my mom. I treasure everything I have now that includes the sound of her voice. I didn't realize she would go silent so soon. I wish I had her teach me every recipe she ever made, and share with me every secret she carried around for decades. I'm lucky that I was SO close to my mother—we traveled all over together—she was my best friend. There was nothing left unsaid between us, but I would love to have her narrative to all of the moments and memories that we shared.

Mom and Dad were married 55 years. On their 25th wedding anniversary, they got a bottle of champagne and a box of all their love letters. They read them one by one in front of a fire. After the words were spoken out loud, they burned the letters. Daddy said the idea was that the two of them would never forget those words—that they would live on in their hearts forever.

My mother forgot the words in those love letters, she forgot that she was in love and married and had children and grandchildren and a rich, wonderful life. How I wish I had those letters.

Joan: What advice will you pass on to your own children if something happens to you?

Leeza: I am not one who borrows tomorrow's trouble today. Yet, I am not naïve. I tell my kids that the reason I am such an advocate in this field is to honor my mom's legacy and to ensure that I do everything I can in my lifetime to scratch the track of this story for our family. I have prepared all of the legal documentation along with my personal wishes to ensure that if and when anything happens to me, they will not have to worry about that painful and burdensome part.

They know that I do everything I can to safeguard my health and manage my stress. Other than that, I believe we get what we focus on. I focus on staying physically fit and mentally active till I'm 100!

Mom gave me simple advice: "Show up, do your best and then let go of the rest." I can't really improve upon that!

Bad news has no regard for timing. Your bubble of domestic bliss is not immune, nor is your job or career. I was happily mothering my children and producing and hosting my own talk show on Paramount's Stage 26 when Mom's stage went dark. My anxiety spread to every aspect of my life and as much as I tried to present a façade of calm and acceptance, my persona never lasted past my driveway, and once home I became as tightly wound up as an angry fist. I snapped at the kids, withdrew from my husband and stayed up until dawn searching and searching for the latest treatments, the slimmest hope.

As Mom declined, I was trapped on a tilt-a-whirl of emotion. I managed to convince myself that if I just did more, she would be okay. The talk show ended its run and I immediately went on to the next stop on my career train, hosting the nightly entertainment news magazine *Extra*. I was all coifed and poised in front of the camera as I delivered the latest celebrity headlines, but the minute the lights went out on the stage, I fell apart. I spent most afternoons leaving through the back door of the lot to wander the neighborhood streets trying to reclaim some control over myself. But bad news can't be controlled and I realized that I was no match for its increasing shadow over my life. My marriage was strained to the breaking point and I was depressed. I needed to let go of the way things were and accept this beast, which had pulled up a chair to my dinner table.

I sought the help of a therapist. It turned out to be more than a lifeline, it was the exploration I needed to reclaim my sanity. Robert, my therapist, provided a safe sanctuary in which to share my feelings. Jamie Huysman, the co-author of my book, was my tether to what would become a new life and a new sense of purpose. He was the friend who always had time for me, who never judged and who always reminded me to be kind to myself. When I was unsure, he was certain. When I was a squishy ball of frayed nerves, he was solid, strong and firm in his belief that I could make a difference. Jamie showed me how to fulfill the promise I made to my mother, to tell her story so that others might be helped and inspired.

Role Reversal

First we are children to our parents, then parents to our children,
then parents to our parents, then children to our children.
~Milton Greenblatt

"I don't want to go." Nan pursed her lips in a pout.

"You'll have a good time."

"Do I have to?" She looked at me with pleading eyes.

I sighed. "Just try it."

It was a classic "first day of school" conversation—an annual ritual for parents and children all over the world.

"But I don't know anybody there." She turned her head to stare out the window at the passing scenery.

My heart broke as I heard the fear in her voice. What could I say to reassure her? "You'll meet new friends. You'll have fun, I promise."

"No, I won't." Unconvinced, she folded her arms across her chest and sulked without a word for the rest of the ride.

A typical conversation on the first day of school. But this day was far from typical. Now I was the "parent," and the "child" was my mother-in-law—77 years old, and the victim of Alzheimer's disease. Nan lived with us, but the stress of never being able to leave her alone required some changes in our family routine.

We were on our way to Nan's first day at the Alzheimer's Day Care Center, a day care program for patients suffering from the debilitating effects of progressive memory loss. The program was designed to help stimulate the patient's remaining cognitive skills while providing respite care to assist the family.

I found a parking space near the entrance and coaxed her out of the car. Nan cast an apprehensive look around. I prepared myself for additional protests, but she didn't say anything else. Instead, she silently walked with me to the building. The program administrator greeted us at the door with a cheerful welcome and led us through a hallway toward the sound of lively voices.

A smiling "teacher" led Nan into a festive room and introduced her to the other participants. I started to follow them, but the administrator, whom I had met during the registration process a week earlier, stopped me. "Don't worry. She'll be fine."

Her reassurance was as ineffective as mine had been in the car with Nan.

"She didn't want to come." I directed my words to the administrator, but my eyes were trained on the closed door. "I think she might be afraid."

"That's to be expected on the first day. This involves a change for her, and change is especially difficult for patients with Alzheimer's. But she'll make friends, and we'll engage her in activities that will interest her. She'll have a good time, and in a few days we'll be part of her new routine."

I remained skeptical. "Maybe I should go in with her to make sure she's okay, or at least stay for a while, just in case something goes wrong."

"You can watch through the window for a few minutes if you want, but it would be better if she doesn't see you. Why don't you go enjoy your day? We'll call you if we have any problems." She gently ushered me away from the door, treating me like the overprotective parent of a kindergarten child.

Enjoying the day was easier said than done. Although we appreciated the opportunity to run a few errands and have a quiet lunch together, my husband and I spent most of the day second-guessing ourselves. Was she having a good time? Would she be angry with us? Was she cooperating with the staff? Did we do the right thing?

Despite our worries, the six hours flew by, and it was time to pick her up. Russ and I waited in the hall and watched in amazement as a smiling Nan stepped through the doorway.

"Bye!" she called out as she turned to wave to her new friends. "See you later."

"Sounds like you had fun today," I said.

"I did. I even met a woman who was in the army with me."

"Really? What's her name?"

"I don't know. But we were in the army together. And there was someone else there who also said she was in the army with us, but I don't remember the second lady—only the first one."

Life had changed dramatically since "I don't know" and "I don't remember" became an integral part of Nan's vocabulary. Memories are a strange thing. We can't see them or touch them, yet who are we when they're gone?

Nan couldn't remember the near past. She couldn't recall what she last ate or when she ate it. She didn't remember when or whether she had taken her medications. She had forgotten how to dress herself and could no longer care for her own needs. She didn't know the current day, month, or year.

But she loved to talk about what she could remember: home milk delivery, green stamps, Lawrence Welk, Jack Benny, her 1951 DeSoto, neighbors who never locked their doors, and gas that cost 28 cents per gallon. She was proud to have been a WAC in the U.S. Army, but she did not consider herself to be a trailblazer or a feminist. Later, as a single mom, Nan worked full-time in the healthcare field while raising her son and caring for her disabled father.

Nan's memory of things long past was sharp and bright as she recalled details buried in the recesses of her mind. Listless conversations about current events transformed into vivid descriptions of experiences from long ago as if they had occurred only yesterday. Her animated stories opened a window into another time and place, and I enjoyed following her into a world very different from my own.

"Will I be coming here again?"

Her question brought me back to the present. "Do you want to?"

"Yes. My friends from the army will be there. I told them I would bring pictures with me."

Our role reversal was complete… and the first day of school was a success.

~Ava Pennington

Can I Do This?

To a father growing old nothing is dearer than a daughter.
~Euripides

My dad and I had never been close. He was a funny old man and, honestly, he embarrassed me. When I was a teenager, I was sure he was way weirder than my friends' dads, with his short, stout body, curly white hair, silly beard, and nerdy glasses. His awkwardness at conversation didn't help.

When I became a mother, I realized how much work it is to be a parent, and my respect for him rose. Still, though, when we visited him, the conversation was awkward. I felt like we never got anywhere meaningful.

And now that he'd been diagnosed with liver cancer and was probably dying, I said he could come and live with me. My older sister was always the one to take on the "hard stuff" in the family, and I wanted to prove that I could do it, too.

My husband, our two young children and I opened our home to my dad one day in March. My brother drove him up, dropped him off, and wished me good luck before he drove the two hours to the town where he and my sister lived. He was as surprised as the rest of the family that I, the baby of the family, a 30-something baby, was going to do this. Even my mom, long divorced from this little old man, was worried it would be too much for me.

I seriously had no idea how hard it would be. We set up a room for him off the kitchen. He settled in okay, enjoying his computer, spending time reading while the children played with their toys on his floor, and eating our good food. And, oh, how he loved to eat. At first, it wasn't a big deal. What was one more plate to fill? But my kids were still young. They needed meals, snacks, monitoring and attention—constant (it seemed) attention.

"Mommy, Max is writing on the floor!"

"Mommy, I'm a fireman!" (Max pours water on the couch, which is apparently on fire.)

"Mommy, I fell!"

"Mommy, I'm hungry!"

"Mommy, I want you!"

I was used to all that. It had been my life for the past six years. It was hard, it often wasn't fun, but it's what I'd signed up for, and I did it as well as I could. But now I had another person in my care 24/7.

"So, what's for lunch?" My dad would sit at the table and watch me cook. He was too weak to help, but happily able to anticipate eating the next installment of whatever I served him. Three meals, three snacks. Every day. "Crackers and cheese? Good." "Spaghetti? Good." "Ice cream? Good." He ate it all with gusto. And somehow, the more he ate, the more resentful I felt.

It got to the point where I wished I could feed my kids without him knowing, without having to feed him, too. And then, of course, I would feel guilty for feeling that way. He was sick. Dying even. How could I be mad at him for liking the food I gave him? It didn't make sense.

My sister and I had always been pretty close, but this was a whole new world for us to dive into. She was extremely grateful that I had agreed to take Dad into my home. She, unlike me, knew it would be very rough. After a long day of taking him to various doctors' appointments, standing in line for him at the pharmacy, feeding him and feeding him and feeding him, and spending (what seemed like) hours rubbing his feet with lotion, I would call Jane on the phone.

"How are you doing?" she'd ask, true concern in her voice.

"I'm exhausted," I'd tell her.

"You're awesome," she'd say.

"Guess what he did today," I'd say, and I'd go on to tell her the outrageous thing he did, and how I managed to keep my cool. "I could do it," I told her, "because I knew I'd talk with you tonight, and we would laugh about it."

Like the time when the doctor entered the room at an appointment, and my dad thrust his jacket at me and said, "Here," in a very rude way. Even the doctor was embarrassed for me. Later, in the car, Dad almost apologized by saying, "Doctors are very busy and important people. When I have an opportunity to speak with one, I need you to be my hook."

"Your hook?" What could that mean?

"You know," he said, "for my coat. You have to be a hook for my coat."

"Um, sure, Dad. Okay."

I'm his hook. When I told Jane that one, she laughed so hard that it got me laughing. She was able to get me to see beyond the painful inconvenience of caring for my dad. The laughing helped me lighten up and lessen the complaining. She listened with a loving ear, never judging, always reminding me that what I was doing was really important, and I would never regret it. Really.

And she was right. One night, I sat folding laundry on the living room couch. My dad sat across from me in his chair. He had lost most of his curls, his skin was loose and pale, and his stomach was distended from the cancer. As I folded tiny shirts with tractors on them and little striped tights, we talked. We talked about the kids, how much they had grown, how great they were. We talked about my husband, whom he adored. We talked about the photos he had taken of the flowers back at his house, and one of a moose that had sauntered into his yard. We talked and laughed, and I suddenly realized I had been given a great gift. For the first time in my life, I was totally comfortable with my dad. In fact, I enjoyed being with him. Slowly, throughout the weeks he'd been staying with us, we had been building up a sweet friendship that had been absent my whole life. Hey, I liked this guy!

The next time I talked to Jane, I told her about it. "Of course, he's great," she said. She and our dad had always been close. "It's about time you found out. It's about time you and Dad had a relationship."

It's about time I grew up, I thought.

I will be forever grateful for the hard time taking care of my dad, and for the love and friendship that formed with him. His lasting gift to me is beyond gifts: my new best friend forever, my sister Jane.

~Lava Mueller

He's Still My Prince

You know when you have found your prince because you not only have a
smile on your face but in your heart as well.
~Author Unknown

"Are you ready?" Dad whispered. Dressed in pure white, I nodded, put my trembling arm through his, and glanced at the crowd in the pews.

The church echoed with the guests' whispers. A soft melody came from the piano while my bridegroom, Gene, waited for me at the altar. The music changed—my sign to begin the walk down the aisle.

My steps were slow, but my heart beat fast as I joined my prince.

"For better or for worse… "

I repeated those words. Back then, they were just words because my focus was on the thrill of my dream coming true.

But nine years later, my world darkened with the reality of the "worse."

"What I can see is a clear deterioration of the retina," the ophthalmologist had said. "You both need to prepare." He paused. "With this retinal disease, no one knows how long you'll have your sight."

Gene held me tight as we walked out of the doctor's office.

"The doctor is wrong. It won't happen. I can see just fine," I reasoned.

But then, after a while, my field of vision began to close in—way too rapidly. Each day became a test of the amount of sight I still had left. One week, I could see the furniture around me—the next, I could only perceive portions of some items.

It's okay, I told myself, I can still see what's important—our three little boys' faces. But nothing changed the reality. We found no surgery, medications or natural treatments to halt the progression of the disease.

I tossed at night. Would Gene still love me? If I were to go blind, how would that affect our future, our marriage, our intimacy?

I tried to brush off those thoughts. But the months that followed ushered in what I had dreaded. One day, as I sat in the passenger seat of the car, with my three little sons in the back seat, I realized I couldn't see the road or the familiar buildings. My whole world was covered by a dark veil.

When we got home, I began to adjust to living my life without sight. I groped my way through accomplishing the basic chores for our sons, for Gene and for myself. Gene's constant support and patience brought glimpses of light into my darkness.

"I'll stop by the store and pick up what we need," he'd say matter-of-factly. "And then I'll get Jason to his Boy Scout meeting."

He took over many chores I could no longer perform, and I took a different place in our marriage. I wasn't in charge of the schedule anymore; I was dependent on his availability and time to take over the driving, pay the bills, and help our sons with their homework.

Navigating through the kitchen became my first priority. Many spilled juices, bumps into open cabinet doors, and burned fingers on hot pots were all necessary steps to my new life without sight.

One evening, I scooped a spoonful of spaghetti sauce. "Okay, are you ready?" I asked, lifting the spoon toward Gene. "What do you think?"

I waited. It was my first attempt to fix a full meal since my blindness, and his approval was vital.

"The best," he said.

Was it really, or was that his way of encouraging me? It didn't matter; he always found a way to lift my mood, to cheer me on and to overlook my mistakes.

"A bit of bleach will take care of this," he said one day when I insisted he tell me what he was doing.

"My T-shirts are a little pink," he said.

"Okay, no more red clothes with white."

Learning and adjusting filled the days and years that swept by, turning the pages of our lives together. Some were stained with the pain of losing our youngest son… Others were wrinkled with adjustments to unexpected financial setbacks… And the pages of my blindness were carefully taped together.

But each page tells of a man who chose to turn the worst for him into the best for me. The sweet aroma of his cologne surrounds me with delight as he prays for my day before leaving for work.

Through the years, he's read dozens of books to me. One day, I interrupted him, "Don't you wish I could do something for you for a change?"

He kissed my lips. "You do for me more than I do for you," he said. "We make a good team just the way we are, and we'll make it to the end."

Now, I look out the window of life, and smile at the fresh and lush scenery. In my mind, I see the beauty of his commitment. I used to grope my way around, but now I take his hand, and my steps don't hesitate anymore; they're secure and confident.

Rather than tears, I now celebrate our days together. Gene saw beyond the ugliness of my blindness and, with his love, turned me into a queen.

~Janet Perez Eckles

When the Helper Needs Help

46

A Note from Joan

I want to introduce you to a woman named Janet Penn. Janet is a vivacious Type A tech-business consultant who helped me design my website: joanlunden.com. Janet is a true "Energizer bunny!" Last year Janet's busy life as a businesswoman came to a sudden halt. She was hospitalized and learned that her life was in peril. Janet needed a kidney transplant.

Janet didn't want her clients to worry and so she told us nothing. I later found out that the reason she didn't want anyone to know or to help her was because she had always been able to do everything on her own. She finally shared part of her story with me, but it was not until she came to a speech that I was giving near her home in New Jersey, that I was able to look her in the eye and ask how she was handling it all.

Her eyes welled up with tears as she told me how emotionally devastating it was to have to accept help from people. The idea that she couldn't cook her meals, wash her clothes, clean her house, and take out her garbage was devastating to her and having to ASK for help was even worse. "Why is this so hard for me?" she asked. "I've run soup kitchens, I know how wonderful it is to 'give care.' Why does it torture me to take it from others?"

I realized that this was probably a universal feeling and I asked Janet if she would share her personal journey with all of you. It is important for us all to put ourselves in the shoes of the person who is receiving care, to truly understand how very difficult this can be for many. Here's Janet's story:

This past year has been quite the journey for me. I am 55 years old, and two years ago, I was diagnosed with two incurable and untreatable kidney diseases that will kill me if I don't undergo a kidney transplant. I am also a very self-sufficient, vibrant woman who never asked for any kind of help—ever. In fact, I have always been the one to help others. Now the roles are reversed. Who would have thought that this kind of thing could happen to me? For the first time in my life I have had to reach out to others for help, both physical and emotional, which has been quite an adjustment and a real role reversal for me. But then again, being diagnosed with two incurable, untreatable kidney diseases is quite the game-changer too.

Here's a little tidbit about me: I am an avid leader and volunteer in my synagogue's Community Soup Kitchen Program, where I have spent a good portion of the last five years providing assistance to the homeless and working poor by delivering healthy and nutritious hot meals for our guests in need. In the past, I have stood in front of our group of volunteers and told personal stories of my own struggles to feed myself and keep a roof over my head, and talked about how we must treat our guests with dignity and respect because, after all, we never quite know when we might be on the other side of the service line... Well, I am now learning what that's like through my illness.

This past spring, I was admitted to the hospital for five days to receive two blood transfusions in an effort to keep me alive while going through the long process of finding a suitable kidney donor and awaiting my kidney transplant. Four days after my initial hospital stay, I was back in for another 10 days because I had developed a life-threatening blood clot and had to undergo immediate surgery to eradicate that problem.

As I was being released from the hospital, my doctor gave me many strict orders. First and foremost: stay home—or else! Along with this was the order of bed rest, which meant no cooking meals, no taking out the garbage, no changing my bed linens, and no showering on my own. How the heck could I obey all of that with a company to run? Well, as it was, I'd been running my company from my hospital bed (have laptop, will travel)... no rest for the weary businesswoman! I had bills to pay, employees to look after, and clients to work for! But who was going to take care of all these things while I was confined to my bed? I thought no one could do all of these things but me.

I obeyed doctor's orders and stayed home for several weeks, and while recuperating at home, I quickly realized that there was a lot I simply could not do for myself at that time. I realized that I had to accept help from others. And even more, not only *accept* the help of my friends but actually *ask* for it as well. This was a life-changing experience, thrust upon me by circumstance and my medical condition. Since I live alone, have no children to care for me, and my mother is in her late eighties and of fair health herself, it was quite the revelation for me to realize I had reached the point where I had to fight my resistance and go for "the ask."

For my whole life I had always been able to "do it all," but now I was on a totally different playing field. Suddenly I had people in my home shopping for me, preparing my meals, cleaning my house, changing my linens, doing my laundry—even bathing me. I was usually the one who would do that for other people! And there I was, having always thought that asking for help was a sign of weakness and vulnerability and that I would never have to do that... boy was I wrong!

For so many years I had been teaching children and parents to be good citizens through social action and community outreach, and yet there I was, not wanting to own the fact that I now needed community outreach directed at me. I now see that it was foolish of me to think that I could survive in this world completely on my own, regardless of the situation. Besides, who really wants to live in that kind of environment anyway? Not I. How self-sabotaging it was for me to pretend my own advice to others, to help those who need it, did not pertain to me. I had to overcome my resistance to this notion and turn to those around me who could indeed help me in the moment. I am forever grateful that they did, and their efforts ferried me through one of many difficult phases I've encountered since my diagnosis.

I thought that if I put my vulnerability out there, I would be perceived as weak, and I didn't want to feel that way. However what I soon realized is that when you are vulnerable (and everybody is) people see that you are in fact human, and you might be frail sometimes but you in fact become so much closer to others because of it. Accepting help from my friends, co-workers, and community created an even stronger bond than I ever knew was possible. These people did not find me a burden to them and it's a big mistake to think that you're not worthy of someone's time. You would be very surprised.

I became even more humbled when numerous people told me that they were willing to be tested for compatibility with regards to my kidney transplant. Ten people offered up their kidneys to me. Ten people offered to be cut into voluntarily to save my life…. Are you kidding me? After all, it's not like giving me the keys to your car… it's giving me a vital body organ.

Who does that? Wonderful people.

The wonderful people who have surrounded me and supported me through the last two years have shown me that it is actually not a sign of weakness to ask for help and to accept it. It's actually a sign of humanity.

~Janet O. Penn

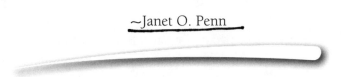

47

Help Line

You can't live a perfect day without doing something for someone
who will never be able to repay you.
~John Wooden

Hot tears seared my eyes. I clutched the phone like a lifeline. "Tom, can you come?" In desperation, I was calling a family friend for help. For three months, my husband had lived in extreme pain. After shoveling two feet of snow off our driveway, Gene had injured his back. He had seen doctors and specialists. They ordered X-rays, bloodwork, MRIs, and physical therapy. They prescribed pills. Nothing relieved my husband's agony.

Each visit to the doctor involved taking more tests, waiting for results, and scheduling yet another appointment. Days turned into weeks. Weeks turned into months. Now Gene could barely stand. He had lost more than 30 pounds. Nights were filled with long hours of prayer since sleep was impossible. An avid reader, Gene no longer had the strength to hold up a book. Because he could barely sit up, I was feeding him by hand.

Our bedroom looked more and more like a hospital. A full-body back brace, an electrical stimulation apparatus, a cane, a walker, a portable commode, and now a wheelchair transformed the area into a steel jungle. The end table held a pharmacy of painkillers, muscle relaxants, and antibiotics.

Both of us were discouraged. For months, I had tried to handle my husband's health needs by myself. Nothing seemed to help. I was not strong enough to move Gene by myself. One night, I spent almost an hour helping him walk from the living room to his bedroom, a distance of only 20 feet.

At my wits' end, I punched Tom's number into the phone. Our children had married and moved out of state. Tom was like an adopted son and still lived nearby.

Strong and capable, Tom was a tree I could lean on in a storm. Just hearing his voice on the other end of the phone was good medicine. I felt even better as I heard him say, "I'll be right over."

Twenty minutes later, Tom stood grinning at our door. Under his arm was a stack of DVDs, treasured movies from his childhood. He greeted Gene and then set up the laptop next to his bed. Together we watched a film that transported us all to a world far from our troubles.

Over the next weeks, Tom helped me get Gene in and out of the car as we went to medical appointments. He listened not just to Gene's pain, but to my sorrow as well. When I needed to go out of town for an overnight, Tom volunteered to stay with Gene.

At last, after Gene spent more than a week in the hospital, the orthopedist discovered that Gene had a staph infection hidden deep inside his spine. No amount of painkillers or physical therapy would ever have cured the infection. For six more weeks, Gene traveled daily to the hospital for infusions of high-powered antibiotics. I drove him there and back during the first weeks, but by the end of the time, Gene was well enough to drive himself. After six long months, the dark curtain over our lives slowly lifted. Today, Gene is able to do everything he wants… except shovel snow.

And Tom? He performed no delicate surgery. He offered no miracle drug. But the hope and encouragement he infused into my caregiver's heart were better medicine than any prescription written by a doctor.

All I had to do was call.

~Emily Parke Chase

Clothed in Love

Turn your wounds into wisdom.
~Oprah Winfrey

I recall sitting in my bedroom, praying for the wisdom I needed to proceed with what I had to do. I had been faced with many challenges in my 70 years, but this could prove to be the greatest. It had become clear that my mother needed more help than I was able to provide for her in her home. There was a 15-mile drive separating us—not a huge stretch, but adding that to my responsibilities with a sick husband was more than I could handle. She would have to come to live with us.

Until now, my mother had rejected the idea vociferously. The mere mention of it would result in a huge argument, leaving us at odds for days. Finally, I just crashed and said that we would no longer discuss the issue. Instead, I resolved to spend more time with my husband and visit my mother every few days instead of every day. Always in control, my mother continued to be firm in her resolve, so I was forced to be firm in mine.

There was another issue that I had to come to terms with. It was something that I hated to acknowledge, but if I expected this to work, I would have to take a look at a deeper, more serious issue. It had to do with the resentment I continued to feel toward the mother who had never shown me affirmation or praise, never a warm hug, never acknowledgment of my talents. How would I be able to welcome her, take care of her, cook for her, see to her social life, and pretend that everything between us was fine?

Finally, my mother capitulated and moved in, making it clear that she would do it her way. "I will stay in my room!" she insisted. "You can deliver my meals there, and I will come out to the living room only if I have visitors."

"But, Mom," I cried. "I have a beautiful sun room and deck! You can watch the snow fall and sit by the fire. You'll love it!"

"I think I know what I love," she responded, not budging from her position.

So the months went on until my husband succumbed to his illness. I was wrought with grief and at the same time angry that he, my best friend, left me alone with my mother. I was over 70 now, and my body was rebelling. More than the physical pain, the emotional pain was dragging me down to a level that I understood to be trouble. I made an appointment with a psychologist.

Dr. Janice and I spent months trying to unravel the reasons for my mother's negative behavior.

"Your mother is stuck in the past," Dr. Janice said. "She's never had a life outside of her own environment. She won't change. You have to change. Put aside your hurt and move along."

"But how…" I began. I didn't have a chance to go on.

"Come on," she said, "you're smart enough to figure it out. Reasoning capacity diminishes in old age, so don't expect your mother to suddenly understand, even if you tell her straight out how you feel."

"So, tell me what to do!"

"Find some common ground," she replied. "Something where you can both come together. If you really want to do this, you'll find a way."

I thought about her suggestion for weeks until I finally came up with an idea. Dr. Jan had said that Mom was stuck in the past. Instead of fighting her, why not join her?

I went to the attic, collected her old photo albums, and placed one on her lap. I pulled up a chair beside her. As we began, the tone of her voice became soft and mellow, full of emotion. There were tears as she spoke of her parents, her siblings, cousins, old friends, all gone now. But there was a good deal of laughter, too, as she recalled the events surrounding the faded pictures.

"Did you know that my father made moonshine?" she laughed. "The cops were always at our door, but it wasn't to arrest him!" She turned the page. "Oh, here's my brother, Tony. He earned a Purple Heart in the war, you know. And my sisters..."

"Tell me about them, Mom," I said, sincerely interested, taking notes on everything she was relating to me.

Finally, we uncovered a large envelope filled with pictures of me as a child. I had never before seen this treasure. They were not casual pictures, but posed and deliberate. Each picture looked like it could have been in a magazine. The outfits—dresses, coats, hats, sweaters—were beautiful. Plain, simple lines were resplendent with inverted pleats, hand-smocking, crocheted collars, and soft gathers. I was totally shocked!

"Mom," I said, "you always talk about how poor you and Daddy were during the Depression. How in the world could you have afforded to dress me in these clothes?"

"Well, you were my little girl. I loved you so much, and I didn't want you to look shabby just because we had no money. At night, after you were asleep, I made clothes for you. Sometimes, I'd take apart one of my sweaters or skirts. I'd save the thread and the buttons to make dresses for you, and cut the sleeves off sweaters to make leggings. I would crochet around collars and embroider little designs. The lovely white wool coat is from the dress I wore on my honeymoon. It took a long time because I had no sewing machine and no pattern."

"But this outfit is fur," I said, pointing to a beautiful little jacket with matching hat.

"Oh, yes, I remember!" she said. "Before I was married, I had seen a fur coat in a store window. I loved it, so my father bought it for me as an engagement present."

I was spellbound. Listening to those stories made me want to hear more. I went to her room daily and began noticing that her demeanor was changing. She was no longer the demanding, angry mother she had once been. She was softer now, happier.

For the eight years my mother was with me, we continued to discuss stories of her past. Sharing the trials of her life and her secret desires, I came to understand that, in her time, outward affection was a sign of weakness. She never understood that there could be a different way.

I think of my mother every day now and of how those old photos gave us a chance to be together before she died. The pictures of a little girl in long curls, dressed in high fashion, are a poignant reminder that my mother, in her own way, truly loved me.

She had given everything to me—literally the clothes off her back.

~Pam Giordano

A Brown Boy of Our Own

The imperfections of a man, his frailties, his faults, are just as important as his virtues. You can't separate them. They're wedded.
~Henry Miller

Brian was born on a humid Sunday morning in the month of August. My labor had been hard; his birth difficult. Struggle defined him at an early age. At three months, Brian was hospitalized with bronchitis. At six months, he underwent a tracheotomy due to the croup. Brian was in the hospital more than he was home when a toddler. Asthma, pneumonia, allergies, ear infections, learning disabilities and eventually dropping out of school followed.

One windy March evening when he was 17, Brian came crashing through our front door in a full-blown psychotic state. His eyes were wild. He spoke nonsense. From that moment on, my role included caretaker.

Paranoid schizophrenia—a misunderstood, highly debilitating and frightening brain disease—was eventually the diagnosis. Psychotic episodes like the first one, plus paranoia, hearing voices, racing thoughts, and a distorted body image are common. This disease not only affects the one stricken, but those in the immediate family as well. We were no exception. It led to my divorcing Brian's father. Brian's siblings felt shame and, at times, hatred toward their brother and each other. To say we've just about come full circle is nothing short of a miracle.

Brian is now 36. Dealing with my mentally ill adult son at home takes an abundance of energy while working full-time and wearing all the other hats I wear. I've tried to remember Brian when his mind was calm — before this monster disease swallowed him up and spit him out in shattered pieces. Most days, that's impossible.

Every three months, I take Brian to appointments with his psychiatrist and counselor. Pills are changed when necessary. His weight is monitored when needed, which is more times than not because of his distorted body image. Periodically, he has me stand with him in front of the mirror. He takes off his shirt and checks his muscles. He feels he is "uneven." Since fearing he was choking awhile back on a candy bar, he continues to stand while eating. He has regular EKGs, blood tests, and physicals.

Brian maintains best with routine. He gets up at a certain time and does the same things as the day before. He goes upstairs to bed at 10:30, arranging his bottle of water and wristwatch just so on the small table by his bed. Before saying good night, he checks and double-checks his framed piece of artwork hanging by the window to make sure it is secure. He wants to be certain that nothing has come in through the panes to dampen this "pen/ink with markers piece" that won "Best in Show." He stands in front of it staring. Then he rubs his hands methodically all around it until he's convinced nothing has harmed this treasure, which he painstakingly and frantically created. Then he'll turn to me — and smile.

After we've said good night more than once and I've said the same things to him over and over in reassurance, I'll start down the stairs until he stops me to ask a question or two. Later, when the house is quiet and I'm unwinding, he'll call down to me to say, "Night, Mom. Love you."

On weekdays, I stop by mid-morning, making sure he's had his coffee and cereal, taken his pills, and is ready for his afternoon of listening to music and doing his jigsaw puzzles. If I'm a bit late getting back home after work, he wonders where I've been. Sometimes he's waiting for me at the door. After I get my coffee, I start dinner. As I work around the kitchen, I hear about every piece he's put in his puzzle and about the music he's heard and the cars that have passed by the window in the kitchen where he stands. I hear in detail about his favorite TV shows he watched the night before. And then the questions start. Some make sense; most do not.

I reassure him that no one can hear us outside, tell him that the refrigerator isn't talking to him, and listen as he talks about having wings and seeing fairies, and spending time in a secret place way up in a giant tree where no one can make fun of him.

On weekends, I take him for rides. We call them cruises. We have a favorite route through the countryside, past Amish farms we've come to consider good friends. We have favorites, like the Pig Farm, the Sheep Farm, Abe Lincoln's and Brown Boy's place. Brown Boy was a rather neglected horse. If he was near the edge of the fence, we'd slow down and talk to him. He seemed to know us. Then one day, Brown Boy was no longer there. We rode the rest of the way in silence. We somehow understood we'd never see Brown Boy again.

I've taught Brian how to cha-cha, do the stroll and the jitterbug. We have favorite tunes and artists. It all depends on our mood. I love to sing along as we dance around the kitchen. Sometimes, we have to stop because we are laughing so hard. In the summer and into fall, we are busy in our garden. Brian has a genuine green thumb. He's in charge. For over two years, he was enrolled in a greenhouse program on the grounds of an area psychiatric center. He loved it. He was up and out every day by 7:30 with his bagged lunch in hand. One night at dinner, he told me the greenhouse was closing, and two weeks later it did. To this day, Brian feels the way he planted the poinsettias was the reason for the program's demise.

I can no longer imagine Brian any other way than what God has given me. He reminds me of life's frailties, while at the same time, life's blessings. I've slowly begun to prepare Brian for the inevitable. I know we won't be doing the cha-cha forever. He's close to his siblings. His little niece is quite special to him. But, for now, we are getting the barn ready for a few goats—and, maybe, a Brown Boy of our own.

~Barbara Briggs Ward

Enjoy This Day

In every walk with nature one receives far more than he seeks.
~John Muir

"Is the dishwasher clean or dirty?" my husband asked.

"Clean. I told you already." I bit my lip. I had promised myself I wouldn't say, "I told you already." Yet those pesky words had escaped my lips for the hundredth time. It wasn't Ray's fault that he'd had to ask the same question a third time within the hour. He was in the early stages of Alzheimer's.

My grandmother, who had this dreaded brain disease, lived with us for a year when I was seven. I'd also watched Ray's mother progress from forgetting where she put things to forgetting the names of grandchildren to forgetting Ray's name. We were with her when she died of Alzheimer's. Facing it again, I was currently reading every book I could find on the disease.

I had an inkling of what I would need to do as a caretaker, and I was terrified. I'd need to remain his confidant and best friend, which I was now. I'd also need to be a nurse dispensing medications, a handyman fixing the closet door when it came off its tracks, and the sole cook, chauffeur, and laundress—roles we had shared since his retirement. How could I do it all?

"Are you all right?" Ray's doctor had asked me as I sobbed into my handkerchief while he explained the various kinds of dementia.

"No." Of course, I wasn't all right. When we met 14 years earlier, Ray and I had planned a life together filled with the things we loved to do—hiking, biking, ballroom dancing. We could share these activities for a while longer, but Alzheimer's disease imposed an end date I'd never imagined.

"You knew, didn't you?" The doctor probably didn't mean his second question to sound so unsympathetic.

I nodded and wiped my eyes. I had suspected Alzheimer's for some time. More and more often, I found myself reminding Ray to take his medications, helping him make lists of the things he wanted to do, and responding to the e-mails that confused him. But a diagnosis based on a battery of tests was so final.

I loved Ray and would do anything I could for him. At our wedding, tears of joy ran down my face through the entire ceremony because I was marrying the man of my dreams. He offered me the kind of love and support I had never received before. Whether it was doing a grocery store run for things we needed, or attending a reading of one of my stories, he was beside me every day in every way.

Now it was my turn to offer him unmitigated, unconditional love and support. I quaked before the task. I knew what a good caretaker looked like. When my mother-in-law had Alzheimer's, she received wonderful care from the staff at her continuous-care retirement home. Every aide was gentle, loving, and patient. Then there was Richard, the man who took care of a friend after she had a stroke. We referred to him as Richard the Angel because he did everything with grace and good humor, from wiping drool from the corner of my friend's mouth to carefully rearranging her feet on the footrests of her wheelchair.

Did it make a difference that they had applied for the job and I was thrust into it? That the patient they cared for was not also the love of their life?

Ray deserved the best caretaker around. But was I up to it?

One sunny morning, when Ray was settled at his computer playing brain challenges, I followed one of the walking paths that meander through our neighborhood. "Dear God, guide me," I prayed. "I'm in desperate need of your help."

"You and Ray can enjoy this day together," God whispered

through the beauty around me. Birds twittered in cedars and vine maples. Fat clematis blooms climbed a trellis in one yard. In another, day lilies in a profusion of reds, oranges and yellows opened their faces to the sun. If Ray were with me, he might bend to smell the fragrant roses that bordered a lush, newly mown lawn.

God's message was clear. Railing against Ray's diagnosis wouldn't change anything. My focus needed to shift to the things Ray and I could still do together. Later, when he needed more help than I could offer, I would trust God to give me other answers.

I knew I would come to need walks like this often, along with an open pipeline to God. But for now I saw the world differently, and felt more positive and hopeful.

When I arrived home, Ray met me at the door. "I changed the ink in the printer, but it won't start. I did what I always do." He sounded frantic.

I kissed his cheek. "I'll look at it, and then will you walk with me?" I asked. "I saw some beautiful yards I want to show you."

"Everything's more confusing today. Yesterday my mind was clear as a bell."

My heart twisted with sympathy. He must be far more terrified than I was about what lay ahead of us. "Tomorrow maybe you'll have a good day again," I soothed as I went to his office. I pushed an ink cartridge into position, prodding it until it clicked, and closed the door of the ink bay. The machine whirred into action.

Ray frowned. "I did all that."

"I know. Let's go for a walk." I took his arm.

He smiled his fabulous, crooked smile. "Just let me get on my shoes."

With tears in my eyes, but a growing peace in my heart, I opened the front door, and we stepped out into the sunshine, comforted by each other's company. Maybe they would find a medication soon that would stop the advance of Alzheimer's, not just slow it down. Meanwhile, we had today. We were out to enjoy it.

~Samantha Ducloux Waltz

Caring for Sophie

If children have the ability to ignore all odds and percentages,
then maybe we can all learn from them.
~Lance Armstrong

Last night, I looked at my daughter, dwarfed by my big bed, as she watched her favorite videotape. And I had this fleeting thought, "Sophie, why are you still pretending to have Down syndrome? I know you're just fooling me. Come on now, snap out of it."

Of course, the disability, while it seems to loom, is actually in the background. I can see that in the twinkle of her eye, and I see that under her confusion and sometimes funny speech she is a genius. Underneath her touch of physical awkwardness is a ballerina, a gymnast, an Olympic champion. But that doesn't change the disability; it just changes the way I look at it.

Caring for Sofe didn't come with a warranty that she will spring up, healed, ready for the next triathlon or doctoral thesis. But in her eyes I see everything important to me. My daughter's care is constant. But so is her progress in caring for herself. We are lucky.

One woman who read a column I had written about my daughter's disability said, "I am glad there is one of us represented out there." The reader wasn't disabled, so what was she talking about? One of us? Sounds odd, but I knew exactly what she was referring to. She was a mom, a caretaker.

"We" inhabit a world that is invisible to those who live on the other side. Those who never heard of a Regional Center or an infant development program. Those who contribute to the March of Dimes to fix other people's problems. Those whose worst fear about their kids is that they won't get into the college of their choice. Those who have never paced the halls of Children's Hospital in a trance of fear and hope. Those whose lives do not revolve around the constant care of 13-year-old daughters.

At 13 years old, my daughter has never crossed a busy street by herself. She has never been dropped off at the mall to hang with friends. She has never demanded Guess jeans or stayed out past curfew.

Still, she is just right. Her own kind of just right. She writes clever stories. She laughs so hard you can't help but join in. She made a party hat for our kitty cat. She screams at her little brother as often as possible. With total abandon, she sings along to Broadway musicals and assigns us all parts. She cooks her own baked beans. Her speech lessons yielded audible words, and her occupational therapy yielded a kid who could run. And just last week, after being shown about 53 times—loop up, loop over, loop through—she learned to tie her own shoes.

When I see a child with a disability who is struggling to speak, or learn, or be understood, or to walk, or to maneuver a wheelchair, I think: That child is familiar to me. I know that child. The disability is irrelevant. Disabilities just make things hard to do. But disabilities remind me of my daughter. And so, of course, I don't cringe or give surreptitious looks or look away. I really want to stop and smile.

When parents like me are out and about without our kids, we can "pass" for "regular parents." When I am "passing" and I encounter a family with a little one who is disabled, I want to rush over and say, "I have a child like yours. I am a parent like you." Sometimes I even do. I don't know exactly why I do, though. Maybe it's because we are comrades in arms—armed against the onslaught of curious looks, doubting Thomases and faulty experts, armed against our uncertain futures.

We aren't in the majority. I am glad of that. This is not a club any of us wanted to join. But we sure could use some open-hearted acceptance of our kids from non-members. If you'd like, we could offer you an honorary membership for that. That's a lot easier than the dues you have to pay to get in otherwise.

In the classic film, *Heidi*, when Clara miraculously rises from her wheelchair, that is only one possible fairy tale ending. A more interesting ending might be young, pink-cheeked Heidi proclaiming to the world, "Accept Clara in the chair. After all, she's just sitting down."

Miracles do happen. I dream of a miracle, a healing for my daughter, and here is how it would go: In a flash of light, the world would be miraculously healed, and be able to see how peachy and perfect my Sophie really is—just as she is.

~Jolie Kanat

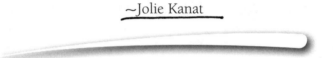

A Time for Change

Change always comes bearing gifts.
~Price Pritchett

My mother-in-law never called me at work, but one day she asked me to come straight home, and that's all she would say. Somewhat nervously, I tapped on the door and entered Mom's apartment, which was attached to our house. Back-to-back on the couch, noses in the air, sat Mom and Mrs. T.

Mrs. T. had been her faithful help—and friend—for 10 years. Not only had she performed household chores, but she had helped take care of my father-in-law after his stroke. When Mom resigned from her RN position, Mrs. T. gave her a few hours of respite with her full-time patient at home. Even after Dad passed, Mom looked forward to Mrs. T's cleaning days as a chance to catch up on neighborhood gossip. After Mom had a stroke and moved into the apartment in our new house, Mrs. T. agreed to come twice a week.

Mom had been complaining about Mrs. T. "meddling." This day, she was highly indignant, accusing Mrs. T. of treating her like an infant. Mom was on her high horse and not about to come off! Taking Mrs. T. gently by the arm, I led her to the door. I thanked her and apologized for any wrong she felt, but let her know we obviously had to have a change.

"Mom, it'll all work out," I promised. "We'll have a new 'normal' around here before you know it."

This change called for more family participation. The

grandchildren made a point of spending part of their after-school day with her. My husband took time to catch up when he was home. I cleaned the apartment on weekends.

One day, Mom became confused and after she couldn't remember her way back from her weekly visit to the beauty shop, she tearfully—but voluntarily—handed over her car keys to my husband. Not long after that, I found her in a befuddled state. Much to her chagrin, I hid the half-dozen bottles of medicine in my kitchen, doling out the medication as prescribed. Her care was becoming too much for me to handle.

It was time for help. We hired a down-home grandma with too much energy to enjoy her retirement. From the first handshake, Edith and Mom connected, despite having nothing in common apart from being Southern grandmothers. Not only did Edith keep the apartment spotless, but she also made all of Mom's favorites—pinto beans with fatback, biscuits from scratch, and fried apple pies.

Finally, we were finding our new "normal" again. Even when I started working full-time, the nights and weekends seemed easier. Edith was happy to stay the occasional weekend so my husband and I could get away. She sometimes just came over on a Sunday to visit. It seemed as though Edith brought sunshine back into all our lives.

It was on one of those Sunday afternoons, absorbed in my preparations for dinner guests, when I heard shouting coming from the apartment. Oh, no, not again! My mind flashed back to Mom and Mrs. T. I dashed through to the apartment. "Go, Dale!" I heard my mother-in-law shout. Edith, a huge Dale Earnhardt fan, had introduced Mom to NASCAR!

Edith became a fixture at our house that summer as we prepared for our twin daughters' double wedding. The ever-punctual Edith came early on the wedding day and tried to keep Mom calm. At the church, Mom's periwinkle skirt kept slipping down, so I safety-pinned it discreetly to the jacket before seating Mom and her ever-present oxygen tank in the front pew. She was too exhausted to come to the reception that we held in the picnic area of our property.

Instead, Mom and Edith watched the comings and goings from her bedroom window.

My prayer had been answered. Many times that year, I'd gazed skyward and prayed, "Please, may Mom live to see the girls married. I just don't know what to do if you call her home that day. Oh, please, please, not that day."

Exactly one month after the wedding, He did call her home. Among the many things we'd discussed over the years were death and her requests. As the days normalized after the wedding, Mom added another request. "Bury me in that wretched periwinkle outfit. It's the most uncomfortable thing I've ever owned, and no one should ever have to wear it again!" Yes, Mom.

~Rosemary Francis

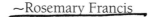

At Maddy's Side

To us, family means putting your arms around each other and being there.
~Barbara Bush

"I can't do that!" I told my sister-in-law Jeanne. My beloved mother-in-law, Maddy, at age 91, had suddenly slipped from needing frequent visitors to needing full-time help, including someone to walk her to the bathroom in the middle of the night. Now she needed someone, this very night. Because there was no time to buy any kind of bed alarm or monitor, what was needed was someone to arrive that night and actually crawl into bed with her, to be there to hear if she tried to get up alone. I could not imagine doing that. It was so private, so personal, so intimate. What if I didn't hear her get up? What if she fell when I was in charge? What if she was as scared as I would be if someone had crawled into bed next to me in the middle of the night?

I called my own sister to discuss the situation. "I can't do that!" I complained.

"Well," she said, "you actually can." And she left it at that.

I thought it over. I thought about all the things Maddy had done for me in the nearly three decades that I'd been married to her son. She had accepted me at first sight. She had supported me when I was the first mother in the family to work outside of the home. She had always treated me like gold.

And then I remembered the closets.

When my husband and I bought our first house, many years

ago, we bought a true fixer-upper, and we had one month to make it livable before we moved in. Every surface needed to be cleaned, repainted, re-wallpapered, or re-carpeted. My father-in-law Johnny had recently retired, so he and Maddy quietly adopted our house as their project. Every day that month, while my husband and I were at work, Maddy and Johnny found a job that needed to be done in our new house, and they did it. Each evening, when we arrived to work on the house ourselves, something new would magically be different. One day, we found the trim painted. Another day, we found the ceilings washed. Once, we discovered the tall weeds outside had been cut back.

But one evening we arrived and could not figure out what Maddy and Johhny had tackled that day. We could tell they had been there, but what had they done? We worked all evening before we figured it out. They had painted the inside of every single closet! Who would think of such a touch? What considerate people! We were delighted.

Johnny's been gone for 10 years, and Maddy has been a big part of my life, supporting me through good times and bad. And now, when Maddy needed me, I thought about all the things she had done for me since the closets.

I called my sister-in-law back. "Of course, I'll be there tonight!" I told her.

I arrived late that night as a caretaker was leaving, put on my pajamas, and quietly crawled into Maddy's bed. A few hours later, she woke up and started to get up for the bathroom. I rushed to the other side of the bed to take her hand. She was surprised, mostly because I stepped on her foot! But other than that, she was just fine with having someone suddenly show up in her bedroom in the middle of the night.

"Who's that?" Maddy asked.

"It's me, Jane, your favorite!" I told her. I like to think that, anyway.

"Oh, hi!" she said brightly. "It's nice to see you!" And she took my hand and off we went.

In the months since that night, my husband and I have spent many days and nights at Maddy's house, taking turns with his brothers and sisters and professional help, making sure that someone is always at Maddy's side. Sometimes, it fits in well with our lives. Sometimes, it doesn't, but we do it anyway. During those times, I just think about the closets. She was there for me then, and I'm here for her now.

~Jane Brzozowski

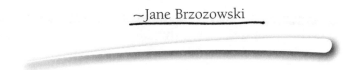

Family Caregivers

Laughter Is the Best Medicine

Mirth is God's medicine. Everybody ought to bathe in it.

~Henry Ward Beecher

The Slip and Slide

Man is the only animal that blushes. Or needs to.
~Mark Twain

Do you remember when you were a kid in the summertime and your dad laid out a sheet of plastic in the yard and squirted water on it so you could run and do belly flops and slip and slide all the way to the end? And do it again and again until Dad said you'd wasted enough water? Ahhh, those were the days, my friend.

Caretakers of Alzheimer's patients rarely get the chance to laugh and giggle until their sides ache, but let me tell you about an evening I spent slipping and sliding with my husband. George got up to use the bathroom about two o'clock in the morning. I heard a frightful crash and raced into the bathroom to find him flat on the floor and using bad language. I helped him sit up after he decided nothing was bent or broken, and the next step was to get him up on his feet.

I was not a weakling; I swam and worked out daily. So, I felt confident that if he gave me his hand, I could pull him up. He reached his arm out to me. I grasped his hand firmly and gave a mighty heave. Well, the reason he'd been in the bathroom in the first place was to use the toilet, and since he had fallen before he accomplished his mission, the floor was now wet and slippery.

My feet went out from under me, and down I went right on top of poor George. After the shock of finding ourselves so intimately entangled, we both began to giggle. The giggle turned into a guffaw, and we were laughing so hard our sides ached. The bathroom floor had turned into a slip and slide.

The initial problem now was worse by a hundredfold. I have an artificial hip and knee, and I couldn't get up. George couldn't get up. We tried, oh dear Lord, how we tried, but we always ended up together in a heap on the floor, laughing as though we had been smoking locoweed until we were as weak as newborn kittens.

It soon became obvious it was time for some clear thinking on the subject. What to do? What to do? George, of course, had the correct answer, "Call 911!" I almost did until I realized I couldn't reach the telephone. It was a wall phone and dangled nearby just out of reach in the hallway. Then I thought maybe I could find something to use as a tool to hook on to the phone cord to pull it down.

It is time now to confess that neither George nor I wear nightclothes. Putting it delicately, we sleep in the "altogether," and my next thought was what the 911 responders would see when they came through the door if I did manage to call them. They would see two old people, wrinkled and soiled, hair standing on end, wallowing around on the bathroom floor naked as jaybirds, and giddy from laughter. I thought, "No way! I can't call 911 even if I can manage to get at the phone." There was no way anyone was going to see us like that. My prudery wouldn't allow it.

But what was the alternative?

After several more attempts, we realized the entire problem was our inability to get our feet underneath us. If we could somehow manage that, we could begin to stand upright. Okay! How to do it?

The back door was not far away, so we decided to crawl to the door and get it open. This was a success, so we continued inching our way out the door and onto the steps that led down to the carport. Aha! Another success. Swiveling our hips enough to sit on the steps, we wriggled our butts down to the step below, struggled to move down one more step, and turned our bodies sideways so we could dangle our legs over the edge.

I won't say it all went smoothly, but after a whole lot more laughter, several bad words, and a great deal of effort, we finally stood erect in the harsh glare of the streetlight not 25 feet away, naked as newborn babes and, by this time, freezing to death.

Lucky for us, the neighbors were all snoozing away, and no one came to see what the ruckus was about. We walked up the steps into a hot shower and fell back in bed. I still can't believe we got away with "prancing" around naked in the middle of the night. Our reputation remained intact.

As a final word to the wise: Put grab bars up in your bathroom!

~Beverly Isenberg

The Beer Hat

Perhaps I know best why it is man alone who laughs;
he alone suffers so deeply that he had to invent laughter.
~Friedrich Nietzsche

There's much to be known about a person by the type of hat he wears. Take for instance my brother-in-law, Ray. He had a beer hat. No, he didn't buy it for himself nor did he drink beer. But who he was could be seen in that hat.

In the final stages of ALS, commonly known as Lou Gehrig's disease, he had lost the use of his arms and legs. The beer hat was a gift from his adult stepdaughter who thought it would give him the independence to drink fluids on his own. A crazy gift to help with liquid intake became a wellspring of joy.

My sons, Jake, age 15, Ben, age 12, and I were helping out for a while at my sister Mary and Ray's home. The hat had arrived in the mail, and Ray was dashing in his new *chapeau*. But it didn't work as his daughter had planned. Sucking the liquids out of the cans was too difficult in his advanced state, and once the contents did begin to flow, he could not stop it. Undaunted by these setbacks, my two sons and Ray put their heads together to devise a plan to create a useable beer hat.

Ray loved a challenge. His creative mind combined with the boys' farm-savvy, machine-repair knowledge and soon the teens were on bikes heading to parts stores in search of one-way valves. It was with heavy hearts that none could be found in the tiny mountain town in which they lived.

Undaunted, Ray "rallied the pack" into a new effort. Searching online through the maze of computer-accessed stores, they were able to locate a special valve that had possibilities. The order was placed with express shipping guaranteed, and the package arrived two days later.

Ray was quickly wheeled outside onto a shady part of the lawn. It was getting warm out, and we had all learned from past experiments that this reinventing of the beer hat could be very wet. Being a great fan of soda, Ray's hat soon sported a can on each side. A tube was inserted into each of them, and then the two tubes were joined, making a type of long, looping straw. The plan was to place a one-way valve somewhere on the straw part so the liquid would flow only when sucked on, and what was in the straw would remain there until it was sipped again. It was easy in theory, but...

There's something about fizzy soda on a hot day, guys needing a break from the seriousness of impending death, and a crazy idea that can create some of the best times of life. My sister and I vanished inside, handing out extra cans of soda as needed, and soaking in the laughter that erupted every few minutes as Ray, Jake, and Ben got doused with sticky soda as each attempt to make it work required another alteration — and another can of soda.

I knew Ray was getting too much sun, but Mary restrained me from interfering. This was their last chance to laugh together. This was the memory that would carry Ray through those next weeks, and the boys for the rest of their lives. Uncle Ray could not do anything but sip on a straw while his two fellow accomplices cut and pieced, fitted and refitted, soaking him and themselves, until "Uncle Ray's Famous Soda Hat" finally worked!

Yes, indeed, there is much that you can learn about a person by the hat he wears. Ray's hat spoke of patience, kindness and a love that went deeper than an ocean full of soda. When he passed to his new life a month later, he still had a bit of a sunburn. For him, it was a treasured reminder of a sunny day filled with laughter and two of the people he loved: my sons.

~Cecilia Egger McNeal

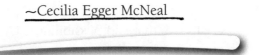

56

Laughing with Mom

The most wasted of all days is one without laughter.
~e.e. cummings

After my mother was diagnosed with Alzheimer's, I learned how exhausting it is to care for someone with this disease. What keeps me going are the funny moments that occur because of my mother's memory loss and confusion.

Yesterday, she said, "I dreamed you had a dog."

I asked, "What kind?"

She said, "A shepherd."

"Oh, a German shepherd?"

She said, "I don't know if he was a German or not."

When Mom doesn't remember a word, she substitutes another one, often with humorous results. She wants to say "education," but instead she will say "constipation." She creates new songs by changing the lyrics. "I Believe I Can Fly" becomes "I Can Fly Like a Pigeon."

Once I said, "Sit down. I want to take your blood pressure."

She said, "I can't. I have too much toxic energy."

Mom has some unusual ideas. To her, it seems like a good idea to wear your nightgown over your clothes if you feel cold. Lately, she's been watching a lot of John Wayne movies. She told me she loved John Wayne and wanted to marry him. I made the mistake of telling her he was dead. After she recovered from the news, she decided she'd like to be buried with him.

Every day holds a surprise for my mother. When I took her to a podiatrist to clip her toenails, she was amazed. She said, "I remember when people did this themselves."

Sometimes, my mother's faulty perceptions are flattering. When I made her a sandwich, she thought I was a genius. She looked at the sandwich as if it was a gourmet meal. "Where did you learn to cook like that?"

I said, "From you."

Mom shook her head. "No, I never made that."

Mom also thinks I'm 30 years younger than I am. She tells me not to worry. She says I'll meet someone soon and get married. She's forgotten I've already been married twice.

I don't know what my mother will say or do today. I hope it makes us laugh. Any day we can laugh together is a good day.

~Laura Boldin-Fournier

57

Humor, 100 mg Daily, as Needed

A person without a sense of humor is like a wagon without springs—
jolted by every pebble in the road.
~Henry Ward Beecher

My husband, Thad, was first diagnosed with testicular cancer in 1981. It manifested itself as a persistent infection of the right testicle with pain on the right side of his body. After six weeks of antibiotics and anti-inflammatory medication, the swelling and lump were only slightly reduced, and a biopsy was scheduled. The biopsy showed a seminoma tumor. Rather than cut into it, the entire right testicle was removed, and an implant was put in its place.

Needless to say, we were frightened. Thad was 32, I was 26, and we had just become parents to our daughter, Francesca, 11 months before. We thought: People this young don't get cancer, do they? Neither of us knew anything about testicular cancer, nor what the operation entailed. I did not want to know. What I did know was that I loved my husband, and we had plans to raise our daughter together, play with grandchildren, and grow old together. And nothing was going to change those plans! I cared for him, not his testicle, and told the doctor as much. Husband alive and well was mandatory—testicles were optional.

When they wheeled Thad into his hospital room after surgery, neither of us wanted to ask exactly what was cut off. The nurse said that as soon as his bodily functions returned to normal, Thad would be discharged. To Thad, that was the sound of the charge, and every couple of minutes he wanted to stand up and try to urinate into the hand-held urinal. As I helped him, I made sure not to look for fear that my face would give away anything that might hurt my husband. It was during one of the attempts that the doctor came in.

He helped Thad settle back down in the bed and asked how he was feeling. Thad said he felt pretty good with just a little pain. Then the doctor pulled back the covers to reveal my husband's resplendent and very naked privates (a complete three-piece set!) basking in the room's daylight!

"Well, what do you think?" his doctor asked me with pride in his voice.

Embarrassed and not having any earthly idea of how to respond, I quipped, "What's not to like?"

The doctor explained. "I want you to appreciate this. I could have given him a small, medium, large or a "wow" testicle. I think I matched his right with the left one pretty well."

It would be 16 years later when Thad and I would meet with this same doctor again to remove another seminoma tumor, this time in his left testicle. His hair was grayer, we were fatter, but the operation was the same. However, the incisions looked markedly different. His first incision was wider and still noticeable after 16 years, while his second incision is barely visible 10 years later. When asked why the difference, his doctor responded, "I got a lot better."

To this day, we laugh when we remember these events. Those were difficult and uncertain days when neither of us thought cancer could happen to us or knew enough to know what to expect. However, in each incident, our doctor used humor to take away some of the fear that we were experiencing. We have used this method of coping time and time again, as we have been caregivers for each other through the myriad of medical issues in our 37 years of marriage. No matter how serious the situation, we have always found a way to get a prescription of humor filled!

~Loretta Schoen

Harvey, Mom, and the Bar

Humor is the great thing, the saving thing. The minute it crops up, all our irritation and resentments slip away, and a sunny spirit takes their place.
~Mark Twain

My mother had an angelic face and a devilish sense of humor—quite the combination. When I was an adolescent, her unexpected puns and punch lines often left me rolling my eyes. Even as an adult, I found myself standing gape-mouthed at many of her sly comments on more occasions than I'd like to admit. However, in her final years, when her already poor health went from bad to worse to failing, it was her sense of humor that carried me through as her caregiver.

No one was off-limits where my mother's biting humor was concerned, and one of Mom's more memorable targets was an acquaintance I'll call Harvey. He was pretty well known in the community—and a regular customer at several bars located throughout the neighborhood. Invariably, each time Mom and I drove out of her development en route to a doctor's appointment or other errand, we would pass one of those old gin mills and spot Harvey's bright red car parked front and center. Mom would always smile sweetly and make her assessment of the situation: "That Harvey. He's not feeling any pain right about now, I'll bet." Then she would nod and wink at me, "All that 'anesthesia,' you know."

Eventually, though, Mom became too weak to climb in and out of my car for even the smallest of trips. Her travels then were limited to medical appointments only, with transportation provided via ambulette where a trained professional could lift and position her and her wheelchair into the vehicle safely. From the back of the ambulette, Mom could no longer view her surroundings as she was driven. Thoughts of Harvey, his bright red car, and his favorite haunts were all but forgotten.

The time also came when even getting out of bed without help became impossible for Mom. Shortly afterward, even sitting up without assistance was difficult. Her doctor suggested some adaptive equipment, including a grab bar at her bedside that Mom could use to pull herself up, allowing her to retain one last bit of independence. I placed the equipment order with the medical supply company, and within a week, the package arrived — without the grab bar. Mom was disappointed, and so was I. That particular item really would have been helpful to both of us. Every few days, I phoned the supplier for an update on its whereabouts, only to get the same explanation: It was on back order.

One day, as I lifted Mom so that she could sit upright and sip some water, she questioned me about the grab bar once again. "Mom, it's still on back order," I explained. "We just have to be patient and wait."

Mom lifted her soft, round face and looked up at me. "I don't have much more time to wait," she said.

I felt my eyes fill with tears. Though I didn't want to accept it, I knew that statement probably was the truth. And in that moment, I felt true helplessness. The grab bar seemed like such a small thing, but still I couldn't find a way to provide it for my mother. All my requests for a rush order on the item continued to fall on deaf ears. Once again, I grabbed the telephone at Mom's bedside and started to dial. "I keep telling those people at the supply house how necessary it is for you to get that last piece of equipment," I said to Mom. "I just don't know what else to tell them."

Mom looked up at me and smiled her angelic smile. Then she

patted my hand softly. "Well, dear," she said, "just tell them I'm like Harvey, and I need a bar."

It took a beat before I caught on to her play of words, but when I did, I started to laugh so hard I almost dropped the phone. Then Mom started to laugh, and we kept laughing together for a good, long while. After I caught my breath, I wiped the tears from my eyes. "You know," I said to Mom, "I think I could use a bar myself right about now." And then we laughed some more.

~Monica A. Andermann

When Your Caregiver
Goes to Therapy

I love being married. It's so great to find that one special person
you want to annoy for the rest of your life.
~Rita Rudner

I promise that my husband, Bob, not only gave me the okay to tell everybody he's in therapy, but he suggested I write this story for two reasons:

1. He feels nobody should be ashamed of seeing a therapist.

2. I'm acting deranged.

Nearly all caregivers are under a lot of stress. Bob's going to therapy because he's having a hard time living with the reality of the huge changes in our lives since my spinal-cord injury.

I vowed I'd never in a million years ask him what he talks about. Here's how it went after his first session.

Me: "What did you talk about?"

He left the room. I grabbed my cane and followed.

"I swear I'm okay about you going to therapy," I lied.

"You're threatened to death."

"I'm not! Unless you talk about me. You don't, right?"

He walked away. I found him in the kitchen. "You didn't talk about sex, did you? That's all every therapist wants to hear about. They're all perverts. That's why they go into the profession in the first place—to hear everybody's dirty stories." I shook my head in disgust. "Can you imagine getting paid to be a sitting peeping Tom?"

He scratched his head and said (sarcastically I think), "Gee. Didn't you have your own therapy practice for 22 years?"

"Yes. That's why I'm an expert at recognizing when people change subjects." I took out a pad and pen. "Let's get back to discussing what you talked about."

"I wasn't talking about that."

I hobbled over to my purse and pulled out a sealed envelope. "Don't read this," I said. "Just give it to your doctor."

He tore open the envelope and read aloud, "No matter what Bob says, I've never pointed out that I can barely walk and he can. I've handled my disability with the courage of Mother Teresa. I have never expressed self-pity in the form of singing all day long, 'Nobody knows the troubles I've seen,' and I do not hum it loudly, heavily sighing between words, while he's sleeping. PS. I didn't start whatever fight he talked about."

He tore up the letter.

"Bob, I just want to know one thing."

"There's never one thing."

"Does he want me to come with you to therapy?"

"I have no idea."

"Oh, no, Bob! He does?" I felt faint.

"I didn't say that."

"I bet he does. I don't want to go," I said. "I'm not mental. You are."

"What makes you say that?"

"Because YOU are the one seeing a shrink!"

He sat with me on the couch and held my hands in his. "Saralee, I like talking to him. It helps me."

"But you could talk to me for free!"

"No offense, but you're a lunatic."

"Oh, if I had a nickel for every time I've heard that. Just try talking to me. I promise on my mother's eyes I'll be objective."

"Your mother's dead."

"Give me one chance," I pleaded.

He sighed, still holding my hands, "Okay. Pretend you're my therapist." I nodded. He said, "Sometimes it's hard being a caregiver."

"You, you, you! Why don't you put yourself in her shoes for a change? Oh, that's right. She can barely walk in her shoes!"

He got up and went to his office, muttering, "I'm not discussing this anymore."

Before his session, I saw him stick a ballpoint pen inside his notebook. He brought that along to take notes. I shuffled to his office and hugged him. I kept my arms around him for a lovingly long time while I gingerly felt his back pockets for the notebook. He softly kissed me and whispered, "It's in my locked desk drawer."

Later, after supper, I said, "Sweetheart. Please forgive me for how I'm acting."

"On one condition," he said.

"Anything. You name it."

"You'll never bring up therapy again."

"Got an alternate condition?"

"Nope."

Caregivers need as much care as the people who are depending on them. If our caregiver wants help, it will actually be better for us, too.

If we're threatened, that's natural. Of course, we're worried about what someone who is close to us is saying about us. But we can help ourselves deal with our fears in a healthy way. Here's how:

1. Remember that a good therapist will actually help improve our situation.

2. Amazon is selling a ballpoint pen that has an 8-gigabyte digital voice recorder inside it.

~Saralee Perel

Queen Bees

When I hear a man preach, I like to see him act as if he were fighting bees.
~Abraham Lincoln

The hill was not very steep, at least not for me. I'm still a young 60, but my two companions are a bit older—94 and 96. These two senior citizens, my aunt and my mother, worked their way slowly up the incline, braced by their canes and pausing a few times to catch their breath. Each year, on this pilgrimage, their climb takes a bit longer and wears them out more, but they never miss it. Little did we know that the hill would be the least of their problems that day.

A cemetery is not the ideal place for a senior outing. But my two favorite elders have a way of making even a trip to the family resting place a laughable, enjoyable time. There were once four Crawley sisters, nicknamed the "Board of Directors" by their children because of their way of meeting life with an incredible optimism. Now there were only two left—my mother, Catty, and her older sister, Rita. Each year in the spring, they took care of their parents' and sisters' graves: cleaning up the grass, watering, and planting favorite flowers for each one. They had done this for years, but were no longer able to do this job or many others without help.

So I became the transportation and their assistant. Even though our trip was late that year because both had been in the hospital followed by a rehabilitation stay, they still insisted that the graves needed their attention. For the first time ever, a nephew had planted the flowers for Memorial Day while they both recuperated, both uneasy not to do it themselves. I thought they might realize that this particular job was just too much for them, but they would have none of that. As soon as both were able to leave the house, we set off. Of course, the graves are up a hill, and the sun beat down as the temperature rose.

They made their way slowly and carefully up the uneven ground. I stayed a step behind, ready to jump if either lost balance. They tottered, wobbled, paused, restarted, tottered some more, wobbled again and laughed all the way, even though I could see they were both in pain.

We reached the graves. My mother and Rita were upset that the mower had left grass all over, obscuring the names of their favorite people. They both insisted on bending down, working at the grass. With both of them bent over hard at work, I first heard the low sound of buzzing.

I saw my mother push against her hearing aid, thinking the buzzing was the battery going bad. Rita shook her head a bit, thinking the buzzing was a dizzy spell coming on. Neither had any idea what was about to happen.

From underneath one of the flowerpots, a line of bees emerged, upset that their homes were being threatened. They didn't come out slowly; they sped out on their mission, about 10 of them, all ready for action.

The little brats came at Rita first. She straightened up really fast and let out a war whoop as she began to flail her arms around her head. One had gotten her in the left ear. Holding her head, she started swinging, kicking her legs, and spinning in circles as Catty came toward her. Of course, that was the wrong thing to do. Now the bees had two targets, then three as I tried to step in. My mother was batting the air around Rita with one hand and started swinging her cane with the other, spinning in circles even faster than her sister. With no thought at all of her aging body, Rita did a Cossack leap into the air to clear the cane that was my mother was swishing wildly. My plan was to swat at the bees, scaring them away, but my mother's batting arm had been reenergized, and I valued my head. Besides, those two 90-plus girls were doing such a great job of hitting the nasty little flyers that they didn't need my help at all. A few more high kicks, full twirls, arm thrusts and ear-splitting war cries (with some rather racy language mixed in, I'm not ashamed to report) soon made those bees head for the next county. My seniors had won!

They realized their victory and sealed the deal with a few more choice invectives about the attackers, then headed back down the hill. I handed each of them their canes, but they just draped the canes over their arms and took the hill in confident strides. I half expected them to break into a chorus-line kick when they arrived at the bottom. They got into the car with no assistance and belted up, and then we drove off from the field of victory.

I could see the fun in their eyes and knew the day was theirs. Rita's ear had swollen to double its size, but she laughed as she looked at it in the mirror. They didn't remember that they were old until the next morning, when complaints registered from all the muscles they had woken up the day before. Getting out of bed was hard for them, but I was glad to assist. The rest of that day was slow and careful, but we all knew that the day before they had been the Queen Bees.

~Anne Crawley

Cue Ball in the Pocket

Every gentleman plays billiards,
but someone who plays billiards too well is no gentleman.
~Thomas Jefferson

When dealing with a disease as difficult as Alzheimer's, it's important to look on the bright side whenever possible. Luckily, when it came to my grandpa, we were able to do just that.

I've read that Alzheimer's patients tend to keep the same temperament they had before they got sick. My grandpa fit this pattern. I'd always known him to be fun-loving and easygoing—except when it came to his Buick, which he was very particular about. When I was growing up, my grandparents often babysat for me, so on nice days Grandpa and I would play catch in the back yard. Later on, we would spend evenings shooting pool at the activity center. He'd grown up in a small Illinois town where the local pool hall was the only center of activity. He'd become so skilled that he could almost always hit a bank shot. He would practice such shots just for fun, to give me a chance to catch up with him.

After he needed more care than Grandma could give him, we moved him to St. Joseph's Home, where the staff of the Alzheimer's ward was cheerful and friendly. The nuns often strolled around giving extra help to patients. There were extensive grounds so that visitors could take their loved ones on walks around the flower gardens. There was a lounge with a pool table.

My grandmother took an apartment across the street from the facility so that she could visit Grandpa every afternoon. Whenever I was in town, I went with her. On summer days, we would take Grandpa outside so that he and I could play catch. Even though his mind wasn't working properly, his hand-eye coordination was excellent. He would still trick me by looking off to the side and throwing the ball right at me. One visitor often brought a dog, and Grandpa would play with it, too, grinning so widely his teeth shone as he threw a stick for it to retrieve.

When I brought my new boyfriend home to Springfield, I wanted Winslow to meet a family member who was so dear to me. Since he was from Sri Lanka, a country where older relatives are usually cared for at home, he had no qualms about accompanying Grandma and me on our daily visit. Together we walked down to the lounge, and when Grandpa saw the pool table, as usual, he wanted to play. I racked the balls and let Grandpa "break." He then started to shoot, often hitting the balls in, while Grandma read a magazine over in the corner.

"He's not playing by the rules," Winslow observed when Grandpa took a shot even after he missed.

"He can't remember them," I explained. "We just hit the balls around."

Despite this handicap, Winslow and I tried a game of sorts, alternating solids and stripes in between Grandpa's erratic turns.

"We have a small problem," Winslow said. "He put the cue ball in his pocket!"

"Fish it out," I suggested, but by then Grandpa had gravitated toward me, so I fished it out instead, put it on the table, and motioned for Winslow to take his next turn.

As we continued our pseudo-games, Grandpa was enjoying himself thoroughly. Even though he sometimes ignored the cue ball, he studied the angles. And even though he hit solids and stripes indiscriminately, Winslow and I were amazed that he made so many more good shots than we did.

The next time Grandpa pocketed the cue ball, Winslow started to fish it out.

"Does your grandpa wear dentures?" Winslow asked, pulling a pair from Grandpa's pocket.

I shook my head "no" as Grandma shouted "Oh, my God!" from across the room.

Winslow and I couldn't stop laughing, and by now, Grandma couldn't either. Grandpa, undeterred, had gone back to his "game."

"Go take them back," Grandma told me. "I hope the nurses aren't mad."

I carefully carried Grandpa's trophy back to the Alzheimer's ward and searched for the head nurse. "Judy, I'm really sorry, but... "

I tried not to giggle as I held up the fake teeth.

Luckily, Judy took things in stride. "You know, they take one another's things all the time."

I did the rounds with her. Most of the other patients were sleeping, and we found dentures in several glasses as we peeked into the patients' rooms. Finally, we reached MaryLou's room, a bright spot full of pillows and stuffed animals. MaryLou was watching TV, not comprehending anything, with a big, toothless grin.

"Of course," Judy said. "I should have known. I think Mike likes her things the best."

I didn't wait around while Nurse Judy sterilized MaryLou's missing teeth.

By the time I got back to the lounge, Winslow was in the middle of a new game with Grandpa, and Grandma had gotten back to her magazine.

"No worries," I said. "The owner never missed them."

"Thank goodness," Grandma said. "It's so embarrassing."

"Think of the bright side," Winslow piped up. "The next time dentures go missing, the nurse will know where to look!"

My grandpa lived another couple of years after the "dentures" incident, and my grandmother cared for him as best she could. The whole family was thankful he could be in such a loving place as

St. Joe's. Whenever I could get back to town, I continued to take Grandpa on walks, play catch, and shoot pool.

But at the end of every session, I always double-checked his pockets.

~D.R. Ransdell

An Unexpected Bucket List

A Note from Joan

I want to introduce to you an extraordinary young woman named Robyn Pring who is the daughter of long-time friends of mine, Dr. Sam Schwartz and the late Diane Schwartz. When Robyn was just 16 years old she learned that her mom Diane had lung cancer. Robyn always took dance classes with my daughters when she was young, so I saw her on a regular basis, but then like many young women she went off to college.

I was quite taken when I learned that Robyn had moved back home to take over the care of her mom when Diane's condition grew more grave. But I never fully understood the full extent of what that commitment meant in Robyn's life until I read her personal account, which you will read below. I am sure that you too will find Robyn's story inspirational.

W e all make many lists in our lifetimes. We list our accomplishments on résumés and our friends on social networking sites. We keep grocery lists, Christmas card lists, and compose an endless parade of daily to-do lists. Most of the time when we have taken the time to write a list, we expect each item to be neatly checked off and soon forgotten by the end. But what happens when a list is left unfinished?

My mother was diagnosed with lung cancer when I was 16 years old. It wasn't long after the epic birthday party my parents threw me that I returned home and was sat down for "the talk." At the time, they promised me miracles. I was to go about my business of finishing high school and getting into college while everyone else pitched in to help her through. I resented this plan, but did as told and eventually she did go into remission, where she stayed for about four years.

When the cancer returned I was halfway through college. My solution was to drop out, get rid of my apartment, and be with my mom, but all the other parties involved seemed to hate my idea and insisted that I stay the course, promising miracles once again. During this period, I rode the train home from New York City every Friday after my last class so I could help out just a little bit. It never felt like enough. My mother was my best friend and in my mind no number of daily phone calls or weekend visits could make up for missing the worst of what my family was going through. All of our dreams came true when she entered remission again. Life would feel normal again, or at least as normal as life can be in any family battling a potentially fatal illness.

Almost five years passed before our world was turned upside down again. We thought she was in the clear, but the cancer was back, bigger and badder then ever. My mother, such a tiny cheerful woman, seemed to have endless fight in her. A five-foot tall super-hero, she had too much passion for life to be taken down by any evil.

But this time felt different. She dreaded the treatments she was now all too familiar with and felt a tremendous amount of unnecessary guilt pulling my father, a doctor, away from his patients again or burdening her own mother, now in her eighties. Though my father was always our family hero, someone had to pay those medical bills and she was desperate to not be alone on the couch with the worst of her thoughts. This time, my parents allowed me to take on the primary caretaker role. Though I loved my job, I gave my two weeks notice the next day. She quit her job to raise me. How often are we given an opportunity to give back to the ones who do so much for us?

My mom and I were always kindred spirits. Our time together had always been filled with adventures, laughter, stories and a deep appreciation for one another's quirky personalities. The first time I took her for her weekly four-hour round of chemotherapy, she found something to joke about at every possible moment. This tiny woman was strapped to a chair double her size, being poisoned by horrific toxins, and yet laughing at bad fashion choices in magazines and baby daddy shows on mid-morning network TV.

During that first session of what would be many, she told me she was determined to heal again, and having her best friend at her side was going to make all the difference. She wanted our time together to be fun. She wanted me to force her out the door and make her live and not allow her to lie in bed, cursing the cosmos. She wanted to make a list of things for us to do while she was recovering and before I went back to work. I happened to have a Betty Boop notebook floating around in my oversized purse. Our brainstorming session began.

By the time we left that day, Mom and I had listed over two pages of things we wanted to do together that neither of us had done before. Some of them were silly like finding stores we always saw on TV but had never been to like HomeGoods and TJ Maxx. Some were places of local historic interest such as the Mark Twain House and Phillipsburg Manor. And some of them were totally out there like the lost, at the time closed to the public, City Hall subway station or a trip to the Andes to sit atop the ruins of Machu Picchu — something she always wanted to do. Our list was filled with adventures that we wanted to have before our lives went back to "normal." I think we both felt blessed to have post-college bonus mother-daughter time that most mothers and daughters never get due to real life getting in the way. I hoped beyond all hope that these distractions and the power of our bond would see her through.

For the next year and a half our routine consisted of chemo Tuesdays, crappy day Thursdays (the day the side effects hit most), a day a week spent with my grandma and the rest of the time was saved for our list or other things we enjoyed doing together. We took in a movie sites bus tour in the city, visited the zoo on a day when babies had just been born, saw the Chagall stained glass windows in Union Church, a Munch exhibit at MoMA and snacked our way through Chelsea Market. We took a great number of three-night girls-only trips to Philadelphia for shopping and Atlantis in the Bahamas. We always left on a Friday and got home in time for Tuesday treatments. Mom even got on a plane to London directly after a treatment to be there in time to watch my future husband graduate from university.

I stood in awe of my mother's strength and will to not only just live, but live well. Her bones and muscles ached, her breath was often shallow, but she kept a smile on her face and an incomparable level of enthusiasm about what she was going to do next. Almost every night, I sat up relatively sleepless wishing I could take her pain away. I'd cry when she looked thinner or if she had been visibly ill that day. The sun would rise as I lost track of time reading about results from trials she was on or the side effects of all the drugs I had to pick up for her. I would have given up anything if it meant she never had to sit in the dreaded chemo chair again. But by mid-morning, I would be back in her service with a master plan on how to get her through the day.

A new to-do list got in the way of us completing our adventures. My wedding was on the horizon and it seemed to be all she could think about. Leave it to Mom to spend over a decade battling cancer and only care about other people. We planned a destination wedding in Rhode Island—as Newport had been on our list and we accidentally found the perfect place while checking it off during a girls' weekend.

The months were filled with food tastings, seating arrangements, dress fittings, and of course lists of the guest and registry variety. I could have gotten married in a decrepit barn filled with spiders and it still would have been great to me as long as my mom made it there. During this period her scans and blood work were not her best. She had done everything right for all this time—treatments, diet, exercise, vitamins and certainly getting out there and living. A few months had turned into nearly two years and she claimed the only reason she was still enduring it was sheer will to not miss my wedding. She got her way.

To me, my mother was the star of our wedding. She looked more glorious than ever in a gold and black lace ball gown, with a long curly wig that she had made just for this occasion. Watching my parents laugh their way through a memorable foxtrot was the highlight of my evening. Every person in that room knew what she had been through to be there that day and they applauded anytime they saw her and I walking together. She glowed with the light of a thousand angels as she danced the night away with almost everyone she ever loved.

As soon as my husband and I returned from our honeymoon, my mother's health took a turn for the worse. Her veins were getting too weak to take treatments, she was rapidly losing weight, and a metastasized tumor in her throat was making it hard for her to swallow. All of this bad news, yet I felt so desperately determined to get her through it. This was my job and I felt like I was failing her. I had been by her side every moment as she had been in my own darkest hours. How could there not be a light on the other side? For the first time in her long illness, she couldn't get off the couch some days and had to visit the hospital a few times. I would take her to multiple specialists, discuss tough issues with her oncologist, deal with visiting nurses, relay information to concerned family members and continued acting my Academy Award-worthy role as the upbeat laidback entertainer. Though I tried so hard to convince myself this was just another rough storm for the weathering, my husband had to see me through nightly maelstroms of tears.

Then came a day when she became tragically weak and urgently needed hydration. I took her to the hospital believing it would be a quick visit. We ended up living there for the next two months. Many days we were supposed to be going home, but then a new infection would pop up or there would be a change on an X-ray. I would come every morning at 6 a.m. and keep her company until 7 or 8 p.m. when my dad would take over for the night. We would play games, watch movies and talk about the items on the list that we hoped to get to someday. She would ask me to take care of my father, my grandma, and the dog, and I'd tell her, "No, you have to get through this to do it yourself." She told me how tired she was of experimental treatment after treatment and made me promise, against my instincts, that should the most recent last-ditch effort not cure her, I was to fight my father on future regimens and let her go in peace. Though she had been a nurse for much of her life, she hated being in the hospital and just wanted to be at home in bed with her dog. I just wanted to get her there.

Mom was set to be released on Valentine's Day to be treated by home nurses. She unexpectedly died hours before she was to go home.

You never expect the people who define your life could ever leave you. You can never prepare for the gaping holes left in your own being once they are gone. For a long time, I felt like I failed her and everyone who trusted me to pull her through. In her last days my mom had told me that though my father has always been her Superman, in the last few years, I was her real hero that made each and every hard day worth fighting for. She said it was hard to give up when I always gave her something to look forward to. I guess I didn't understand this for a long while.

The doctor's treatments gave her 12 years of life, my father's endless doting and research landed her on these miracle trials and all I did was hold her hand through the worst and pester her to get out of the house every day. We didn't make it to Machu Picchu and I couldn't even get her home to her dog. I wasn't anyone's hero. As I began to heal, it started to make a lot more sense to me. My mom didn't want another doctor—she needed a friend and constant companion, something simple we all hope to have in our lives.

We spend so much time tied up in our own responsibilities that there are too many dreams and to-do lists that end up left behind.

The earning potential of our jobs, all the broken things that need fixing, and the trivial obsessions we each take on can stand in the way of the connections we all starve for as human beings. We never have as much time as we want with the people we love so how you utilize the time you are given can make all the difference in the world. Maybe I reopened doors she thought had been closed, or maybe I just did my duty as daughter and best friend, but something about the time we spent together turned part of the worst period of her life into some of her favorite days.

With Mom gone, my responsibilities began to grow by the day. My husband and I gave up our home to move in with my father, another great person who should never have to be alone. I started up a home-based travel business so I can continue to have the freedom to be with the ones I love. I still take my grandma out once a week and I did take care of my mom's elderly rescue dog with every ounce of love I had to give. When our treasured pit bull, Sweet Pea, had to be put to sleep, I made sure it was done while she rested warmly in my mother's bed, the way she had wanted it for herself and never had. Every day I try to do at least one thing Mom would have done. I leave new socks on my father's desk, help friends out of binds, sort out family affairs, perform random acts of kindness, and make charity donations, always in her name and honor. The capacity of her heart was tremendous, and though I doubt I could ever quite live up to it, a daily effort is a good starting point.

And about that list we made… there are still a few things left unchecked but sometimes on weekends I round up my father and husband and we'll cross something off in her honor. Outings such as Dinosaur State Park and the covered bridges of New Hampshire are spent talking about the better times, as we know she is somehow there to share them with us. Every year on the anniversary of her death, I run away from here, but not in the traditional sense. To mourn the anniversary, I choose to celebrate her life and dreams by going somewhere she would have wanted to see. The first year, it was Machu Picchu, the next, the pyramids of Egypt. I stare upon the wonders and I can feel her warmth encompassing me. I feel her smiling as Dad and I carry out the dreams she never had time for. I hope she knows I never would have done any of these things if she hadn't encouraged me to follow my heart. At the time we made our list, I did not know what a Bucket List was. Even if I did, I wouldn't have classified it as one because I didn't think she was going to die. Had we known that was our own bucket list, maybe I would have pushed to do the grander things with her that were left unchecked, but I have a feeling she wouldn't have changed anything about those days we spent conquering the world by each other's side.

~Robyn Pring

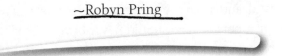

63

Sense of Humor Needed

Laughter and tears are both responses to frustration and exhaustion. I myself prefer to laugh, since there is less cleaning up to do afterward.
~Kurt Vonnegut

Mom is getting more difficult. Lately, we waste so much time arguing and not getting anywhere. I know it is impossible to reason with a person suffering from Alzheimer's, but sometimes I get so frustrated that I can't help myself.

This morning is one of those times. Mom is scheduled to go to adult day care, which gives me a respite for a couple of hours. I will be able to go to my dentist appointment and shopping. We are running late as I am trying to get her out the door.

"Come on, Mom. It's time to go," I say.

"Wait, I want to change my blouse," she says.

"You can't," I state. "It's too late. Besides, what you have on is fine."

"No," she insists. "I don't like this blouse."

"There's nothing wrong with what you have on," I say abruptly and then I shout "WE HAVE TO GO NOW!" as I pull on Mom's arm to get her out the door.

Mom is not happy. And neither am I, especially since I haven't had a good night's sleep for a couple of weeks.

Finally, I drop Mom off at the day care. I'll be able to have a few hours to myself.

I know Mom can't help being so difficult. I feel bitter, too, that

Alzheimer's disease has kidnapped the wonderful mother who loved and cared for me all of my life and left this imposter.

The day flies by, and I feel satisfied with all I have accomplished. It's time to pick up Mom, and I brace myself to resume our futile arguments.

Mom is waiting for me when I arrive.

As we get in the car, I ask pleasantly, "Did you have a nice time today?"

"Yeah, it was fun," she says with excitement.

"That's good. Today was exercise class. I know you love that," I say.

"Yeah, that was fun."

"Did you have a good lunch?" I ask warmly.

"Yeah, it was good."

Then she spots the chocolate candy I have in the car. "Would you like some candy, Mom?"

"Yeah, I'll have a piece," she says, reaching for a miniature Hershey bar. Mom still has a good appetite. And she craves sweets.

Then Mom says, "I'm glad you picked me up instead of that lady who took me this morning. You're the nice one. That other lady who took me this morning is such a bitch."

I am a little shocked at her statement. Then I start to giggle.

"You are right. That woman is a bitch. Everyone says that about her."

"Well, what's wrong with her? Why is she so mean?" Mom asks.

"Oh, who knows? She probably has all kinds of aches and pains. And she just doesn't have a sense of humor like us," I say.

"Well, even if she has aches and pains, she should learn to be a little nicer," Mom says with indignation. Then we both start laughing at that bitchy woman.

"From now on, I'll try to be the one to take you and pick you up," I say.

"Oh, good, 'cause I like you," Mom says.

"I like you, too," I say.

Mom smiles at me. Then I say, "Let's have another piece of candy."

"Good idea," she says.

For the rest of the way home, I find myself smiling at this situation. I vow to take my own advice. The best way to deal with unpleasant situations is with a sense of humor. Even with Alzheimer's, Mom's still teaching me so much about life. She makes me laugh at myself, which keeps me from taking the situation too seriously. Today, I learned not to be like that lady who drove Mom this morning—the one with no sense of humor.

~Lucille Engro DiPaolo

64

Showered with Love

Pure water is the world's first and foremost medicine.
~Slovakian Proverb

I'll never forget the year that my husband's 91-year-old mother came to stay with us in Tennessee. She lived in Delaware and had suffered from several small mini-strokes, and the doctor advised her not to live alone any longer. That was when her two sons decided she should move down south with us until we could sell her Delaware home and get her into an assisted-living facility not far from us.

Grace was a ray of sunshine in our lives! She had so many tales to tell of growing up in a large family of seven children, and most of her stories would make us laugh. She had a wonderful sense of humor and a formidable spirit, believing that when God closed a door, He usually opened a window. No matter what hurdle she had to face, she'd find a way over it, even at 91 years of age.

One incident I recall was when I was trying to convince Grace that it was time she started taking showers, instead of trying to climb in and out of a tub. She had never taken a shower in her life. Our first shower experience was a memorable one!

I took Grace into the bathroom and told her to undress and wrap the towel around herself, and I'd come in and help her get into the shower. When she called to me that she was ready, I entered the bathroom and turned on the water to get it to a comfortable temperature for her. Then I pulled back the shower curtain, handed her the soap, gave her a washcloth, and helped her climb into the tub.

The first thing I heard were her screams when the water hit her smack in the face! "Beverly, WHAT DO I DO?"

"Mom!" I yelled. "Back up a little!"

All I heard were some blubbering noises, and then a "kerplunk."

"I dropped the soap, Beverly!" she bellowed as if I were down the hall in another room.

"Mom, I'm right here... I'll help you find it," I reassured her as I opened the shower curtain.

The water was hitting her smack-dab in the forehead and bouncing off all over me. I tried to guide her frail little body backward as I reached down for the soap, but by now I was washing my own hair in the process!

"I don't want my hair wet," she blubbered.

"It's a little too late for that, Mom," I replied, handing her the soap. "Do you need help washing?"

"I don't like this. I don't know how to do this... I can't SEE!" Grace had her eyes closed as the water hit her neck area and splashed up into her face.

"Why don't you turn around?" I suggested, as I noticed my shirt was now soaking wet.

"I don't want my hair wet," she insisted.

Okay, what to do now?

"Mom, give me the soap, and I'll help you."

"No. I can wash myself. Just stop the water from hitting my face."

There was water all over the bathroom floor at this point, and I had to step carefully so I wouldn't fall and end up in the tub with her! I urged her to back up even more in the tub until the water was just hitting her knees.

"Okay, Mom," I said. "I'm closing the curtain now, and you finish washing. Then step up into the water to get the soap off, okay?"

"Okay."

I left her alone. Grabbing extra towels, I mopped up the bathroom floor and waited. It wasn't more than three or four minutes before she yelled, "I'm finished, Beverly!"

Reaching in to turn off the shower, I looked at Grace and said, "There, now, wasn't that refreshing?"

Then I noticed she was covered in soap.

"Mom, didn't you rinse off the soap?" I asked.

"I don't want that water in my face," she replied.

Gently, I turned on a little warm water and used the washcloth to get the soap off my sweet mother-in-law. She looked as if she'd been dragged through a ringer washing machine, and I could tell she was thinking that her first shower experience would undoubtedly be her last!

We managed to get her out and dried off, and snuggled into her nightgown and robe. She had survived, but she did not enjoy it one little bit.

Grace was with us approximately a year before we got her into a wonderful assisted-living facility just 10 minutes away from us. The nurses and aides there were so good with her, and she learned to love her showers. Maybe I just didn't have what it takes to handle shower duty! Or maybe she just learned after a time how to maneuver in there — and with her shower cap, she did not have to get her hair wet!

We miss Grace. She lived in the facility for about five years until she had to be transferred to a nursing home. Our sweet Grace passed away last August at the age of 98 and eight months old! When I tell my beloved stories about her, I never fail to include her first shower episode that I was so privileged to experience with her.

~Beverly F. Walker

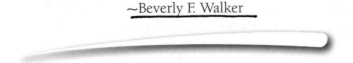

Chapter
6

Family Caregivers

Perseverance

Fall seven times, stand up eight.

~Japanese Proverb

Milkshake Miracle

We do not remember days; we remember moments.
~Cesare Pavese, The Burning Brand

I looked forward to a visit with my mom, who lived 2,000 miles from my home in California. Since Mom was 80 and suffered from Alzheimer's, I realized how important it was to see her again—soon.

Mom received loving care from the Sister Servants of Christ the King at a 40-bed, basic-care facility in Edgeley, North Dakota. She occupied a simple room, spent most of her day doing simple things, and seemed to be "all right," considering that dementia had set in.

When Mom appeared in the lobby, I smiled, hugged and kissed her, and said, "Nice to see you, Mom."

She didn't know who I was! Not a clue that her son (fourth of her five children) was with her. I was devastated.

Stressed out, I spent several hours trying to connect with my mother—talking with her, walking around the grounds, looking at family pictures in her room, chatting with the nuns—doing whatever I could think of to help Mom recognize a member of her own family.

While I was aware that Alzheimer's is incurable and is a leading cause of death in America, I still hoped for a recognition "miracle"—something that would shake Mom loose from her semantic memory problems.

But nothing I said or did worked, and, reluctantly, I returned to my hotel for an overnight stay. I spent several hours worrying and wondering what I could say or do that might bring Mom around. Nothing occurred to me.

But driving to Edgeley the next morning, I suddenly had a "Eureka moment." I thought of something that might jar her memory.

When I arrived at the St. Joseph's Manor, I greeted Sister Teresa and waited for Mom. While waiting for another nun to bring Mom from her room, I obtained permission from Sister Teresa to take Mom downtown for an hour or so. I wanted to treat her at a restaurant — in this case, the Edgeley Coffee Shop (just about the only restaurant in the little town). I drove Mom the few blocks to the café.

After we were greeted and seated, Sandy the waitress asked for our order. While Mom was looking at the menu and peeping out the window, I took Sandy aside, quietly told her of Mom's dementia condition and my plot to jar her long-term memory, and ordered two strawberry milkshakes.

When Sandy delivered the milkshakes, Mom took one sip, looked me in the eye, and said, "This is good, Bobby." She'd recognized me at last, calling me Bobby (as she always had while her memory was intact). I was ecstatic and thanked Sandy for being "in on it."

There's a simple explanation for Mom's recollection. When I was a boy, Mom and Dad and us kids often piled into the Chevy, drove around town, and nearly always stopped at the Polar King for milkshakes (Mom's favorite treat). I'd hit upon one of Mom's episodic memories.

Talk about stress reduction! A serendipitous event allowed me to reconnect with my mother — the last time, as it turned out. Mom died two years later of complications from Alzheimer's. But I had managed to connect with her one last time — thanks to a strawberry milkshake in a little café in Edgeley, North Dakota.

~Robert J. Brake

A Journey of 4,000 Miles

The greatest explorer on this earth never takes voyages as long as those of the man who descends to the depth of his heart.
~Julien Green

The anguish that I felt at the onset of my mother's Parkinson's disease grew more profound as she deteriorated. She had always enjoyed a life full of multiple and diverse activities, and her accomplishments were numerous, ranging from award-winning golfer to licensed pilot. She loved the outdoors and all of nature, and was deeply involved in social and civic activities. She truly loved people, her community, and being on the go.

As my mother's condition worsened over the years and dementia also developed, she was less able to do the activities she loved so much, either indoors or out. My father did his best to care for her, but with his own health declining, it was becoming more difficult. It got to the point where he couldn't even get her outdoors anymore.

I lived near my parents through all of this, but frequent business trips took me away a lot. I always stopped by my parents' house when I was in town, though. With each visit, I made sure to get my mother out and about even when she was eventually confined to a wheelchair. While her movement was more restricted due to the disease, I still promised myself to help her enjoy her favorite activities in new ways, whether it was watching a golf game at the course rather than playing, or sniffing roses in the garden rather than cultivating them. I knew these activities brought joy and enrichment to her life by the small gestures or sounds she could still express.

When my father passed away at 79 years old, my mother had been experiencing Parkinson's for 20 years. He had done an admirable job of caring for her with love and patience. But it had come to the point where she could no longer move on her own or take care of herself in any way. Determined for her to stay in familiar, comfortable surroundings, my dad had hired nursing professionals to come in the home part-time, and he was there for her the rest of the time. I came by to help when I could. Now that my father was gone, though, a critical decision had to be made: Should we keep my mother at home or move her to a nursing facility?

With the cost of full-time home care exceeding our budget, my sister living out of town, and me working full-time, my sister and I decided to move our mother into a care facility. It was with great anguish that I accompanied her to the new place and left with a heavy heart and tears in my eyes. For two days, I couldn't sleep as I thought of the fresh air, blooming flowers, singing birds, and neighborhood activities my mother loved so much and would no longer enjoy. And so, less than 48 hours and two sleepless nights later, I returned to get my mother out of the care facility and bring her back home. I had made the decision to quit my job and move into the family home to become the primary caregiver for my mother.

I decided to take this caregiving journey with my mother all the way to the end, and I vowed to take an active approach, not only tending to her care needs but also enriching her days with the activities and interests that brought her such happiness. That meant getting her outdoors among nature, people, and the bustle of neighborhood activities. Even though her movement and expressions had become quite limited, I knew her heart could still feel love and joy, and this active approach would give her a richer quality of life. After all, she had done so much in giving me a happy, active life as I was growing up.

As I reflected on my idea of the active approach, I thought of the great quote by Lao-tzu, "A journey of a thousand miles begins with a single step." And so I began the full-time caregiving journey with my mother with a single step that became a long walk. Soon, I was planning each day to include three long walks outdoors—in the morning, the afternoon, and early evening. I carefully scheduled my mother's feeding and other care activities so there was plenty of time for our walks. I also allowed some time to get her ready for our outings. I would lift her into the wheelchair and then prepare her for the day's weather—a sweater if it was cool, sunscreen and sunglasses on sunny days, and layers of coats and blankets on cold days. Then, we were out the door and on our way.

Fortunately, we lived a couple of blocks from the village, with its assortment of shops, parks, and services, and the terrain was all flat. Each day, I pushed the wheelchair along, taking my mother into shops, the bakery, the library, or the grocery store. Sometimes, we went to a park or a playground to watch the children.

During these outings with my mother, we were truly in the bustle of neighborhood life. One hot summer day, I pushed her through the sprinkler in front of the municipal building along with some neighborhood children. On several summer nights, I took her to the church lawn to watch the firefly display along with some young families. And on Halloween, I pushed her along the sidewalk with all of the little trick-or-treaters. There was a special joy and energy to these activities that I just knew was stimulating to her.

I continued this active approach of caregiving for three years. I figured with all of our walks we went some 4,000 miles. As the disease progressed, we had to stop occasionally along the way to soothe my mother's coughing or address other health issues that had started to develop. But we never quit our walks. Sure, I felt tired sometimes with all of this physical activity and the physical demands of at-home care, but I remained devoted to getting her out and about. Along the way, we talked to lots of wonderful people and made many new friends of all ages. On one of our walks, we met a woman who would one day become my wife.

One cold winter night, my mother passed away peacefully at home in her own bed. While I felt a great sadness at her passing, I also felt a tremendous gratitude for the journey we had taken together. Because of those walks, my mother's later years were rich with stimulating activity, colorful experiences, and new friends, despite having a debilitating disease that kept her from moving or functioning on her own. And because of these walks and the whole caregiving journey, the bond between my mother and me grew deeper. My understanding of love was changed forever. I had given up a job and an independent life, but had gained a profoundly meaningful experience.

~Rick Semple

Seizing Opportunities

Look at a stone cutter hammering away at his rock, perhaps a hundred
times without as much as a crack showing in it. Yet at the hundred-and-first
blow, it will split in two, and I know it was not the last blow that did it,
but all that had gone before.
~Jacob A. Riis

"Please don't take him from me. I just want to hold him
a little longer. I don't care if his heart has stopped beating." These were the words I cried to the doctor as my
less-than-one-day-old son lay wrapped in a blanket in my arms in a
small waiting room off the neonatal intensive care unit. This was my
first baby, and our family and many of our friends had gathered in
the waiting room where they had just been informed our baby had
died.

Spencer was born on December 29, 1999, and I knew the
moment he was born something was wrong. We did not experience
the birth of our baby as we imagined it would be, where my husband
was allowed to cut the umbilical cord and the baby was placed upon
my chest to hold. Our baby was not crying, and his Apgar scores
were zero.

Doctors and nurses flew to the rescue to work with him, taking
him immediately to the neonatal intensive care unit. He had suffered
a stroke and asphyxia (lack of oxygen) during the birthing process.
We were informed he had lung, heart, and brain damage. A little less
than 24 hours later, he had a seizure for which he was medicated,

and he went into respiratory arrest. The medical team exhausted every rescue measure available to them, and finally called my husband and me in to have an opportunity to hold him for the first and last time.

His heart rate was 18 beats per minute. My husband and I huddled together over this precious little boy, hoping for a miracle but praying for God's will to be done. The doctor kept checking his heart rate in order to call an official time of death. The third time he checked, I knew something was different. Convinced my son had died, I begged the doctor not to take him from me. However, the doctor informed us he was not dead; he was alive. His heart rate was back over 100 beats per minute—a miracle.

He returned to the NICU where he continued to improve. For two weeks, we had every test imaginable run on him. Finally, we were released from the hospital, but were told the damage to his brain was in the area of speech and motor skills, and he would probably never walk or talk.

Every new mom comes home from the hospital with her baby knowing she will be the primary caregiver for her little bundle of joy. For some moms, though, especially those of special-needs children, the job is a bit bigger and more demanding. Such was the case with my son, Spencer. At a few months of age, we began therapy. We did speech, occupational and physical therapy several times a week. I was working a full-time job at a major university, but I had to quit to care for my son and make sure he received the therapy he needed. He eventually sat on his own, crawled and learned to walk, although it was later than most. He learned to sign more than 200 words. Then one day we experienced another miracle when he began talking. By age three, he was completely caught up to where he was supposed to be in both speech and motor skills.

Then, on a cool day in March 2003, he had a seizure. We weren't sure what was happening at first. We went to the hospital where he was medicated to stop the seizure. Afterward, he could not move his right arm, and the right side of his face was drawn, causing his speech to be slurred. We thought he had experienced another stroke.

After a few days in the hospital, he returned to normal and came home. A few months later, he had another seizure. It was then he was diagnosed with epilepsy.

Over the past eight years, we have lived a life of uncertainty, not knowing when a seizure might happen or how severe it might be. Spencer has been on more than 10 different medications and currently takes 19 pills per day to attempt to control his seizures. He has been evaluated for epilepsy brain surgery, but it was determined he was not a candidate. His seizures and the side effects of his medications have caused him to regress in his speech and motor skills. He has been in occupational, physical and speech therapy off and on for most of his life.

In order to advocate for my son, I have had to educate myself about epilepsy, medications, and treatment options. I have changed doctors, even traveling halfway across the country looking for the best one. I have met with teachers and school administrators to make sure he receives adequate accommodations. I have fought tirelessly to educate others and try to end the stigma surrounding epilepsy. I have even gone to our nation's capital to lobby for changes in health care. Has it been a battle? Yes. Has it been worth it? Absolutely. In doing these things, I've changed my son's life and hopefully helped change the lives of other people who suffer with epilepsy. And I have taught my child a valuable lesson: to advocate for himself and others.

He understands that seizing is not just what happens to him, but something he can do. He can seize every opportunity to make a difference in the lives of others through his experiences. He is active in a group of advocates for epilepsy to educate others and bring awareness. He has traveled the country with me, visiting more than 20 states to present educational programs. He has participated in the National Walk for Epilepsy in Washington, D.C., for three years and has put together teams for local awareness walks in the state of Georgia. He has been to Capitol Hill with me. Because I didn't give up, he won't either.

There are times when I am weary and worn down from being

the caregiver of a child with an invisible chronic illness. During those times, something always seems to happen to give me one more day's strength and the will to push forward. A few years ago, I was at a breaking point. Spencer had been in and out of the hospital for 17 straight months. One day, the phone rang, and I received the most wonderful news. We had been selected to receive a seizure response service dog from an organization called Canine Assistants. Lucia, our dog, is a constant companion for Spencer. She is trained to alert us if he has a seizure and has even developed the ability to detect some of his seizures in advance. It's like having an extra set of eyes and hands—or in this case, paws—to take care of Spencer. She has given him confidence and a sense of security, and has given me assistance and assurance.

A few things I've learned as a caregiver through our experience is to seize opportunities to help others, to never give up, and to take help where you can get it, even if it comes from a dog.

~Amy Wyatt

68

Pressure Perfect

The difference between perseverance and obstinacy is that one comes from a strong will, and the other from a strong won't.
~Henry Ward Beecher

Twice I passed my mother in the hall without recognizing her. My own mother. It wasn't just that she looked like all the other nursing facility residents, dozing in their wheelchairs or staring vacantly at nothing. Dementia had changed even the lines and shape of her face until she no longer resembled the person I knew and loved so well.

Or was it dementia?

Our journey had begun a few months before with odd symptoms. Mom leaned to the side when she sat or stood and seemed unaware of it. Her toes curled, and she walked awkwardly on the side of her foot. Though she'd had mild cognitive lapses over the previous year, her memory suddenly took a nosedive. Always a voracious reader, she could no longer follow a story and stopped checking out books from the library. Driving and cooking became impossible. By the time my dad and I realized how much she had declined mentally, the checkbook was in a shambles. I was surprised their utilities hadn't been cut off because of late payments.

Then the falls started. In poor health and with balance problems of his own, my dad could rarely help her up. Calls at four in the morning began with, "I'm sorry to wake you, but..." Mom had always been the one to take care of everyone else, and it was heartbreaking to see her sitting on the floor, helpless.

Visits to the doctor uncovered a few problems that were quickly treated, but nothing slowed her decline. A neurologist asked her age, did a cursory mental test, and proclaimed dementia. But something kept nagging in the back of my mind. She was deteriorating so rapidly, and what about the odd motor symptoms? Was this really simple dementia?

I knew something else was wrong. One night, while praying for wisdom and guidance, I recalled a friend years before whose father had fallen repeatedly and been diagnosed with a treatable condition I had never heard of. What was it? The words leaped into my mind. Normal pressure hydrocephalus.

I raised the possibility at the next visit with the neurologist.

The doctor shook his head. "She doesn't have normal pressure hydrocephalus."

"How do you know?" I asked.

"Her MRI doesn't indicate it."

Fortunately, I had done my homework. "But I thought an MRI couldn't definitively rule out NPH."

"Well," he said, backing down, "we could do a special test called a cisternogram, but you'd have to take her to a neurosurgeon for that."

"Okay," I said.

At the neurosurgeon's office a few weeks later, I again asked about normal pressure hydrocephalus.

"She doesn't have NPH," he said.

Déjà vu. "How do you know?"

"Her MRI doesn't show it, and besides she can lift her feet when she walks. Patients with NPH usually shuffle."

"But sometimes she can't lift her feet. She says it feels like they're glued to the floor."

He didn't appear swayed. "We can do a cisternogram if you really want."

His emphasis on the last words made me feel like a bad daughter, as though I would be putting Mom through an unpleasant test just to satisfy my own curiosity. "I'll talk to my dad."

Before we could make a decision, a fall landed Mom in the hospital. When she came home, my dad exhausted himself trying to follow her everywhere to make sure she didn't fall again. I helped all I could, but I couldn't be there 24 hours a day. Finally, I made the hardest decision I'd ever had to make.

"Dad, we have to put her someplace she can be constantly supervised." Mom's primary doctor had suggested a skilled nursing facility where she could get physical therapy and perhaps regain her strength. The facility doubled as a nursing home.

I expected arguments and tears when I told Mom what we were doing, but she just nodded and said, "Okay." She settled in without a whimper. Her mental state had deteriorated so that she hardly seemed to notice the change.

Barely able to walk when admitted to the nursing facility, Mom continued her swift downward spiral until she could no longer stand and rarely spoke, only answering one or two words to questions. One day I happened to be in Mom's room when the facility's doctor made rounds, and I unloaded on her, explaining my suspicions of NPH.

"We are just beginning to understand normal pressure hydrocephalus," she said. "The learning curve is going straight up. I wouldn't blame you at all for pushing for the test. After all, you only have one mother."

Her words were music to my ears. Though it was probably futile, I had to do everything possible to give my mom a chance at returning to a normal life. We would do the cisternogram — whether it labeled me as a bad daughter or not.

After completion of the three-day test, we returned to the neurosurgeon's office to learn the results. Expecting the doctor to repeat the diagnosis of dementia, I was surprised to hear him mention surgery. "But she doesn't have normal pressure hydrocephalus, right?" I asked.

"Yes, she does."

Thank you, Lord!

Seven months after our ordeal had begun, the neurosurgeon inserted a shunt to drain excess fluid that pressed on Mom's brain. Three days later, she began making complete sentences. Her sense of humor returned, and before long, we were enjoying lively conversations. Despite intensive therapy, Mom only regained limited mobility, but she was able to return home to live with Dad, her husband of 56 years. God's mercy and a daughter's stubborn persistence overcame what seemed like a hopeless situation.

A few days later, I asked Mom how she liked being at home again.

"Oh, didn't I tell you?" She patted my hand. "It's lovely!"

~Terri Cooper

69

Don't Take It Personally

A Note from Joan

When I married my husband, Jeff Konigsberg, I married into a large loving tight-knit family that spends a lot of time together. Jeff's Grandma Rosie quickly became a favorite of mine, as she was a shining example of an eternal optimist who always looked at life through her "rose colored glasses" (this is something that my mom always suggested to me as I was growing up—in those exact words). When Rosie was in her eighties, she was still getting herself dolled up every day, never missed her hair appointment at the beauty parlor and was still going into the gym several times a week.

Despite her efforts to stay healthy, one day Rosie had chest pains and learned she needed double bypass surgery. Amazingly, at 90 they deemed her healthy enough to have this surgery, and she made it through with flying colors. However upon returning home Rosie just wasn't recovering well. Jeff and I flew down to Florida with his parents to cheer her up and get her moving again. When we got to her home, I opened up all the drapes in the house and the sliding glass doors that went to the pool area and the sunshine came streaming in on her. I knew that she liked milkshakes so we had stopped to get her a chocolate Frosty. It wasn't long before Rosie was her smiling self, looking through picture albums and laughing and reminiscing about wonderful times spent together. Our "cheer up" operation complete, we returned home.

Despite Rosie's wonderful optimistic outlook, she missed her family and she wanted to return to New York to be with them. We once again flew to Florida to scoop her up and bring her home. She literally was singing out loud on the flight home and chatting up the flight attendants like she hadn't had a chance to talk to strangers in ages. We moved her into a beautiful senior assisted home where she had a lovely one-bedroom apartment and was surrounded by old family friends from her younger days and of course all of her children, grandchildren and great-grandchildren. She was once again coming to every family function, holiday gatherings and birthdays, dressing up to the nines and smiling ear to ear.

We all felt comforted by the fact that we had given Rosie a renewed happiness, a loving secure last chapter. My mother-in-law Janey visited Rosie daily, and took care of her every need and desire. While moving Rosie back home made Rosie's quality of life much better, it unfortunately did not necessarily do the same for her loving daughter Janey. They had always had an extremely close and loving relationship, but Rosie was becoming more demanding as she grew older and it seemed like Janey could never do enough for her. I have heard about this happening often — sometimes the elderly turn on the family members who are closest to them. It can be very hurtful and it is hard to put in perspective and not take personally.

As the family was planning Rosie's 100th birthday, she developed pneumonia and in less than two weeks she passed away. Janey has since struggled with the guilt of the sometimes tense final days together. As someone who watched the whole situation unfold, I know that my mother-in-law Janey was a wonderful daughter to her mother, who at times could really be tough on her. I admire Janey for her fortitude and her willingness to hang in there anyway. I interviewed Janey for this book, and as you will see below, she is still being hard on herself.

Joan: Janey, what was your relationship like with your mother in the early years?

Janey: Extraordinary! So extraordinary, that unless you were there, you almost wouldn't believe it. We had THE MOST fun relationship. We never had the mother/daughter tension that many people experience. We went shopping together, we went out to lunch together, we laughed together, and I was the envy of all my friends. In that time, most mothers looked like "mothers" who stayed at home with their aprons. My mother was young and beautiful, she played golf and bridge and loved her friends, and many of my friends were jealous of our relationship.

Joan: Your father passed away when you were pregnant with Jeff, which I know was unbelievably difficult for both you and your mother. Your mother eventually remarried. Was that hard for you to accept?

Janey: After my father passed away my mother had an extremely difficult time. She was 50 years old, vibrant, beautiful, the matriarch of her family, and was now alone. She had no interest in dating and was in a very tough place for a while. It took her a long time before she was ready to date again. Then, when her friends introduced her to Bill, a member at their club, she got swooped up and married him within two months. While Bill was enamored with Rosie, he was less taken with her family and he soon after moved the two of them to Florida.

Joan: About five years ago, the day came when you moved Rosie from Florida, back to New York, where she was again able to spend her days surrounded by her children, grandchildren, and great-grandchildren. How did you feel about finally being able to bring her back up to live in your town?

Janey: I was ecstatic to have her back! I thought that it would be just like it used to be. I knew she had limitations now; she could walk, but with a walker for longer distances and a wheelchair for even longer distances, but for general day to day... she could still walk! (Even when she got to be 99 she could still wake up in the middle of the night and get to the bathroom with a little nightlight!) She was still as fashionable as ever—she had pants in every color, one to go with each of her happy, colorful printed tops, and of course perfectly matching jewelry, make-up, and accessories. I thought she was still the same old mom. But when she got back, the complaining started immediately.

I wanted to create the perfect environment for her. I looked at 12 different assisted living facilities before I finally decided on the place I thought would be perfect. It was beautiful, bright, and happy and it didn't feel like an "old people's home," which I knew she wouldn't stand for. I was so excited to show her what I picked... the perfect Rosie place. When I brought her in, she looked around and just said, "I'll think about it." That was the beginning of what it was going to be like having my mother back.

Mom was thrilled to have left Florida, but she wasn't doing so well at adjusting to her new life. She complained about everything: the food, the care aides, the food shopping, everything. I would walk in with five bags of things for her and I would leave with a list.

She was always out of something! It wasn't enough that she had a container of oatmeal. And it wasn't enough to have a backup container of oatmeal. She had to have a backup to the backup container of oatmeal. (The big joke was that she had us buy her toilet paper. I would always bring her the toilet paper and the aides would say "but this senior center provides toilet paper!" But Rosie didn't like the quality, so she stockpiled her own!) I think that when she became dependent on others for her household items, she developed a fear of running out of things. Now in retrospect, I can understand that.

Joan: Your relationship with Rosie became strained, was there a tipping point for you?

Janey: My family and my grandchildren are my life, I love love love being with them and watching them grow and experience their lives. But I do know that they will soon be uninterested in us as grandparents. Kids grow up, they have their own lives, they become teenagers, and I get that. So I cherish this time with them, while they are still young. I started to feel like Rosie was taking a lot of this time away from me. I also wanted to tell her everything that was going on with the kids because I thought she would so appreciate it, but I felt that she became very self-absorbed. I would tell her about something one of the grandkids said, or about a soccer game that morning, and she would just say, "That's nice…" I got no validation from her. Now, she probably took that story or anecdote and shared it with all her friends at dinner that night, bragging about her great-grandchildren. But never to me. It was very frustrating because I wanted her to care so badly the way that I do. That was hard for me.

Joan: I think there's a natural tendency to want to live in the present, and have our elderly parents also live in the present with us and frankly be like they used to be. But sometimes older people have a hard time connecting with what is going on now; however they have a great ability to connect with the past.

Janey: I wish I had realized that then. But I wanted her to be there with me in the here and now… she had just moved all the way up from Florida to be with us! But she wasn't the same person who I remembered and she just didn't really connect with me the same. I think I might have felt scared to bring up the past because my brother had died and I thought it might upset her.

Joan: Did you ever resent her or lose your temper with her?

Janey: I never lost it with her. There were a few things that ticked me off. Like when she thought I wasn't telling her things — keeping things from her — and I felt accused of lying. She thought the doctor would tell me things about her health and I wasn't telling her. One time she found a wrinkle on her face and told me that she *knew* she had had a stroke and I just wasn't telling her. I felt like saying, "Mom, you're almost 100, you might have a wrinkle!" but I didn't, because I didn't want to make her feel bad.

There was one day when my husband Donnie and I were driving in the car with her and she turned and yelled at me, speaking to me like I had never heard her speak before. When Donnie tried to defend me, she snapped at him too. We had never spoken to each other like that in our whole lives. I thought that when she came back up here to New York it was going to be just like it used to be. I thought we would go to the deli and get her favorite sandwich and we would have fun. But there was a tension there that we had never ever had before.

It became uncomfortable to be together and I am so sorry about that. It wasn't pleasant for me and so I didn't go just to hang out. I went when I had a reason to be there, something to bring her or somewhere to go with her. I'm very grateful that I didn't lose it with her, but I also didn't run to see her if I had an hour free here or there. When she had lived in Florida, I used to send my mom little things to her house for no reason. I would send cards, pillows with sweet sayings, just little things to make her smile. And there I was, living right around the corner from her, not looking forward to spending extra time with her because I knew how she would behave and how hurtful it would be for me. How could this have happened?

Even when you and Jeffrey would invite her over for Sunday night dinner, while I loved that she would be with the family, I knew what it meant for me. Jeff was amazing to do that, but I knew on those nights that she would miss the scheduled aide to put her to bed and that it would fall on me. And that was really a tough job. Besides having to get her make-up off, make the change into pajamas, get her into bed, etc... there were her preferences, everything had to be a certain way. The blanket like this, the chair like that, the water filled a certain amount—those late nights were difficult.

Joan: We all knew how hard it was on you and that she really loved you deeply. You did a great job caring for her despite how difficult it was for you. We were all amazed at how healthy Rosie remained, and we were all planning a 100th birthday bash for her in a few months, but one day she complained that she was feeling sick. Tell me about that.

Janey: Rosie really wanted to make it to 100 so badly—she had her outfit all picked out and was excited for her party and all the attention. And it seemed like she was going to make it. If there was one thing Rosie had till the end, it was her health! She really was in great health, but she always thought something was wrong. She would complain about her eyesight all the time even when the doctor told her that her eyes were better than many 80-year-olds! (Rose was 99!) However one day she complained about her breathing so I took her right over to the doctor. She was diagnosed with bronchitis but the doctor told me that he didn't want to put her into the hospital because he was afraid that if he did, she might become dependent and exhausted and never come out as is common with many elderly people. He put her on a massive dose of antibiotics but told me that "this might be it," which totally shocked me.

Joan: But about a week later, she was taken to the hospital in the middle of the night. After only a few days in the hospital Rosie succumbed to the pneumonia. After her death, you were feeling very sad about how strained the relationship had become in the final months and it seems like you are still wrestling with unresolved emotions. Tell me about how you felt and how you are dealing with it.

Janey: I felt grief stricken about her death, and about our relationship at the end. And I still am. I remember watching a video at your house that you and Jeff had made of her in her final months talking to the camera. At one point you guys are talking about how great it is that she is back up living near her family and how "you get to see your daughter every day!" She responded with, "…well, not every day…." That killed me. I did see her probably every other day… but I was not there with her every day the way I felt I should have been. I know everyone says I am being hard on myself, but I can't help how I feel.

I feel that I shouldn't have only gone there when I needed to, and I shouldn't have TRIED to talk so much about the current things that were going on in our lives. I should have gone and talked to her about the past — about all the wonderful stories she had to tell and all the wonderful times we had shared together.

Joan: But Janey, that's with a lot of reflection, and most people don't know this before they have gone through it.

Janey: Yes, I know. And with reflection Donnie and I have also come to realize that some of the things we rolled our eyes at with her, she might have been right about! We laugh that as we get older we now understand some of what she would say. We'd say, "Rosie, you should go to lunch with your friends," or, "Rosie, you love reading the paper; go downstairs to the daily talk about current events." She would respond, "You don't know what it's like to be 99." Well, she was right! As you get older, you get tired from things that you used to do unfazed. Not to mention, she wanted to take her time to pick out her outfit, put on her make-up, get her jewelry on, and all of this took time and energy! She also thought that some of the other women didn't need walkers, and she did. Those things can make a person feel bad, and with some time and reflection we now understand that.

Joan: So how are you dealing with these reflections and regrets?

Janey: I can't say that even after two years that I feel much better about things with my mom. I wake up in the middle of the night thinking about it. I went to the cemetery to talk to her to try to tell her. I just feel that I could have been a better daughter at the end.

Joan: But you brought her back to be with her family and many people grow old all alone, without the loving care of their families!

Janey: Not in our kind of family. You are supposed to be there for each other. I was there for her physically, I did her chores and took her where she needed to go, but I don't think I nourished her enough emotionally.

Joan: But aren't you coming to that conclusion in retrospect?

Janey: I don't want you to think this totally consumes my life. It doesn't. I am grateful for all the wonderful years we had together. I have so many happy things in my life, and I am grateful and happy. But I do think about this every day. I do wake up in the morning and wish that I could turn back the time and have a chance to do it over.

Joan: If you were going to give our readers one piece of advice about caregiving, what would it be?

Janey: I would say talk about the past. You tend to want to have the elderly person you are caring for live in the now... You know, fawn over the grandchildren, and talk about current events. But long-term memory is usually their greatest attribute, so keep talking about the past and all the joyful times you shared together, and just the things that bring them pleasure. I tried to focus on the present, but in the present, Rosie wasn't really herself. Now I realize that I could have talked about other things that she probably would have connected with more and taken her mind off of herself.

Also, there are so many things I wish I had asked. There are so many things that I don't know about her life. I wish I had asked her about when she first met my dad and about their first date. Things like that that I will never get to know about now.

In retrospect, yes, I am dealing with more guilt than I could have ever imagined. But I am also grateful for the unbelievably wonderful years that I spent with my mother. I've thought about it a lot since her death and I understand a lot more now. I just wish I could have had this insight when it mattered most.

Joan: Janey, thank you for sharing such valuable insight with our readers. I think your story will be able to help thousands of other adult children of elderly parents who are dealing with their changing relationships, and learn not to take some of the negative changes so personally. Unfortunately they seem to be a fact of life in many end-of-life relationships.

70

Loving Words

Patriotism is not short, frenzied outbursts of emotion,
but the tranquil and steady dedication of a lifetime.
~Adlai E. Stevenson

As my father napped on the couch, I sat down in his favorite chair and looked out the window. The American flag blew in the warm breeze of the summer afternoon from its post on the front porch railing. Smiling to myself, I thought of the many times Dad had gotten up from his chair that day in order to unfurl the flag after the breeze had wrapped it around its pole.

We had flown an American flag at home for as long as I could remember, and Dad was always a stickler on flag etiquette. Flags should be brought in at night, unless a light shone on them. They should be brought in out of the rain or high winds, although a mild breeze was okay. Even with his advancing Alzheimer's disease, Dad made sure the flag flew unobstructed, no matter if it meant him getting up from his chair numerous times throughout the day.

I shifted my vision to the numerous flowers blooming throughout the front yard and willed myself to find the one that was causing my dad to fret. "That flower's not right," Dad had insisted for the second time in as many minutes as he pointed out the window earlier that day. "Which flower?" I asked. But Dad just pointed out the window, frowning. I had taken Dad outside, and we walked around the yard together, stopping to admire each blossom and bush. As nothing seemed amiss, we went back inside, only to have Dad point out the window moments later saying, "That flower's not right." I was frustrated with myself for not understanding what Dad meant.

Several months earlier, my husband, two daughters and I had moved into my father's home, when it had been determined that it was no longer safe for him to remain at home unsupervised. Although he was still considered to be in the "early stages" of Alzheimer's, each day brought new challenges for all of us to overcome. For example, while Dad could dress himself appropriately each morning, he could not find the words to identify a shirt or a pair of pants.

So, much like a new mother learns to identify with the developing language of her offspring, I began to learn to decipher my father's decreasing communication skills. Earlier that spring, I had purchased six young chicks to raise in Dad's back yard. As I placed a chick in his hand, Dad had gently stroked its soft down and listened in wonder as I described how it would soon grow to be a chicken, and we would enjoy fresh eggs at breakfast. Days later, when Dad had asked to see "the babies," I knew he was referring to the chicks. I learned that when Dad said, "I'm going up top," it meant he was going upstairs to his bedroom for the night. And I knew he wanted to watch baseball on television when he asked, "Are the Phillies working?"

My focus was brought back to the window as the breeze picked up the folds of the flag again. I hoped that whatever concerns Dad had with the flowers would be forgotten when he awoke from his nap. It saddened me to see the defeat in his eyes those times when he realized I couldn't understand him.

Later that day, as we walked around the block enjoying the gorgeous weather, Dad seemed to be in better spirits. He most enjoyed looking at the historic homes in the neighborhood, and he stopped every so often to ask me to read out loud the dates etched on them. Our walk coming to an end, I headed into our driveway, but stopped as I realized Dad wasn't keeping pace with me. I was curious as to why he had stopped in front of the new house that had been built just across the street from ours. Walking toward our new neighbors' porch steps, Dad pointed and said, "That flower isn't right." Frowning and a bit hesitant, I was about to tell Dad that there weren't any flowers on the porch. But then I watched with a smile as Dad walked confidently up the steps to the pillar where the flagpole was mounted. He gently and carefully unfurled our neighbors' flag so that it, too, could wave freely in the breeze.

~Lori Lefferts Davidson

Date Night

Worries go down better with soup.
~Jewish Proverb

The atmosphere is swank and intimate, the dragon roll artfully arranged. The aroma of sweet sushi rice, tangy wasabi and fresh, grated ginger makes my mouth water. Sitting across from my husband at a cozy table for two in a neighborhood sushi bar, for the first time in more than a year, I should be celebrating the moment.

Instead, my mind is at home. On my middle daughter, Elena.

I check my cell phone for the third time since sitting down. No messages. Maybe I should call home anyway. Elena's flirting with another infection, and I don't want our sitter to be blindsided if a fever suddenly hits.

My thumb is hovering above the call button when Phil clears his throat. He's studying me over the top of his glass of Chardonnay.

"What?" I ask, suddenly feeling guilty.

"It's hard to turn off, isn't it?" he says. "I mean, I'm having a hard time relaxing, and I have more practice than you do. At least I get out of the house every day. But you..."

"Live, eat, sleep, and work with my boss?" I say.

Phil smiles and sets down his glass. "Something like that."

Our 19-year-old daughter doesn't actually sleep with us. But we keep a baby monitor in our bedroom for when she needs help in the

314   Perseverance : Date Night

middle of the night. And since I'm Elena's primary caregiver during the day, I'm really on call 24 hours a day.

A couple strolls by our table. Their steps are light, and they're sporting goofy grins as if one just shared an inside joke with the other. We used to be that couple. Carefree. Playful. I catch Phil watching them, and wonder if he ever imagines what our lives would have been like if Elena had never gotten so sick.

It happened one July. The day hot and humid, the sky so bright it hurt to look at it without squinting. One minute Elena, then nine, was playing dress-up with her sisters and cousins, the next she was curled up in a fetal position in her yellow Disney princess costume, screaming and holding her head as if it were about to explode. We begged her to tell us what was wrong. She groaned before slumping in Phil's arms, limp and unresponsive.

We didn't know it at the time, but Elena had suffered a ruptured brain aneurysm. Two weeks she lay in a coma, but by the grace of God she returned to us. She needed to learn how to walk, talk, and be nine again. Against all odds, she did it, graduating from wheelchair to walker to cane in less than a year's time.

Unfortunately, Elena's learning curve stalled. Ten years later, she is stuck at the second-grade level educationally, and unlike the majority of her old friends who are now heading off to college, she needs help with the most basic of things—toileting, eating, dressing, navigating stairs, and taking a shower.

Elena's health continues to be a challenge as well. She is living with aneurysms in her head and kidney. She will need a kidney transplant in the near future. She has developed Moyamoya, a rare, progressive neurological disease in which blood flow to the brain is compromised, leading to symptoms of strokes, TIAs, headaches, and seizures. Neurosurgery is needed in order to slow the degradation, but frequent illnesses have prevented Elena from having the procedure.

If I could leave my job at the office, I know things would be better. But my "office" is my home, and my "job" is my daughter. Quitting is not an option.

"Are you okay?" Phil's brow is furrowed, and his smile no longer lights his eyes. I shake my head, afraid if I answer I might start crying.

Away from the regimen of Elena's daily routine, with its round-the-clock medicine, therapies, and blood pressure checks, there's nothing left to distract me from the reality of what we've lost. Seeing the couple we used to be before we became caregivers doesn't help. It makes my regrets palpable, gives them a seat at the table with us.

The server refills our water glasses. "Anything else I can get for you?" she asks.

I want to say "Yes!" The family life we signed up for. The career I put on hold. A future we can look forward to. "I'm good, thanks," I say instead.

"Do you ever wish things were different?" Phil asks when we're alone again. "I mean, you know, do you ever wonder what things would be like if we were a normal family?"

I practically choke on my water before thunking down my glass. "Every day," I say.

"Really?" he says, and I don't even need to hear the relief in his voice to know what he's feeling. His face gives him away.

"Really," I say, and I'm struck by the irony of the situation. All this time, I'd assumed I was alone in my thinking. All this time, I'd been wrong. To be fair, we've been living in crisis mode for so long, we've barely had time to breathe, let alone share our feelings. But now I'm convinced we need to try harder.

For the first time since sitting down, I relax. I reach for my phone, but this time I'm not checking messages. I create a new to-do list and label it "Date Night."

I spear a piece of sushi and pop it into my mouth. "I have a request," I say, after savoring the bite.

"Name it," he says.

"Can we do this again next month?"

~Kim Winters

The Language of Silence

Love cures people — both the ones who give it and the ones who receive it.
~Karl Menninger

It was a beautiful day on August 13, 1996, when I returned home from attending the first seminar of the new school year. Shortly after I arrived, the phone rang. I recognized my mother's trembling voice as she spoke. "You need to come to the hospital right away. Your daddy's had a stroke. He's conscious, but he isn't talking to us."

Daddy's health had begun to deteriorate some time ago, and he was admitted to the hospital for a colon hemorrhage three days before my mother's call. He would have been released the next day.

My husband and I left immediately to make the two-hour trip to the hospital. As we sped along the interstate, a flood of emotions hit me as memories of my father's voice sped through my mind. "Daddy's speech silenced?" I asked myself. The man who taught me to write my name, who sent me an Easter card signed "Daddy" when I was four, and later drilled me on my spelling words was speechless. As a storyteller, he could make you laugh or make you cry as we sat around the woodstove on a winter night. Enchanted, I listened time after time as he told about the day of my birth on a frosty Easter Sunday morning.

After what seemed like days, we turned into the parking lot and found the spot closest to the hospital entrance. I ran up the stairs to his room where he lay amid a tangle of wires. Brushing back tears, I touched his hand, but his only greeting was a smile. I knew he recognized me. As the nurse suctioned out his mouth, she said, "Who is this pretty girl?" but he remained silent.

Only a week before, I had driven him and my mother through the countryside where he grew up. Each home and family prompted a story. Now my mother and I sat with him through the night and into the next day, and I saw the depth of grief in her eyes. The test results showed he had suffered a massive left-brain stroke, which left him paralyzed on his right side and a victim of aphasia—the inability to speak and process language. Doing research, I learned that one out of three stroke patients experiences aphasia. The recovery of speech depends on the severity of the stroke. Daddy's stroke was severe.

He did manage to say two sentences in the first few days. When I asked him what time it was, he looked at his watch and said, "It's twenty till one," which was correct. Another day, he said, "I'm not going to get any better." That prophetic statement was the last sentence I would ever hear him speak. Yet, he seemed to be aware of his surroundings most of the time.

When I asked him what time it was, he would immediately look at his watch. If I told him it was raining, he looked toward the window and watched the rain splashing against the windowpane. When I asked him to look at the sunset, he watched the sun until it dropped over the horizon.

Daddy spent 17 days in the hospital, and each day was like a cliffhanger in a TV serial as I called my mother, waiting for any change in his speech and physical condition. The physical therapist and speech pathologist continued to work with him, but he made no progress with his speech or motor skills. All he could utter was an occasional "yeah," "oh," and "good." So, he was moved to a nursing home.

I became angry, frustrated, and bitter. I missed him the way he was before the cruel stroke silenced his conversations with me. My heart broke as I watched him struggle with frustration when he could not release the words he wanted to say. Then I started thinking of ways to communicate with him by means other than speaking, and my anger dissipated. One of my aunts gave me an idea when she said, "Reckon he could write something?"

I gave him a notepad and pen, but he could only make a few straight lines. They made no sense to me, but maybe they made sense to him, and I encouraged him to continue making marks. I longed to teach him to write his name as he had taught me to write mine, but maybe he already thought he was writing his name.

Though it meant separation from my family, I went home every weekend to be with my parents. If my dad couldn't speak, my presence would comfort him, knowing he was not alone.

I drew pictures of objects on white index cards with a black marker. They included a sketch of the van he used to haul produce to market. I cut out pictures of fruits and vegetables, which he had grown on the farm. I set up a flannel board on his bedside table. Pointing to the pictures and repeating their names, I asked him to say them, but he remained mute.

When he looked at pictures of family members, he would sometimes cry and sometimes smile. I always wondered what he was thinking in his silence during the times he was connected.

I read children's books to him, changing the conversations to show the grandfather as a main character doing the speaking. He smiled when I read *All the Places to Love* by Patricia MacLachlan.

One day when my sister was home she told me, "He absolutely loves that book *Country Road* by Daniel San Souci." She and other family members continued to read to him and show him the cards when I couldn't be there. As I wheeled him outside to look at the trains on the railroad track, I retold the hobo stories of his youth when he hopped freight trains to find harvest work.

Sunday was the hardest day of the week because I knew I would have to leave him and my mother until the next weekend. Before I left, I took him to the church service in the activity room where I hoped to keep language alive through the preaching and singing.

Daddy stayed in the nursing home for nearly three years with no change. I realized it was not just he who benefited from my visits.

I found myself enjoying these activities and looking forward to the weekends. Karl Menninger says, "Love cures people — both the ones who give it and the ones who receive it."

As I held his hand, one late winter morning in March, he turned his face toward the light in the window and breathed his last breath. I feel he was taken to heaven at that moment. Twelve years have passed since the day he left us. Though he was silenced during his last years on earth, I know he was healed and made whole again. And I wonder now what story he is telling to entertain the angels.

~Janet N. Miracle

73

Adjustment

The leaves of memory seemed to make
A mournful rustling in the dark.
~Henry Wadsworth Longfellow

Late afternoons Mother wanders
the corridors of the nursing home.
She looks for a way out
to a place where she
can recognize herself.

She's gone from her narrow kitchen
once brightened with pink Formica
where she stood for hours in front
of her old gas stove, satisfied
stirring stews or soups, roasting chickens.

Now she can't boil water, the simplest
of tasks. She spends her days wandering
through rooms of other patients,
fills a shopping bag with treasures —
someone's pair of cheap earrings, a borrowed
polyester dress two sizes too large, a terrycloth
robe with tears at the hem. The nurses and I
laugh when she tells us she's tired,
having spent the day shopping.

But late at night I can't laugh
when she grows restless again
and walks the corridors. She
and the others pass each other
again and again trapped like fish
in this waterless bowl. Outside
are flowers and a bench in the garden
where she's not allowed to go.

Each night she re-hides her purse
in a new spot under her mattress,
packs earrings, a dress and a robe
in her pillowcase, ready for her escape.
I know she's standing by the phone
but can't remember anyone's number.

~Sandra Berris

74

A Season to Be Strong

A Note from Joan

I first learned about Penelope Vazquez and her journey of family caregiving from the woman who is in charge of my Resurgence skin care Line at Murad, Marina Randolph. Marina's husband is a professional dancer who tours with major musical performers. Marina shared with me the story of one of her husband's fellow dancers, who had a tragic accident while performing on stage, a ruptured brain aneurysm.

He had only been married a few years to Penelope Vazquez and they had a new baby—their first child, Elijah. Life came to an abrupt halt for this fast-paced young couple who have had to face multiple surgeries and have had to make some very tough personal decisions since his accident. This is a story of true love and devotion and a young woman's strength and perseverance.

I'm 28 years old and my husband and I have been married four years. We have traveled the world dancing professionally. We were performing off-Broadway together when we found out I was pregnant with our first child. We had made a point to really enjoy each other in the first years of marriage and we were ready to settle down and start a family. It was the beginning of a new season in our lives.

We were celebrating our first Father's Day together with our 10-month-old. My husband woke up to breakfast in bed and received a gift that my son and I made for him. It was a good start to the day. My husband hadn't been feeling well five days before. He came home from dance practice and was throwing up and having terrible headaches. We weren't sure what was going on but didn't pay too much mind to it considering injury is very common to dancers. We had plans to take him to the doctor on Monday morning, but we weren't going to let it ruin our first Father's Day together.

On our way to church, shortly after breakfast, my husband starting acting a little weird. He didn't feel like driving and wanted me to hold our son. It was during the service that I was called from the nursery because my husband had passed out. I knew something was terribly wrong when I looked into his eyes as he was being helped onto a gurney. He was completely pale. I immediately felt a knot in my stomach and began to cry.

My first instinct was to start praying with whoever was around me. We were taken to UCLA where we learned that my husband had had a ruptured aneurysm. He had suffered from two ruptures, the first being at dance practice five days before and the second at church when he passed out. He had been walking around with a bleed in his brain, not feeling well but functioning.

I was in shock and couldn't believe this was happening to us. My husband is a good person. Patient, loving, generous, selfless, a leader, wise, humble, humorous and a very talented dancer and actor. He had never been sick in all the time that I had known him and now this horrible thing had happened.

My husband had a third rupture on the table during brain surgery and they were unable to operate. They had to go in with a different plan and you can imagine my reaction when they called me for my consent. All I wanted to hear was that everything went well but that wasn't the case. And I'd like to say that it got better after that but it was only the beginning of a long summer of surgeries, setbacks and multiple complications.

I could see that this was going to be a long road and my husband would only want me to be strong and apply our faith. We are both believers and my husband has spent a lot of time sowing wisdom, patience and faith into me. He has prayed for me and has set the bar for what kind of wife he wants me to be by being an example as a good husband. Not having my husband to lead me through this because he isn't neurologically all there was tough. So I had to change my attitude and thought process. I had to step into a leadership position. It is difficult to see your better half in a vulnerable position. I had to make medical decisions to save his life and on top of it all take care of our baby, bills, home, work, etc. I could have easily had a mental breakdown but I wanted to handle this circumstance the way I know my husband would have if the roles were reversed.

My family, friends, and I stayed with my husband throughout his whole time in ICU. My husband wasn't alone for nine weeks. It was important to keep him surrounded by people who loved him and who would pray over him. I didn't want him to feel alone or fearful and wanted him to know what he was fighting for. My son's first birthday came and I organized the biggest first birthday that I had ever been to, but I wanted my husband to be a part of that too. Although he may not remember it, we opened presents and sang happy birthday to our son Elijah in the ICU room. Even the doctors and nurses came in to join us.

My son took his first steps at the hospital. He was growing before my very eyes and it made me sad that my husband was missing that. I didn't want anything else in our life to have to suffer because of this circumstance. I had been breastfeeding at the time and I had no intention of stopping. It added a little more stress to worry about pumping and then eating right so my milk wouldn't dry up, but I was determined to keep some sort of normalcy for my son. One of the harder decisions I had to make was sending my son off with my mom for several weeks. Would that ruin our bond? Would I have to stop breastfeeding? Would that traumatize our son? These were the questions running through my mind, but I had to prioritize and although my baby needed me, my husband needed me more.

Since my son was with my mom, I was able to be more present with my husband. Not just physically but mentally as well. I supported him as he was beginning his physical, occupational and speech therapy. He had to learn how to walk and talk again. His progress improved when I was there for his therapy, so I tried not to miss any sessions, but that became more challenging over time. I had to start working and that pulled me away from spending as much time with my husband.

Eventually my son came home and I had to balance learning how to be a single mom, take care of the house, work and go back and forth to the hospital to support my husband through his rehabilitation. Sometimes I wish there were five of me, and one of me would be sleeping on a beach somewhere, but I know this is just a season in my life and I have to keep pushing through.

A lot of people tell me I'm strong and that they couldn't do it if they were me. The truth is that when you're put in this position, you just do it. You have no other choice but to step up. It's hard and ugly but it builds character. I know I can handle anything after going through this and I look forward to taking that nap on the beach with my husband by my side.

~Penelope Vazquez

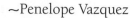

75

Wrestling with Perseverance

Think left and think right and think low and think high.
Oh, the thinks you can think up if only you try!
~Dr. Seuss, Oh, the Thinks You Can Think!

My boys love to wrestle. The youngest is the toughest — Ben uses all of his stout, muscular three-year-old body to bring his older brothers to the ground. My middle one, five-year-old Knox, is more cerebral; he gives play-by-play of who's doing what and whether he's stuck. My oldest just enjoys being in on the game. His secret weapon? The ear-twist. James Dylan's fingers are unusually long and contracted, making for a unique pinching grasp sure to elicit lots of yelps from his stepdad and younger brothers.

James Dylan's name has been shortened to "Dee." He was diagnosed at age 10 with a degenerative neuromuscular disease. We called him James Dylan when he could say all three syllables. Around age six, we shortened it to James D, as he said "Nane D" back then. By age nine, he could only say "Dee," so that's what we've been saying for the past six years. Because Dee doesn't know how not to smash his brothers during wrestling matches, Daddy Stan usually takes him down first and lets the others pile on top. It's a sandwich that always brings a smile to Dee's face and mine, too — until I think they've had enough. Then I plead with my husband to let the boys up.

Letting up is not something I am accustomed to doing when

it comes to my eldest child. For eight years, he was my only child, and his development was my focus. He is developmentally delayed. I fought the school system's label of mental retardation because from my experience that was the one label that caused educators to give up hope of progress. Fighting prejudice against his inabilities became another focus because I knew my son. His sense of humor, the light in his eyes, his antics to get what he wanted made me know that he could and would learn to be more independent than doctors and teachers wanted me to believe.

Then the seizures began, and his balance deteriorated. Although I was still taking him to physical, occupational and speech therapies and doing exercises at home, including an oral-motor program a speech pathologist friend designed, his word list shrank from 150 to 45 recognizable words. He went from wearing leg braces to help him walk at age three to needing no help at age five to needing leg braces again at age 12. Something was wrong.

Then I saw the evidence with my own eyes. The MRI done when the seizures began showed a cerebellum with a nearly normal cauliflower-like appearance, but just three years later, it looked like an oak tree in winter. Too much space. The neurons that typically renew themselves were refusing to do so. My son with the limited self-help skills would sooner or later have no way of helping us help him.

Each summer until he was 10, I attempted toilet training with vigor. This was going to be the year, I would tell myself hopefully. Each year, I would feel we were making progress. Each time I picked up packages of diapers, I would say to the clerk, "I don't think we'll need these much longer. He is becoming more and more successful." But when I learned that his condition is degenerative, I was tempted to give up. And I did for four years. If he couldn't stand on his own or pull up his pants by himself, what was the use of teaching him to use the toilet? Mess after mess, I would cry inwardly to God, "Why? I am going to have to do this for the rest of his life. Why can't he learn just this one skill?"

And God answered as He often does in unexpected ways. Today, I did something I haven't in four years—I pulled out the toileting schedule. Dee really has been more successful lately. Maybe we can try this again. My old optimism is coming back. God has given me hope. God is persistent in that way, giving me small, unexpected victories to help me persevere in my care for Dee.

A few weeks ago, Dee underwent a surgery to remove two of his salivary glands and ligate two others, leaving only his sublingual glands intact. For the first time in his whole life, I do not have to change his shirt four to six times a day. He does not carry a rag, handkerchief, or sport sweatbands to wipe the saliva from his face. Occasionally, if he is listening to relaxing music or bending down, a line of saliva will begin to form, but with a tactile cue, he will wipe his face or use his lips to bring the drool under control. He appears more alert and more talkative to others, though he is the same boy he was one month ago. It is only the perception others have of him that has changed. They now see him as I do: a bright-eyed, handsome, friendly teenager. And their excitement about his "new" potential has encouraged me to challenge him once more. The more I expect, the more he will accomplish. And I unreservedly believe he will master the art of staying dry, provided I trust God for the patience to persevere.

Perseverance is something Dee certainly possesses. I've been known to try to sleep in as I am not a morning person. But Dee rises with the rooster, even before the summer light. One morning, he was hungry and wanted me to get up to find him something to eat. He first said, "Eat. Eat." Then he turned on the light in my bedroom. Then he opened and shut the microwave door in the kitchen. When that didn't work, he found my keychain on top of the microwave and hit the alarm button on my car key. I jumped out of bed and poured that boy some cereal after I stopped the alarm. I know my neighbors did not appreciate the 5:30 alarm, but Dee enjoyed watching his mama move 10 times faster than usual.

My mother used to repeat the old adage, "If at first you don't succeed, try, try again." With Dee, it's try, try, try, try, try, try, try... again, just as God in His mercy and everlasting love forgives, loves and teaches me again and again. Though the lessons may be trying and sometimes especially so, teaching my son to become independent is an endeavor worth every try.

~Ginny Layton

Losing Gracefully

Loss is nothing else but change, and change is Nature's delight.
~Marcus Aurelius, Meditations

How do you spell old age? L-O-S-S. I know. I was there to bear witness.

After my father-in-law's unexpected death that Independence Day, Velma decided to move to Colorado to join her three sons, to immerse herself in their families. But the cost of love and companionship was high: My mother-in-law traded her rural hometown, her beloved house, and most of her worldly possessions to be with us.

In the process, she chose to leave behind other members of her family—her brother, sister, nieces, and nephews. She waved good-bye to her pastor, her girlfriends, her old classmates, her long-time hairdresser, her Sunday school class. She uttered her final farewells at the headstones of her parents, grandparents, and younger sister.

And her husband.

It was my privilege to spend time in Kansas that winter, helping her dismantle the household she'd established decades earlier when her boys were young, her days full, and her dreams rosy. The idea of old age and ill health in those years was still so distant it hadn't even seemed possible.

"What do you want to do with these?" I nodded toward the kitchen counter where rows of vases stood at attention, soldiers waiting for orders.

She blew a tired breath. "Box 'em. The hospital auxiliary will fill them with flower arrangements."

"And those?" I pointed at mountains of craft supplies, rainbows of embroidery floss, and packages of straight pins glinting like mica.

"Well, I was thinking some of the ladies at church might use those up. I've already set aside my scraps and quilting books. They go with me." When she reached for a stack of crocheted doilies on her desk, her hand trembled—a symptom of the disease we suspected but was as yet undiagnosed.

Each closet held surprises. The white Tonka truck my husband treasured in his childhood. A vintage game of *Chutes and Ladders*, still in its original box. Brittle photographs of ancient relatives. We unearthed a lifetime of memories and a flea market's worth of goods amassed throughout six decades of marriage.

"Look here." Velma leafed through her wedding scrapbook. "These gift cards came from Germany, relatives we hadn't heard from during The War." Two heads, one copper and one silver, angled over the pages as we identified signatures and sighed over photographs.

She pawed through boxes and sorted file cabinets, handling each old receipt and rereading every yellowed letter. After a thorough romp through recollections, she left them behind—along with almost everything else she owned.

"No room for any of this in my new apartment at Good Samaritan."

She was right, of course. Space in her new quarters was limited. Even so, I was stunned at how easily she deserted the possessions she'd spent her entire life accumulating and treasuring and storing.

Velma loved her new digs and segued smoothly into assisted living. She contacted old friends from the 25 summers spent at our local campground. She made new friends at the facility, engaged a hairdresser, and purchased yards of fabric to quilt. She attended church services, sang, and sewed baby quilts for her professional caregivers.

But more loss was on the horizon. In a few short months, the doctor diagnosed progressive Parkinson's disease. It wasn't long before Velma's physical needs outgrew the parameters set by the assisted-living facility. As a family, we stepped in to take up the slack. As she steadily declined, we drove her to appointments, escorted her on shopping expeditions, mediated with doctors, oversaw dentures, nursed her through a broken hip, purchased an electric cart, gave her "driving lessons," sat with her at the hospital, and hosted her graduation to a wheelchair.

One by one, she lost her motor skills. Toward the end, we did for her the things her muscles were no longer capable of. We spoon-fed her; we painted her fingernails with her favorite polish — Creamy Carnation — and clipped on her favorite jewelry; we dialed the phone and held it to her ear; and we wiped spittle from the corners of her mouth, straining to catch the words she struggled mightily to speak.

Through it all, she kept up with family near and far. She knew which of the nursing home staff were on vacation, who was expecting a baby, whose teenager was having trouble in school. She read her hometown newspaper and celebrated each victory of the Denver Broncos.

By the time she died, Velma had lost so much — her spouse, her home, and her health. But, ever gracious and accepting of life's circumstances, she set an example for us all. Without complaint or grieving, she willingly gave UP a lot. Yet she never gave IN.

The real loss, I came to realize, wasn't hers... it was ours.

~Carol McAdoo Rehme

Is There a Doctor in the Family?

Good instincts usually tell you what to do long before your head has figured it out.
~Michael Burke

Recently, my mother-in-law, Sylvia, was diagnosed with ovarian cancer. She chose, for reasons of her own, to keep this news to herself for three months. By the time she let her children in on her little secret, she had also made another decision. She didn't want any treatment.

I know 85 years is a long time on this earth, and my mother-in-law was "feeling fine" (her reported reason for keeping mum). And if treatment was going to cause her to suffer and not buy her significantly more time, then I'd be all for this plan to just run the clock out on her life.

But she was operating in a vacuum; we all were. We needed information. That's where I came in. I'm the doctor in the family. Being a pediatrician, ovarian cancer is not one of my specialties. But I do know how to search the scientific literature to answer certain questions: What is her prognosis? What is the recommended treatment? What are the side effects?

I came up with good news. With chemotherapy alone, her life expectancy could increase by as much as 36 months. And though her blood counts might decrease, putting her at risk for infection, other side effects she dreaded like nausea and hair loss were less likely. I called her, armed with this new information. She agreed to see the oncologist. I was elated.

But was I cherry-picking my data? I was supposed to be objective; I'm a doctor. But I'm also a daughter-in-law who desperately wanted her mother-in-law to live. Was I simply putting a rosy spin on grim statistics, hoping to nudge her gently toward treatment just so I could have her for another few years? Was I being selfish?

I kept searching. An Australian study found that chemotherapy was well-tolerated by fit elderly patients. An Italian study concluded that older women with ovarian cancer were not being offered appropriate chemotherapy by physicians who falsely believed they wouldn't tolerate the drugs' side effects. These reports sounded promising.

My sister-in-law, Marilyn, and I took Sylvia to her appointment. The doctor summarized their interactions thus far.

"Last time we met, Sylvia, you didn't want any treatment. You were feeling pretty well, and you didn't want to lose your hair. What changed?"

Sylvia arched her eyebrows in my direction. I smiled sheepishly. He answered our questions. How much time did she have without treatment? (Maybe six months.) What about with it? (A year, maybe more.) What about side effects? (Low blood counts. Infection.) Nausea and hair loss? (Not so much.)

Sylvia took it all in, seemingly unconvinced. Silence filled the room. I told her about the Italian study with the elderly women not being offered treatment. We waited.

"Well?" her doctor asked. "It's up to you, Sylvia."

"I'll take it," she announced. Marilyn and I looked at each other, stunned but delighted.

The doctor led us all down the hall and showed us the room where Sylvia would have her treatments. Full-length glass windows looked out on a small, tree-lined courtyard. Half a dozen fairly healthy-looking patients sat hooked up to their IVs. They watched TV or worked on laptops. The doctor boasted about the presence of WiFi. We snickered among ourselves.

"I'll bring a book," Sylvia said.

We chose a date with the receptionist and penciled it into our calendars. Then we left. We walked out into the chilly autumn air. Clouds were gathering. It felt like snow.

In the car headed home, we shared our surprise and pleasure with Sylvia.

"What changed your mind?" I asked.

"It was that article you told me about, the one where the women were being denied treatment just because they were old." My feminist mother-in-law would be damned if she was going to let someone write her off just because she was 85!

We dropped Sylvia off at the Jewish funeral home in town. Another one of Sylvia's friends had died. She waved off our offers to go in with her.

"I'll find a ride home," she insisted, wrapping her scarf around her neck and heading inside.

Marilyn and I ate lunch at a Vietnamese restaurant downtown. We reveled in Sylvia's acceptance of the chemo and marveled at her spunky reason for acquiescing. We clinked our thick white cups of green tea together in a toast to Sylvia.

"Thanks for coming, Cal," Marilyn said. "She wouldn't have agreed without you."

But driving home alone, my doubts began to creep in. Had I only seen what I wanted to see in the studies I'd looked at? I knew that if Sylvia did well and had a few more good years with us—a few more vacations at the beach, another couple of Passover dinners—I might be credited with the bonus time. But if she suffered... if I was wrong... if her hair fell out... if she got an infection... if this didn't buy her much time at all... I'd be held responsible for that, too. By her. By my husband. Or maybe just by myself.

It's been six months now, and so far so good. No hair loss. No nausea. No infections. Her CA-125 levels are falling nicely. We know we have to lose Sylvia eventually. But we have her with us for now. I don't take any particular credit for her longevity. I'm just glad to have her here, each day a gift.

~Carolyn Roy-Bornstein

Chapter 7

Family Caregivers

Blessings

All that we behold is full of blessings.

~William Wordsworth

Family Meals:
The Whole Family
Approach

A Note from Joan

I first met Michael Tucker and Jill Eikenberry when they were starring together on the hit television series *L.A. Law*. I was always intrigued by this couple, since as actors they worked on so many professional projects together. Therefore it did not surprise me at all when I learned that they had collaborated on a book about a very challenging chapter in their personal life.

Michael and Jill made a decision to leave behind their Hollywood life filled with glitz and paparazzi, and move to the quiet countryside of central Italy to live in their dream home, a 350-year-old stone farmhouse. However not too long after the dream life had begun, it was abruptly interrupted. What happened next led them to reexamine their lives and reinterpret the meaning of family. Michael has written a wonderful book about their family journey called *Family Meals: Coming Together to Care for an Aging Parent*. I had an opportunity to talk with Jill and Michael about their experience in family caregiving and how it changed their lives.

Joan to Michael: Michael, this idea of living in a farmhouse in the Italian countryside was really a lifelong dream of yours and it took you years to talk Jill into it. Jill finally agreed and you guys went over there and then all of a sudden one day you got a call that changed everything. Tell us about that call.

Jill: The call was from a friend who told me my mom's husband had died at 91. And I unfortunately had been awaiting this call. In fact it was hard for me to go to Italy that particular summer because I was worried the call was going to come.

Michael: When the phone call came, it was of course, at a chaotic time. We had houseguests, and this and that, but we picked up immediately and went to Santa Barbara to where Jill's mom, Laura, was living.

Jill: My concern for my mom was I felt that she was starting to lose it mentally. In fact, her husband had been saying for years it was worse than anybody knew. I thought he was kind of looking over her shoulder all the time, making it sound worse than it was. What I found out after he died was he had been covering for her, and in fact it was a lot worse than we thought.

Joan: And I know how hard it can be when you live far away, as you know we have similar situations—since I am in charge of my mom's health and she lives on the West Coast and is exactly the same age as your mom, Jill. How did you go about deciding how to handle this? These are decisions that would affect how you all live the rest of your lives. Do you bring her to you? Do you have her live with you? These are hard decisions, family decisions. They can't just be your decision.

Michael: We actually tripped into these decisions. They were sort of forced on us as we were bumbling through this. At that time, there was literally no one to take care of Jill's mother. They wouldn't let her back into the assisted living because she needed full-time care.

Jill: And I'm an only child. There was no other place for my mom to go, and I was just beside myself. What do I do? Michael and I had to go back to New York for some work that we were doing. We left my mom in a hospital temporarily while we tried to figure out how we were going to solve this problem. We went out to dinner with our son Max and I was just hysterical, and Max said, "Mom, Grandma has to come here. She has to come to New York."

Joan: So you settled in New York, which is something you guys are happy with — you've lived in New York on and off over the years and you were able to get your mom an apartment across the hall from you.

Michael: Well, eventually we did. Actually at first we moved Laura to a senior living center. And this was not the right place for her. I think it was really the low point for Jill. Jill went to visit her, and she was with her all the time. Her mother would look at her and say, "What have you done to me? You have ruined my life. I have no friends." This was very hard for both of them.

Joan: Michael, it was hard for you too, I can see.

Michael: Yes, hard for me too… One day I came home and I saw the real estate guy who sold us our apartment outside my door. He was showing the apartment across the hall. I asked if he was selling that apartment and he said, "No, this is a rental." So we took it, and we moved her in across the hall and we got her aides so she has 24-hour care.

Joan: Though stressful, you tell the story in your book about how through all of this, you reestablished a wonderful closeness with your children and brought them into the family caregiving process.

Jill: I don't think if you asked me five years ago whether this could ever happen to our family that I would believe it.

Michael: Allison, our daughter, prepares all of Laura's meals in our kitchen, which has made me so much closer to my daughter than I've ever been.

Joan: Jill, how has this family caregiving solution been for you?

Jill: At first it was a 24-hour job for me when my mom came to New York. I could think of nothing else. But gradually what I discovered was that the aides, these extraordinary women from the Caribbean, knew my mother better than I did. They knew what to do for her since they specialized in dementia. They accepted her for who she was now. I was still trying to make her who she was then. And it was always so hard for me, because I would see a little spark of my mother and I would suddenly rush in and be disappointed over and over.

Joan: So what advice would you give to other families who are dealing with parents or other family members who just can't take care of themselves?

Michael: My advice, and it's one of the stronger themes in the book, is that while you have to take care of your parent, you also have to live your life. Don't give up one for the other. This was our struggle.

Jill: My advice is to try to figure out a way to let go of your expectations, of what was, and embrace what is. There are some wonderful things about my mother having been able to lift off the burden of that personality she was trying to carry around for so long. And now there's contentment on her face that I know comes from having let go. And so if she can let it go, I better be able to do that too.

Joan: And the book, *Family Meals: Coming Together to Care for an*

Aging Parent, is filled with more heartwarming advice like this. Thank you for sharing your story.

79

The Unexpected Blessing

Caring is the essence of nursing.
~Jean Watson

"I'm sorry, Adaline," the doctor said sternly yet with compassion, "but it's no longer safe for you to live alone in your house. You need to move into a smaller place without stairs. You simply can't handle another fall down those stairs."

"I see your point, but I'm not eager to leave the house," my husband's 85-year-old mother responded with a crack in her voice and tears in her eyes.

Accepting his advice was not easy for Adaline since she had lived in her home for 62 years. And it wasn't just any house; it had been built by her father when she married Herbert, her husband of 51 years. Both my husband Tom and his sister had been born in the house, and our three girls had spent innumerable days there playing in the attic and basement. The memories imprinted in the walls were countless and precious, but Adaline knew she had to part with the home if she wanted to live to see age 86.

We prepared the house for sale and moved Adaline into a ranch condo that was next to an assisted-living and nursing home facility. She had the freedom to live independently, but could eat at the facility when desired. She only lasted there two years when it became too much for her. Next came assisted-living, followed swiftly by the nursing home.

It was during these latter years of moving her to progressively smaller and simpler living quarters that I assumed the role of primary caregiver for Adaline. I didn't necessarily choose the role; it chose me.

"I think I should be the one to take Mom to her doctors' appointments," I announced to Tom when Adaline's health began to decline and the doctors' visits increased. "As a nurse, I feel that I will know the questions to ask the doctors and will understand what is going on with Mom's health."

"Okay, but that's a lot of driving," Tom said, thinking of the one hundred miles I would have to drive for each visit.

"Yes, it is, but I feel like this is something I should do for her."

I happily delivered Adaline to visit after visit, but soon their frequency took a toll on me. Realizing the sacrifice of time and energy I was making to help her, she developed a much-appreciated sense of humor to help us through each visit. While we were sitting in the waiting room for one such visit, I noticed bruises on her arms. When she saw me looking at her arms, she said, "You should have seen the other guy!"

During another appointment, Adaline must have seen the fatigue I felt from working full-time and spending three to four hours driving her to doctors' appointments two or three days each week. I'm sure she felt like a burden to me because she said, "They just can't get rid of me. I thought about walking into the middle of the lake to drown myself, but with my luck, someone would save me!"

Chuckling, I responded, "Mom, you know I don't mind taking you to your appointments. It's part of my calling as a nurse." Adaline appreciated my response because she had also been a nurse. For many years, she and Old Doc Miller had driven around together on the country roads of southeastern Iowa, delivering babies in people's homes.

While driving her to the cardiologist one day, I asked, "Would you like to go to Long John Silver's on our way back?"

With a twinkle in her eyes, she responded, "Oooh, Long John Silver's. Wouldn't that be a treat?" It was her favorite restaurant and one that she hadn't visited in many years. When we arrived, Adaline got renewed strength in her 91-year-old bones. She moved her walker up the ramp and through the restaurant door without a hitch. She even managed to use the restroom by herself! This visit was a memorable one. I got to experience her youthful side one last time and was privileged to be the one to share her last meal at Long John Silver's with her.

Adaline's character provided much appreciated comedic relief, too, without her even realizing it. One Halloween, Tom and I visited her at the nursing home. She was in the dining area with other residents where they were decorating Halloween cookies, or at least that's what she had been doing at one point. All that remained of her cookies by the time we arrived were crumbs stuck to her face and spilled down her shirt. We suppressed our laughs as we looked at her innocent expression and asked if she wanted another cookie.

All of the laughs I experienced thanks to Adaline helped to sustain me through the last 10 months of her life when she had seven separate hospitalizations. We spent countless hours together in the emergency room where we chatted about lighthearted topics. Although she was far more tired of the hospital visits than I was, she maintained a positive attitude and joyful spirit, even when the nurses struggled to start an IV in her barely visible veins. Her attitude helped to pull me through the hospitalizations, each of which was emotionally and physically exhausting.

Although Adaline Valentine strove to make it to one hundred, which would have been six months longer than her father had lived, this was not to be. She died the day after her 92nd birthday.

While she may have felt like she was a burden to me, my time with Adaline during her countless doctors' appointments and hospital visits was a great blessing. Although I didn't realize it at the time, she helped me discover that my calling now that I'm retired is to assist the elderly. Since her death, I've gladly assisted two other elderly family members when their health deteriorated. I can only hope that someone will care enough to do the same for me one day.

~Janet Zuber as told to Heather Zuber-Harshman

80

Words to the Wise

It is impossible to speak in such a way that you cannot be misunderstood.
~Karl Popper, Unended Quest

Mom is in bed when I visit one afternoon, her eyes open, her hands twisting the blanket like a kid who's had enough of her nap. She smiles when I walk in.

"Hi, Mom, how are you?" I say and think about my friend who decries such pleasantries, thinking they are inane and not designed to inspire a meaningful dialogue. I certainly expect no direct response from Mom, but the greeting makes me feel normal.

"Do you have any...?" Mom says, raising her head.

She looks at me expectantly, and I say, "No, I don't have any today."

"How are," she says, and I feel a little thrill at this social nicety.

"I'm fine, Mom. How are you?"

"I know what you mean," she says, looking out toward the hallway.

I am excited by Mom's little monologue. Alzheimer's has erased most of Mom's considerable vocabulary, and this spill of words is a treat. As I stroke her arm and smile at her, I realize I am literally listening to my mother's last words.

In the movies, the last words are profound gems of wisdom, uttered upon a deathbed. Those words are a raft to hang onto so you don't drown with grief. Though my mother is lying in bed, she is definitely not dying. In fact, given her vast years and advanced Alzheimer's, she's relatively physically healthy.

"Well we item," Mom says. "All right."

She no longer needs a listener's approval. She no longer checks for understanding. The words tumble out, like the random winnings from a nickel slot machine.

"So, but that's," Mom says, as I touch her leg.

"Well, we," Mom laughs.

"Why."

"Oh."

"That's right."

Each word is an independent contractor, a one-act play. Mom's words require interpretation, involvement, imagination, and curiosity. Unlike last words in a deathbed scene, Mom's words do not neatly sum up her life or philosophy. Still, these words are gifts. Many visits go by with the barest scraps of language. I get out my pen and paper and write down every one of my mother's last words.

"Okay."

"I don't know."

"I paid."

"But her," Mom points to the blank wall.

"There you are," Mom says, and she may be referring to me.

"Uhuh."

"Yeah."

"I'll try."

As I write, I imagine she is giving me a secret code, sending me a message from the last cognitive bastion of her brain. "I don't know. I paid. I'll try." What depth, what meaning, what spiritual significance these simple phrases might have.

"Since I set up a peg," Mom blurts out. I know she is only partially revealing her intriguing hidden agenda.

Across the hall, a television set blares out the *Jeopardy!* theme. The receptionist pages the head nurse. The cleaning cart bumps down the hallway. Two nurse's aides walk past, talking about vacation time.

"No," Mom says. She looks right at me and smiles.

"No what, Mom?" I ask.

"But she didn't," Mom says.

As I memorialize my mom, I listen to the *Jeopardy!* contestants. Their brains are bursting with all kinds of fascinating data. Full, well-formed sentences flow seductively from their mouths. They are wealthy in concept and language. Mom used to be rich in language, rich from reading, from painting, from going to movies and concerts, from listening to others. She was eager to get into conversations.

I think of times when Mom visited me, and we'd stay up late, drinking coffee, eating cookies, and talking. It was ordinary conversation, unadorned cotton cloth. But now, those casual talks seem like intricate embroidery on plush velvet.

"Where did I get," Mom says.

"You can."

Jan, the activities director, drops in. "Hi, Frances," she croons to Mom.

Mom smiles and says, "There just."

"Mom's really talking a lot today," I say.

"She's doing so well," Jan says. I feel a small sense of pride. I have seen my mother praised for many things—her cooking, her friendship, her gardening, and her oil painting. Today she is being praised for smiling and saying a few words. She is being praised just for being who she is.

Jan looks lovingly at Mom as Mom says, "They don't. Oh, really."

"I'm gonna," Mom says after Jan leaves.

"I'm going to leave soon, Mom. I love you, Mom," I say, leaning down to kiss her cheek.

"Yeah, I know that."

I leave quickly, wanting to hang onto that last quartet of words, wanting to believe those words are true, and they are just for me.

~Deborah Shouse

They Call Me Chuck

How far you go in life depends on your being tender with the young,
compassionate with the aged, sympathetic with the striving and tolerant
of the weak and strong. Because someday in your life you will
have been all of these.
~George Washington Carver

In his prime, Grampa Charlie stood at 6'3" and weighed in around 220 pounds. He'd graduated from Central Washington Normal School and taught school for two years outside Tacoma. Then he earned a law degree from the University of Washington, but he never used it. In his heart, he was always a farmer.

Gramps liked working with his hands, to till the earth and watch things grow, and took pride in baling his own hay to feed his dairy cows.

"Take a bite of this," he said long ago, slicing off a portion of an apple with his pocketknife. "Know what kind of apple that is?"

I shook my head.

"Smell it," said Gramps.

Dutifully, I sniffed the apple, but it didn't reveal any useful clues.

"That's a Gravenstein," he explained. "Sweeter than a Macintosh. Comes on right after the Transparents and earlier than the Kings. Gravensteins are best for eating off the tree and for making applesauce."

I chewed my piece of apple and nodded thoughtfully, trying hard to remember everything he ever tried to teach me.

Fast-forward a few years, and now Gramps and I claimed the same alma mater. He gave me his old brass school bell "to call the kids in from recess," and his rubber-tipped pointer "so you can point to things on the map without getting in the way."

Another decade went by, and it nearly broke my heart when Gramps, at age 94, needed to move into a care facility where there were people who were better equipped to help him with his day-to-day challenges.

Gramps was a World War I veteran, and we found the perfect place for him to be with other men with his background. At first I worried that the people we entrusted his care to wouldn't really listen to him; that he'd be just another old war vet.

When I went to see him one day and found his bed empty, I asked at the closest nurses' station where I could find him. "Chuck's out back," I was told.

"Chuck? Who's Chuck?"

"Well," said the young nurse's aide, "we already had a Charles and two Charlies, so your grandfather said we could call him Chuck because that was what they called him in college."

"I never knew that." I smiled and shook my head as I went out the back doors.

"Chuck" was sitting in his wheelchair on the lawn, gazing out over the water.

"Hey, Gramps!" I called.

He turned and smiled. "Lookie what they did for me." He gestured to the nearby mason wall of the rest home.

A 10-foot row of colorful sweet peas had been planted along the wall, and the prolifically blooming plants were climbing up a trellis. A sign next to the flowers read: "Chuck's Pea Patch."

Without a word, I sat on the lawn next to my grandfather, the sweet smell of summer washing over us both.

"They really care for you here, don't they, Grampa Charlie?" I finally choked out.

"They call me Chuck," said Gramps. "I like that."

I liked that, too, and I never gave another thought to the quality of his care.

~Jan Bono

Foggy Blessings

*Being considerate of others will take your children further in life
than any college degree.*
~Marian Wright Edelman

I was driving one day with both my teenage girls in the car. An intersection was ahead. The "fibro fog" was thick that day, and as I looked at the traffic light, I couldn't figure out what it meant. The light was green, and my mind was blank—what did that mean? Approaching the light, panic rose in my chest—what was I supposed to do: go or stop?

"What does a green light mean?" I asked my girls.

They both shouted, "Go! Go, Mom, go!"

So I went. This was the first time I realized how serious the effects of fibromyalgia could be on my judgment. I had noticed lapses in memory or judgment, but at this moment in time, I realized how vulnerable I really was and that the consequences could affect my children in a significant way.

This was a turning point—I gave the kids, who were both licensed drivers, permission to "call me out" on my driving. If I seemed too tired or spacey to drive, they could tell me to pull over and take over the driving. Nowadays, I am better at telling beforehand if I am too fatigued or my mind is too cloudy to drive, and the girls accompany me on errands.

This turning point was one of many leading to a transition and change in my relationship with my kids. I am the mom. I am supposed to take care of my kids, not vice versa. I am supposed to be someone they can depend on, a financial safety net, the stable rock in times of trouble or turmoil. I was supposed to be the vibrant, active mom who participated hands-on in all their activities, the mom who filled up the van with kids, transporting them from one place to the next. But instead I struggled to make it to their plays, concerts, and award ceremonies. I would frantically go down a list of friends and people available to acquire rides to doctors' appointments and social events. I struggled to make it to the grocery store, and dinner became whatever was "easy."

I don't know if other parents with chronic illnesses feel like failures. I know that I have felt that way many times. More and more frequently, I find my kids taking care of me. Massaging sore muscles, making sure I eat, carrying in the groceries, opening jars, catching me before I trip, repeating what they have already told me. They find the memory loss and lack of concentration very annoying. My younger daughter commented on how I never used to watch movies more than once, but now that I can't remember them very well, I'm okay with watching them again. "It's like you're seeing them for the first time, Mom," she laughed.

It's times like those, when we can laugh about how our life has changed, that seem so precious. It's times when my daughter is rubbing my purple swollen feet that I realize how much she loves me. I mean, really, teenagers have much more entertaining things to do than take care of their sick mom. When my older daughter stepped up and taught her sister how to drive on the freeway — a job I had failed to do — I was so proud of her and so grateful she was there to pick up the slack without having to be asked. I have watched my girls take responsibility when they should not have to, but they do anyway without complaint, with love, kindness, and compassion. They are gentle and tender in their manner, and their love shows through so completely. I realize what strong women they have become, and I am grateful for that — not the means, but the consequence.

Although I feel like a failure having my kids take care of me, I see how close we all are. I see how compassionate they are to others who are ill. And I see how much they love me in spite of my deficiencies. These are some powerful blessings.

~Nancy Engler

One in a Million

Sometimes even to live is an act of courage.
~Lucius Annaeus Seneca, Letters to Lucilius

"What's harder, being the caregiver or being the patient?" I asked. My husband, Michael, and I stated in emphatic unison: "The caregiver." We both had the "opportunity" to occupy the roles of patient and caregiver. We understood, implicitly, the impact—physically and emotionally—of caregiving.

We lay on the bed holding hands. He shivered under the covers. I was on top of them, warm enough to break a sweat. I watched the shadows race each other across the ceiling as early evening began to settle in.

I leaned over and kissed my husband's clammy forehead. As I did so, I caught a chill. It had nothing to do with the ambient temperature. It was a warm, beautiful early evening in late spring. But the frigid fingers of knowledge running up and down my spine caused me to shiver. Knowing that the man I married—the man who fathered my children and lit up my world—was rapidly losing his battle with cancer literally left me cold.

"Do you want me to bring your meds to you, or do you want to try to join us at the dinner table?" I already knew his answer to my question. There was no possible way for Michael to get out of bed, but I wanted him to know that no matter the circumstances, he was still part of our family.

Michael was diagnosed with a cancer of the adrenal gland. A slow-moving deadly cancer, it comes with no symptoms until the end stage… stage IV. "Stage IV adrenal cortical carcinoma." The oncologist rolled the words off his tongue as smoothly as a marble rolls off satin. It took me six months to be able to say the name, and I usually choked on each word.

Michael was doomed the moment the diagnosis was made, and because of this cancer's rarity, he was "one in a million." There was no known cure.

My own diagnosis came two years before Michael's. The name was easier to say, but just as likely to stick in the throat. Strep A necrotizing fasciitis, more commonly known as "the flesh-eating bacteria," had waged microscopic war on my body. I fought hard and eventually won, but my legs below the knees, my right hand, and the left side of my chest were collateral damage. I ended up with a new identity in my victory — "triple amputee." But I held onto my life.

From the beginning of my illness, Michael was with me fighting as hard as I was to keep me alive. And it was he, my loving, devoted husband, who had to make the heart-wrenching decision to keep me alive by sacrificing my limbs. He was at the hospital every day and night. He kept me company, made me laugh, and dried my tears. He became my courage, my cheerleader, my caregiver. Now, it was my turn to fill that role.

I placed my fake feet on the floor and rose from our bed. I walked to the threshold of my bedroom door, when I heard his words, raspy and weak, in the immortal wisdom of Jed Clampett of *The Beverly Hillbillies* fame, "Y'all come back now, y' hear?" Chuckling, I turned and looked at my husband. He looked small and wasted; his skin, once a beautiful dark olive color, was now waxy and pale. His hair had taken a beating from the brutal chemotherapy. The dark, thick curls that had adorned his head for 44 years had been replaced by white baby-fine wisps. Only his beautiful crystal blue eyes remained unscathed by the ruthless, heartless hands of cancer. I gave him my assurance that I would return after our two little boys were tucked securely in their beds, and then I turned quickly so he wouldn't see my tears.

It was excruciating to witness Michael's swift decline, and I knew that it wouldn't be long before he was no longer with us. But as his caregiver now, I wanted to give back to him what he had given to me. I emulated his behavior, trying in desperation to walk in his caregiver shoes and keep my tears at bay. Like me, he did not need to see the profound sadness in those we depended on to be our courage.

And it was courage that kept me balanced, courage that moved me forward. There were days when I felt as if I had one foot in the world of the living and the other on the grave—and this day was one of them. I knew I could lose my balance and fall at any moment. But the three people I loved most in the world were depending on me to stay on my feet. Falling simply wasn't an option.

I reached the kitchen to a chorus of "Mommy, can you do this?" and "Mommy, can you do that?" I smiled at my two precious children. They were so innocent and unknowing of what was to come. It wouldn't be long before I would have to pick up the pieces of two little, broken hearts. So I reveled now in their everyday little-boy antics. Even in my desolate sadness, looking at my two little boys, I could not help but feel blessed.

Michael and I utilized every moment of the time we had left together to talk about our children... about us. I promised not to allow my disabilities to interfere with our children's growth and self-esteem. He wanted them to know above all else that he loved them, that he didn't want to leave them. I held him in my arms and dried his tears, as he had done for me.

We reminisced, we laughed, and he took me places with his words and touch that I had never been before. We spoke our language of love and truth and passion to each other. Our souls were intertwined, becoming one in total honesty. It was beautiful, and lovely, and amazingly freeing. I got to know and understand my husband on a deeper level, a soulful level, and that was truly the gem unmasked in the last moments of his life. It was the last and most profound gift he ever gave to me.

I have come to realize that the hardest thing about being the caregiver is being the one who has to live through the dying, being the one who prays the caregiver's prayer… "end the suffering." But even with all of the physical and emotional exhaustion and heart-ache that comes with taking care of someone who is desperately ill or dying, I have also come to realize that the gifts received through this process are overwhelming, plentiful, and permanent.

Over time, my grief has dissipated, and I have kept my promises to Michael. I remain astonished by how I survived such profound and enduring losses. But I know, without hesitation, that I would do it again. It is easier being the patient than the caregiver; Michael and I were correct. But being the caregiver is invaluable, life-altering, and transcending. It is one of the most amazing gifts of all.

~Cindy Charlton

84

Never Too Old to Want My Mommy

A mother's arms are made of tenderness and children sleep soundly in them.
~Victor Hugo

December 16, 2009, was the worst day of my mother's life. It was the day I told her that her 36-year-old daughter had stage III breast cancer. I will never forget the look of devastation in her tear-filled eyes as I told her. Seeing my mother sob uncontrollably broke my heart. It was one of the few times in my life that I saw my mother weak and vulnerable.

Since I had been diagnosed with advanced breast cancer, the doctors had a heavy-duty plan of attack to beat it, which would mean a double mastectomy, five months of chemotherapy, ovary obliteration, and five weeks of radiation. It also meant that a fiercely independent single girl who lived alone was in serious need of some help taking care of herself.

Thankfully, I was blessed with my own personal army of family, church, friends, and co-workers who had offered to help me out with whatever I might need, including meals and rides to doctors' appointments. But as grateful as I was, there really was only one person who I wanted by my side—my momma. My mother lived more than 300 miles away, but didn't even give it a second thought. She was going to be my primary caregiver, chauffeur, personal chef, nursemaid, communications liaison, counselor, and shoulder to cry on. No one else in the world could fill her shoes. It was a job that only she could do.

The night after my first chemotherapy treatment is forever imprinted in my memory. I was never so sick in my entire life. I couldn't even keep down a glass of water. And after hours spent in the bathroom, I weakly lifted myself into bed, weeping, "Please, God, take this away from me. Please make me feel better." At that moment, my mother crawled into bed with me, wrapped her entire body around me, and cried with me. Just like when I was a little girl, her arms enveloping me made it better.

Over the next six months, my mom traveled back and forth between two homes and two lives just to take care of her 36-year-old little girl. She sat by my side for almost every chemo treatment and made me grilled cheese sandwiches in the middle of the night. She ran to the pharmacy when I was in severe pain and the video store when I wanted to be entertained. Basically, she put her life on hold to take care of me, her baby.

I think about what my mother sacrificed while I was going through such a tumultuous time in my life. She was attending to my every need, both physically and emotionally, but who was attending to her needs? Who heard her cry in the middle of the night when she sobbed for her daughter? I know what my mother would say if I asked her that question. She would say, "That's just what you do when you are a mother." And for that, I am eternally grateful.

~Tiffany Mannino

85

The Three-Year Gift

Humor is an affirmation of dignity,
a declaration of man's superiority to all that befalls him.
~Roman Gary

When I asked my boss for a week's vacation to move my 85-year-old dad the 100 miles from Vista to my home in Torrance, California, he said, "Don't do it. You will be miserable."

Widowed at 75, my independent, proud dad lived alone. He learned to clean, do laundry, and cook wholesome, nourishing meals. He called the contents of packaged foods "chemical equations." It seemed incongruous then when he asked to come live with us.

"I could help you," he said.

We soon learned that it was Dad who needed help, and in his oblique way he was asking. In the process of moving him, we discovered his life was unraveling. Some bills were unpaid, others paid twice. His clothes hung neatly in the closet, but hadn't been laundered. His car had numerous dings and dents from "those careless people driving too fast." I felt chills when the bank teller in Vista said, "I wish there were more children taking care of their parents like you are." Guiltily, I realized she was more aware of my dad's decline than I was.

Dad came to live with us just as our lives changed radically. Bob, my husband, had just been laid off after 33 years in an engineering position. Although he was looking for employment, he became Dad's caregiver. We settled into a new rhythm — I went to work and Bob took care of Dad. As predicted, my boss was partially right. I was miserable at times and frightened as I watched Dad disintegrating in front of me.

At the dinner table, he'd ask randomly, "Where did the little boy go?" or "Did you see where I left my tool chest?"

We learned that when Dad said, "I never touched it" or "I didn't see it," they weren't lies, but the results of dementia.

Dad's desire to help resulted in some hilarious but upsetting times. He "helped," all right. For example, when our refrigerator was making weird noises, he thought the noises were coming from the telephone. When Bob came home, he found a very puzzled telephone repairman talking to Dad. The next day, Bob left Dad home for a short time, and this time Dad solved the problem. He now knew the refrigerator was the problem and stopped the noise by opening the freezer door and wrapping it in blankets. It became apparent that leaving Dad home alone was not an option.

When he "helped" in the garden, an area of former expertise, he cut down the dead-looking center of my tomato vine, carefully cutting up the dead leaves and vine to make mulch. However, he left the eight-foot living part of the vine, loaded with green and red tomatoes, detached and hanging on its stakes. I was furious and yelled at him. He looked like a whipped puppy. Shame and guilt washed over me as I realized that Dad's dignity and self-esteem had to be preserved despite the dementia and its effect on his behavior.

There were great moments when the dementia took a back seat and my funny, sweet dad was with us. When he came in from the garden one day with blood running down his sleeve, I asked, "Dad, why are you bleeding like that?"

"It's the only way I know how."

He had always been funny, extremely intelligent, and loved to play with words. When I showed him how to de-bud the fuchsias, he said, "You only have to show me once."

"Yes, Dad, I know. You catch on fast."

"Right, now I'm bud wiser."

In the evenings after dinner, rather than watch what he considered the "sordid" programs on television, he would take out his violin and beautifully serenade us with all the old songs. He could play anything he heard. Knowing what an impoverished childhood he had had, I asked, "Dad, where did you learn to play so well?"

"There was always a fiddle on the farm," he said, as if they were as common as the overalls he wore.

One night when he seemed bored, I asked, "Why don't you play your fiddle?"

"Because my shoulder hurts."

Thinking he might need a doctor's appointment, I asked, "Why does it hurt?"

"Because it's 87 years old" was his matter-of-fact reply.

When he regressed, I would panic, wondering how long we would be able to keep him with us. What adjustments would we have to make?

Bob was a blessing. As Dad's caregiver, he engineered features to preserve Dad's safety without impugning his dignity, watched over his personal hygiene, and found his ever-disappearing hearing aids.

When we found Dad sitting outside in the cold, damp morning air at 3:00 AM, waiting for the newspaper, Bob installed an alarm on the door. After Dad wandered away, we purchased an identification bracelet.

Bob secured a position teaching seminars that required his absence for two to three days at a time. Knowing we couldn't leave Dad alone, we discovered the Salvation Army Senior Day Care Center. The staff was excellent, and there were activities all day long. We thought we convinced Dad that he was there to help, just as he used to help at the senior center in Vista, but he wasn't fooled. The sad and wistful look on his face as he stood staring at the locked gate when I came to pick him up each evening broke my heart.

At 88, Dad suffered a heart attack, so a temporary pacemaker was installed. Somehow, it became disconnected. At the hospital, a crash team rushed in to keep Dad alive until the surgeon arrived.

When I saw them pounding on him, I cried, "Stop! I promised never to do this to him. He has a do-not-resuscitate on file."

The irate doctor yelled, "This is not a heroic measure, and you are asking me to violate serious medical and legal ethics."

The permanent pacemaker was inserted, and Dad was in great pain from the broken ribs. I was concerned, watching him vacillate in and out of reality, saying, "Oh, Joy, look at those beautiful white clouds and sailboats."

When I expressed my fear, the doctor told me Dad would be fine and probably go home the next day. He said, "Go home and let the nurses do their job."

When the call came at 6:30 the next morning, I was stunned. I yelled into the phone, "You told me he was going to be okay, and he died alone!"

I was heartbroken and angry. There was so much left unsaid.

Despite everything, the three years that Dad lived with us were a gift. If I could return to the first day Dad came to live with us and exchange anything, it wouldn't be him, but the anxiety and fear that I always felt that kept me from enjoying his presence. We miss him, but his love, sweet spirit, "help," and puns live on in our minds and hearts.

~Joy Feldman

Richie

Never be afraid to sit awhile and think.
~Lorraine Hansberry, A Raisin in the Sun

Empty nesters—the baby boomers, alone at last. Somehow, empty and alone did not happen for my wife and myself. And in many ways, though there is sadness attached to this alternate reality, something good has emerged.

I recently read about what it means to be back under the watchful eye of your parents from the point of view of several recent college graduates. Let me tell you the story from my perspective.

My son is now 30, and he is brilliant. There is no other way of describing his intellectual capabilities. At two, he could pick up a record, find the cut on the album that he enjoyed, and put the needle to the appropriate sound. At six, he was teaching 10-year-olds in his elementary school about the latest on the computer. He wrote music and words for a song for his fifth-grade play. He graduated near the top of his class, had an outstanding academic career at Dartmouth, and was a star in his graduate program in public policy at Berkeley.

And he has spent the past five years, from the moment he called to say he was too sick to finish the last term of his studies and took a plane home, in the bedroom down the hall from myself and my wife.

This is not easy to write about, and it makes me feel a bit irritated with those young graduates who good-naturedly grouse about the difficulties they have in finding a world not ready, willing or able to accept them. But this is not about responding to them, nor about pitying myself or my son. This is rather about the benefit that has come from his unexpected return.

You see, empty and alone connotes that there is something missing. And what my son, in his mid-twenties and in his diminished physical state, brought back into our lives was an intellectual curiosity and questioning. Events of the world that seemed to swirl around my life without focus suddenly started to have meaning. Here was a young man, with all his passion for those who have been trampled in the rush of the few and the privileged to reach the top of the food pyramid. Here was my son, making me turn my attention to all that was wrong in so many arenas. Here was this young mind, challenging me to take issue with a world that had lost its compass. For you see, my son brought to me the gift of compelling me to think.

As my intellectual horizons broadened upon my son's insistence, I found that I took a real interest in exploring parts of our universe—and my own mind, which had long been ignored. The sports pages no longer were the only focus. Soon, the news and opinion pages took center stage. My discussions with my son, while often still about the Yankees, more and more centered on matters that mattered in more fundamental ways. And I began to write about my reactions to the world around me.

Now I write almost every day. It is a role that I could never have fathomed and never would have taken on had illness not forced the return of my son to a nest he wanted nothing more than to abandon. And while he acts as my in-house editor, and responds with the most gentle of criticism to my less stellar efforts, my son's "this one is good, this is very good" is for me the sweetest of all sounds.

There is much more bad than good in watching a son turn 30 under your watchful eye, in a bedroom intended for many things other than his permanent residence. He can and should be spending the incredible gifts he was given on a world that could sorely use his skills and his passion. I know that each day he hopes and waits to feel the pain disappear, the strength to return to his muscles, and the weight that so mysteriously and dramatically dropped to as mysteriously and dramatically return. And maybe tomorrow will be that day. And there will be no happier moment for his mom and me than waving goodbye as he begins a life that has been placed on hold.

But if and when he does leave, it will be a sad time, too. For I have grown to be a more complete and mature person because of his presence. I have discovered things about myself that make each day of my life more full and interesting. So while I curse the fates that have been unkind to my son, I also thank them. I wish nothing more for my son than good health and a productive life, but I will be forever grateful for his unexpected return that made an empty nest much fuller.

~Robert Nussbaum

An Inconvenient Blessing

There is no moral precept that does not have something inconvenient about it.
~Denis Diderot

"I just visited with your mom," said the hospice nurse. "She told me she wants to come live with you now." The nurse's call interrupted a project at work, and I had difficulty making the mental shift from my job to my personal life.

"But that's simply not possible," I stammered. "We both work full-time, our house isn't suitable, and we have two busy teenagers."

"I can understand that; I'm just reporting what she said. You'll want to discuss it with your husband and with her."

We weren't trained to care for a terminally ill person. How could we possibly bring Mom into our home and add her needs to our busy schedule?

I phoned my husband Larry and relayed the conversation. His response echoed my objections. After a brief discussion, we agreed to visit her after work and tell her that we would have to find another solution.

It was difficult to concentrate on my work for the rest of the day. Although we had already agreed to refuse her request, I kept looking at the situation from every angle. When Mom was widowed nine years earlier, we had promised her that when she needed help, we would be available. We had kept that promise, responding to various needs over the years. I hated to deny this new request, but couldn't see how it could work.

A little more than a year before, she had broken her hip. This put in motion her long-planned move from California to Portland, Oregon, to be near us. Always independent, Mom loved the small retirement apartment we found near us that fit both her tastes and her budget. After living apart for many years, we were grateful that she was now close enough for us to visit her regularly, take her shopping, and include her at meals and family gatherings.

Within a few weeks, however, she had been diagnosed with inoperable stomach cancer. She was immediately assigned a hospice nurse, but after several months she had stabilized enough to fly to California for a granddaughter's wedding. Now, a year later, it was obvious that her body was failing. We were pursuing options for additional care when the nurse's call came.

On our way to her apartment that night, Larry and I rehearsed how we could gently tell Mom that her request was impossible. For part of the drive, we were silent, struggling with our thoughts. We must have reached the same conclusion because when we walked through the door of her apartment and she said, "I want to come home with you," we said, "Okay, we'll find a way to work it out." Her appreciation was gratifying, but we still had to figure out how to add her care to our busy lives.

She was now considered "terminal," but did that mean days, weeks or even months? Bringing Mom into our home indefinitely was a huge responsibility. We weren't sure if our family was emotionally or physically ready, but we were certain we had made the right decision.

Within days, friends and family came up with unexpected solutions. One friend built a free-standing privacy wall, and our dining room became Mom's cozy bedroom. Her dresser and rocker fit snugly next to the rented hospital bed, making the space comfortable and familiar. Her bed faced the woodsy back yard, giving her a view of the squirrels and birds in the tall firs.

Our biggest dilemma was her daytime care. When I mentioned my plans to interview caregivers with our 26-year-old daughter, Rebecca, she said, "I'd love to take care of Grandma!" Her compassionate and levelheaded personality made her ideal for the task.

We moved Mom in and started a new routine. Hospice workers assured us that they would visit regularly and be available day and night. Larry spent extra time with his mother, recalling memories and reflecting on her life. Our teens, Jennifer and Josh, took time to talk to Grandma and include her in family activities. We adjusted commitments so that someone would always be home with Mom. I slept on the couch so I could respond quickly at night.

While we were at work, Rebecca cared for Mom and provided companionship. She played piano and sang hymns, read the Bible with her, and reminisced about holidays and vacations at Grandpa and Grandma's.

After a couple of days, Rebecca said, "Grandma keeps saying how much she misses the cat she left in California. Maybe we should try to get a 'foster' cat to keep her company." Within two days, I brought home a cuddly kitten. In the mysterious way of some animals, kitty knew her assignment. She would allow us to pet her, but as soon as we put her down, she headed for Mom's bed, scrabbled up the sheets, and snuggled down next to her. Her comforting purr and soft warm body were a constant soothing presence for Mom.

What had appeared to be an impossible challenge became a blessing. Mom understood the difficulties we faced and didn't take it for granted—she thanked us daily.

The blessing we felt did not ease the difficulty. Each of us felt the disruption and stress. We had moments of near panic as Mom's body began to shut down. We often felt uncertain, not knowing what to do. The hospice staff constantly reassured us and guided our journey.

We quickly realized that her stay would be short. In her first week with us, she was strong enough to sit on the couch and enjoy a visit from Chuck, her son from Tennessee. After that, her strength rapidly waned. Just two weeks after we brought her home, there was a dramatic decline. She was still alert, but eating and drinking less, retreating into her private world. She roused only when one of us spoke to her or touched her. The kitten stayed faithfully at her side, providing constant comfort.

One evening, we phoned her daughter JoAn in California so that Mom could say goodbye. After their conversation, Mom seemed restless. Her eyes would open briefly and find their way to the clock on the wall. Late that evening, we prayed at her bedside, verbally releasing her and expressing our love. She seemed to fall asleep peacefully.

Larry went upstairs to bed while I stretched out on the floor near Mom and dozed off. Barely an hour later, I woke up, aware that something had changed. I checked on Mom and immediately knew that her spirit had left her frail body.

It was just after midnight. When we called JoAn, she said, "Mom knew! She was waiting to join Dad on his birthday." I glanced at the calendar; it was February 16th, the day Dad would have turned 84.

~Carolyn L. Wade

Like Mother, Like Daughter

And mothers are their daughters' role model, their biological and emotional
road map, the arbiter of all their relationships.
~Victoria Secunda

I can still remember the day my mother came home from the hospital after her first operation. It was a sun-filled day, the weather at odds with the atmosphere in the house, which was morbid and tense. I had just left college to become my mother's full-time caregiver — a decision I was already beginning to question as I surveyed the volume of medical supplies that had accompanied my mother's return. It was daunting to be faced with the prospect of looking after someone who had looked after me all my life.

With one operation down and three more to go, my mother was already unrecognisable to me. The warm, plump woman who had raised me had been replaced by a pale waif-like creature. The pain and stress had dulled the brightness in her eyes, and her trademark dimples had disappeared in her sunken face. Fragile had never been a word to describe my mother, but now it defined her. For the first time, the enormity of what I had taken on struck me.

The first few weeks were the most difficult. Like a newborn, she required constant care and attention. Her wound had to be dressed every day. She couldn't feed herself, clean herself or even get out of the bed.

I wasn't sure how to cope with this role reversal. I was so used to my mother being the caregiver, the provider, that I couldn't bear to see her so weak and helpless. I really didn't know how I was going to cope. However, nothing tests character like necessity. It turned out the thoughts of being responsible for my mother's health were far more challenging than the reality. Over the next few months, my mother slowly began to improve. Under my care, she began to live again. I watched the twinkle come back into her eyes as she regained the strength to do small things for herself. We celebrated the little things that we had previously taken for granted — simple things like when she finally had the strength to lift a teacup to drink by herself or when she could sleep through the night without waking from the pain.

One of the happiest days was a sunny day in July. It was a couple of weeks after her final operation, and her recovery had been slow and complicated. When I brought the breakfast tray down to her that morning, she turned to me and said, "It's a pity to be stuck inside on such a nice day." I bundled her up in a scarf and coat and brought her outside.

I will never forget the look of pure joy on her face as she looked up at the blue sky. It was the first time in a year that she had been able to go outside and enjoy something as simple as the heat of the sun on her face. She looked at me, put her hand over mine, and smiled — a smile that said much more than words could express. In that moment, I realised how much I had gained from becoming a full-time caregiver for my mother. I had become more mature and responsible, and I had discovered strengths that I never knew I had. Our relationship had evolved from the traditional one of mother and daughter. I gained a newfound respect for my mother. Through caring for her, I learned to appreciate how wonderful she really is. Her remarkable inner strength, her uncomplaining nature, and above all her ability to smile through the pain are qualities that I can only hope of inheriting.

Caring for my mother has been a turbulent journey full of both tears and laughter. Although we both felt like giving up at times, ultimately, it has brought us closer together and allowed me to count every day we have together as a blessing.

~Anna Fitzgerald

Who Would Have Thought?

My mom used to say it doesn't matter how many kids you have...
because one kid'll take up 100% of your time so more kids can't possibly
take up more than 100% of your time.
~Karen Brown

I t's 10:00 PM, and the game is on. The Phillies are winning
7-4, and Wayne is fed, changed, and resting comfortably. He
is the last survivor of our three musketeers—Wayne, Dylan
and Adam—three terminally-ill "total care" children whose feeding
tubes, wheelchairs, and hospital beds transformed the first floor of
our home. I have just hung up the phone from a rare conversation
with my older brother. "I still think you are nuts," he said, referring
to my life as the primary caregiver to our children, adopted from
foster care with a range of special needs. "You gave up so much—all
the career options you had when you graduated from college, all
the money you could have made—for what—to still be changing
diapers in your fifties?" I chuckle to myself as I settle in to relax and
enjoy the game. I am not sure what exactly I gave up, except maybe
for sleep. I am bone-tired at the end of each day from the physical,
emotional, and spiritual demands of our unusual family. Before the
inning is over, I am drifting off in my chair.

•••

"Where's Wayne?" asks Raj.

"What do you mean, 'Where's Wayne?' He was right here!" I look toward the next campsite and there he is, sitting with two campers, reaching for their food. I walk over to get him and apologize to the older couple.

"How old is he?" they ask.

"Six," I say.

"He's such a beautiful child." I thank them and note that I would have called him to come back to our campsite, but he cannot hear due to his degenerative illness. Soon, he won't be able to walk either.

As Wayne and I return to our campsite, Renee asks if today is our Great Adventure day. "No, it's our beach day. Tuesday is Great Adventure and Wednesday is when we go into Chicago to meet up with Lilly and Fisher at the Sears Tower and go on the city tour."

"Oh, that's right," she responds. By now, all the kids are up and begging for breakfast. Out come the Pop-Tarts and cereal. SueAnn grabs the milk from the cooler, saying, "We need more ice," as she carries it to the table. Trish and Abel help dole out the food.

"Yeah! Beach Day!" says Todd as he spills his juice.

"Good job," I tease, adding, "It sure is, so let's all remember who we are in charge of because we're heading down in a few minutes. We need to get the three little kids' diapers changed and everyone fed. Flory, make sure Dylan's oatmeal is not too hot for him," I add as I check to see if JD is still in the van.

"Hurry, hurry! Everyone into the van! He's coming!" I holler.

"Who's coming?" Aaron asks.

"The buffalo!" I scream, hustling the kids into safety. As the older kids pile in, I grab Wayne and Adam while David scoops Dylan out of his wheelchair and hoists him inside. I slam the sliding door of the 15-passenger van, scaring Alysia, my five-year-old with cerebral palsy.

"It's just a buffalo going by our tents," Joelle says reassuringly to Alysia. It's a normal thing at Yellowstone; there are signs all over the place that say "Don't feed the bears and buffalo," with pictures of stick-figure people getting mauled.

"Hey, Dad—let's do it—let's feed them!" urges Jose, the dare-devil. "We have some hot dogs in the cooler."

"Sure, that sounds like a great idea," I say, playing along as the giant creature approaches our tent. "You coming with us, George? Isaac?" They are both eager to join the fun as I teasingly open the door of the van just a bit to the screams of the other children.

"Now make sure you kids stay off the paths because there are rattlesnakes around here," I tell the kids as they pile out of the van. The rest area in northern New Mexico had signs all over warning of rattlesnakes in the area. After another long night of driving, 629 miles to be exact, I needed to pull over for a break and to feed the kids breakfast. "Don't wander off, and make sure you all go to the bathroom. I need to change a few diapers, and Mom is going to get us some breakfast."

"Okay, let's eat!" Sue hollers, and the younger kids come running to the picnic tables.

"Pull up your pants, Abel!" ("Teenagers!" I mutter to myself.) "Geeta, push Adam over here and make sure you unlock the brakes on his wheelchair."

"Where are Jose, George, Isaac, and Chelsea?" David asks in sign language. I look around and don't see them. Oh, no—they didn't!

Just as I am about to speak, Chelsea comes running down the path, shouting with enthusiasm, "He caught one! He caught one! Jose caught a rattlesnake—it's on a stick!" she announces.

At this moment, most parents would freak out at the sight of their children emerging from a path with a long rattlesnake hanging from a stick, but not us. Sue tells me to grab the camera as she instructs Jose and the others to stand in front of the "Beware of Rattlesnakes" sign for a picture. She urges the kids to gather closer together just as the flash goes off.

• • •

"What? What? What's that flash?" I am feeling a bit disoriented before I realize it is just the light from the TV. Darn, I fell asleep in my chair again, and my back is killing me. Once again, I will have to wait for the morning paper to find out if the Phillies won or lost. But what a dream I was having.

I sit for a few moments reflecting on my dream. I smile to myself as those memories of five cross-country summer camping trips flood my mind and heart. "We sure had fun," I say aloud to no one in particular. The kids still reminisce about those trips when they come over for Sunday dinner. They all tell the stories from their own perspectives, and speak so fondly of their memories of Adam and Dylan now that they are gone, and Wayne who probably has only a year left to live.

Life has changed, and the kids have all grown up. Many are now raising kids of their own. Who would have thought that Sue and I could have pulled 22 kids together from all different backgrounds and so many needs and make one family?

Maybe my brother is right; I probably am a little nuts to have dedicated myself to this life. But what did I give up, really? In spite of my exhaustion, I can only be grateful for the riches I have gained. Who would have thought?

~Hector Badeau

The Hidden Blessing

Give thanks for unknown blessings already on their way.
~Native American Saying

For as long as I can remember, Grandma has been a blur—a 4'11" tornado in an apron. Persuading her to sit down for a one-on-one talk was like nailing Jell-O to the wall.

When I went to her house, I had to keep up with her or eat her dust. She called our visits "chat and runs." In addition to working full-time at a department store, she had my invalid grandfather and a large home with two acres of land to care for.

Hers was not a life for the weak.

Retirement didn't slow things down much. Household chores and Grandpa-duty kept her darting to and fro like a moth courting a porch light.

"The more I do, the more that needs doing," she declared.

In the summer, I helped her in the garden. Weeding, harvesting and hauling veggies up to the house weren't drudgery because we did them together.

Afterward, we'd sit under a big maple tree, snapping green beans, shelling peas or peeling potatoes for dinner. I cherished our quiet moments.

For a little while, she was all mine.

As we worked, Grandma would tell me about her childhood: tales of her family and friends, their barnyard shenanigans, hay rides, and school dances. I especially enjoyed hearing about her beloved pig, Billy.

"I bottle-fed Billy from the time he was a tiny runt so he grew up believing I was his mother. That silly pig would walk on a leash like a dog and then pull us kids around in a cart like a horse. Did I tell you he could predict the weather? Daddy always knew a storm was brewing because Billy would be terribly upset."

She was the most interesting person I knew.

Then a few years after Grandpa died, Grandma began to change.

It started with lost minutes that quickly progressed to lost days. She'd fix breakfast and find herself sitting upstairs on her bed hours later with no idea how she got there or what happened in between. One morning in mid-November, she clung to her street-side mailbox, shivering in a thin terrycloth robe, terrified as cars whizzed by. A worried neighbor helped her back into the house and called Mom.

"I'm afraid it's Alzheimer's," the doctor said.

Heartsick, Mom and I believed that telling Grandma would only make matters worse and perhaps hasten the inevitable.

"The doctor prescribed some new medicine that should help you with your memory," Mom chirped.

"It had better work," Grandma grumbled.

That was it, no third degree. For a woman who possessed the sleuthing skills of a bloodhound, she quietly and uncharacteristically accepted what she was told. She must have suspected the worst, but was afraid to ask.

Who could blame her?

After selling her house, Grandma moved into an assisted-living facility down the street from Mom. Surrounded by new friends, she was off and running again, a social butterfly involved in the facility's many activities. She planted a little garden outside her bedroom window, and even found time for romance.

"Guess what? I have a boyfriend," she said, smiling mischievously.

"Oh? Who might that be?"

"Bert Kowalski. He's the only man at Sterling Villas who still drives his own car. He took me to Humpty Dumpty's last night for ice cream."

"Wow, sounds like a hot date," I laughed.

"I'll have you know he's considered quite a catch. The ladies at Tuesday morning bingo were pretty frosty after word got around," she chuckled.

Other than a few episodes of disorientation, Grandma was doing remarkably well.

Then, without warning, the bottom dropped out.

One day, she was fine. The next day, she nearly set fire to her kitchen after forgetting to turn off a pot of boiling soup. She fell in the bathroom two mornings in a row and lay there for hours, bewildered, unable to remember how to get up or to pull the nurse call cord just above her head.

The next heartbreaking step was a nursing home with an Alzheimer's unit, where exits remain locked for resident protection until a code is entered into a keypad. It was regarded as a prison by a woman who was always in charge of her own life.

The first few months were horrible. Grandma's moods alternated between fits of anger and tearful pleas to go home. I can't even imagine how unbearable it must have been for her to be held against her will.

Eventually, she grew accustomed to her surroundings, helped by regular visits from Mom and me. It isn't always easy to find time to run to the nursing home in the midst of my own busy day, but it's clearly a sacrifice worth making. When we're together, she feels more normal again; she can be mother or grandma, needed rather than needy.

With no more "chat and runs" to worry about, I can sit shoulder to shoulder with my precious grandmother, leaning my head against hers. We talk. We giggle. We peacefully sift through old photos. She doesn't always remember names, but she usually knows titles. Aunt, uncle, brother, sister, mom, dad; recalling the part each had played in her life. The pictures seem to jog her memory, keeping her sharper than she might otherwise be. They also seem to help lessen her confusion.

"Who is that man wearing the dark suit and the funny hat?" I asked.

"That's Grandpa."

"And the pretty lady in the flowered dress?"

"It's Mother," she said, lovingly rubbing her thumb back and forth across the figure.

It's a relief to see Grandma's eyes brighten when I step through the door because she still knows who I am. I dread the day she won't. But for now, her hugs are still capable of crushing my bones and melting my heart; hugs I never take for granted.

There are signs that she's nearing the end of her journey. Mom and I can see it, feel it. Grandma is less hungry, sleeps a lot, smiles and speaks less. It's harder to interest her in short walks or a fresh batch of yellowing snapshots, once a source of delight. She's fading, drifting to a place where we won't be able to reach her and there's nothing we can do about it.

How does one prepare for such a loss?

For years I've longed to hear that someone has found a cure for Alzheimer's, but it remains an unfulfilled wish. Life can be brutally unfair, and so much of what happens is beyond our control.

But how we look at our circumstances is in our control.

A wise friend said, "At first glance, we may not like the cards we're dealt. But upon careful reflection, we'll usually find something good in every hand, a hidden blessing."

Mourning the woman Grandma used to be would have meant missing out on the woman she's become: more affectionate, gentle and trusting than ever before. We have hours of once-elusive quiet time to spend together; opportunities to gather dozens of new memories to cherish and hold onto when she's gone.

Perhaps that's the hidden blessing.

~Michelle Close Mills

Chapter
8

Family Caregivers

Saying Goodbye

We only part to meet again.

~John Gay

Safe Journey

It is good to have an end to journey toward,
but it is the journey that matters in the end.
~Ursula K. Le Guin

My father and I sat on the couch watching a DVD of a Josh Groban concert. My dad turned his head toward the bank of floor-to-ceiling windows overlooking our small lake. His neck stretched to look over and around me as he smiled that crooked smile of his, the result of a cerebral stroke he had in 2004.

"What are you looking at, Dad?"

"Well, look at all those ships out there," he replied.

As a registered nurse, who has taken care of many terminally ill people, I was aware of the hallucinations and visions that accompany many people during the death-and-dying process. They occur days, weeks and sometimes months prior to their death. I had decided, a while back, not to interfere since Dad enjoyed his hallucinations and didn't fear them, so I stopped trying to orient him to reality and let him enjoy his visions.

Many were very entertaining to both of us as he described them in detail. At times, there were golfers playing on the lake, moving trucks on our island, and fishermen on the curved walking bridge catching whales and pelicans. One of my favorites was the arrival of a Big Top Circus with all the animals. He described in detail the rising of the tent, the display of elephants, and all related circus activities. But today was a heartfelt hallucination.

"What kind of ships?" I questioned. "Battleships, cruise ships, submarines?"

He hesitated a bit. "No, sail ships," he replied, "about 20 or 21 ships. Some are small dinghies; a few are very large with many sails looking old and tattered. It looks like a parade of ships. The people on the ships are waving at us."

His eyes lit up with pleasure; this vision was clearly fun for him. I looked over the lake to see if there was something that would trigger this scene in his mind's eye. There was a huge, leaning oak, reaching out over the lake some 30 to 35 feet, almost horizontal with the lake's surface, with lots of Spanish moss dripping from the branches and swaying slightly in the gentle breeze. Perhaps those were his sails.

"Dad, do you remember Kristen Beth, your granddaughter?" I asked.

"Oh, of course, I remember Kristen. How could I forget her?" he said with a smile and giggle. He loved Kristen, who died of severe asthma at age 21 — the only time I saw my father cry.

"Well, you know, Dad, if Kristen was still alive, we would be celebrating her birthday today. She was 21 when she died, so maybe this is her birthday parade of 21 sailboats. This is her parade, a gift to you."

I thought for a moment and recounted the last words I whispered into Kristen's ear before she was taken to the operating room for organ harvesting and donation. "Have a fun and safe journey, Kriss, and wave to me when you see me. I love you beyond the moon and more and will miss you."

He continued to look at our lake, nodding his head, and murmured, "Well, if this is her gift of a 21-sail-ship parade because she lived 21 years in my life, then I will give her, you and your mother an 87-ship parade each year on my birthday." I smiled and asked if he would wave to me as he passed by. He simply replied yes with a definite nod.

My father passed away 10 days later at home as planned, while listening to his favorite music from Mitch Miller, Linda Eder and Josh Groban. While my mother sat at his side holding his hand, I leaned in to whisper in his ear.

"Have a fun and safe journey, Dad. I love you beyond the moon and more. And don't forget to wave to me when you pass by on your sail-ship parade. Bring Kristen and our beloved yellow Lab, Maggie."

As promised, each year on May 3rd, I stand in front of our bank of windows overlooking the lake. I imagine the parade of 87 sailboats. And then I smile and whisper, "Thanks, Dad, for being a part of my life. Your golden threads are woven tightly in my life's tapestry. I love you." I wave to my imaginary vision, indelibly painted in my mind by my beloved father.

~Peggie L. Devan

Unexpected Caregiver

A Note from Joan

Larry Shaps was 31 years old, single and living in Atlanta, Georgia. Larry had established roots there and had a wonderful circle of friends and thought he'd never leave. However one day Larry got a call from his older brother Scott saying, "I need help." Scott had been diagnosed with ALS, also known as Lou Gehrig's disease — a progressive illness that affects the brain and spinal cord. Scott was living in New York with his pregnant wife who he said was having a difficult time coping with her husband's dire diagnosis.

That call from his brother Scott would change Larry's life forever. It didn't happen immediately, but ultimately it turned into a 10-year ordeal. Larry uprooted his life, and so did his brother Robert, who was living with his family in Massachusetts at the time. Both brothers would end up moving to New York to care for their ailing brother, Scott.

I think it's fair to say that most of us expect that we will end up taking care of an ill or aging parent one day, but not necessarily a sibling. When I met the Shaps brothers and learned of their family caregiving journey, I asked if they would share their story with all of you. I felt privileged to have the opportunity to interview Larry and Robert, and I will forever be inspired by their story.

Joan: Larry, tell me a little bit about your brother, Scott, his ALS diagnosis and when you first learned of it.

Larry: It took a long time to get a confirmation that he had ALS. Scott was having symptoms but they had to rule out other things so it was a long process. During that time when Scott reached out to say, "I need help," I knew he was scared. He was nervous and needed our support.

Joan: Scott was married when he took ill, and both of your parents were alive at the time of his diagnosis. You were the youngest of four brothers, and yet you say that you were "the obvious choice" to be Scott's primary caregiver. Why was that?

Larry: I was the single one at the time; my brothers Robert and Michael both had a lot of responsibilities with their families and their careers, and my parents were dealing with their own health issues. So it seemed logical that I would be more involved.

Joan: However, Scott was married at the time. Why didn't his wife Kathy take over Scott's care?

Larry: In the beginning Kathy was there for Scott, but she was also a new mom and as things progressed she couldn't do it anymore. I attended many ALS support meetings with Scott and we learned about the dynamics of couples dealing with this illness. It seems that there is no gray area when it comes to supporting a spouse with ALS. There's a point where they can handle it or they can't. If they can't, they check out.

Robert: We were surprised and disappointed that our sister-in-law decided she couldn't do this anymore. We knew we had to step in.

Joan: Larry, when did you realize that you were going to have to uproot yourself and move from Atlanta back to New York?

Larry: I thought about it for a long time. I needed to be able to support myself. It just so happened that I was approached with a job opportunity in New York so that I could move back and be near Scott.

Joan to Robert: You and your family were living in Massachusetts where you were a school administrator. However you were also finishing up your doctorate degree at the University of Pennsylvania at the time, traveling there on weekends. That's a lot for anyone. How did you incorporate Scott's needs into all of this?

Robert: It was not a good situation. I was completing my studies at the University of Pennsylvania. However I was also traveling with Scott to see experts in several cities while we were trying to determine the diagnosis. Scott was the warmest, nicest person on earth so the idea that he was diagnosed with a terminal illness was overwhelming, and when he asked Larry for help, we sensed what it meant and asked, "How can we do this together?" Fortunately I moved to New York for a job opportunity.

Joan: We often hear that caregivers are working full-time at another job, which makes it even more difficult being torn between work responsibilities and caregiving. You had your job and also your studies on the weekends. How did you juggle it all?

Robert: That was the hardest part for me. Though we had wonderful caregivers, I never knew if I would be spending my weekends working on my doctoral dissertation or in a hospital with Scott. Often he would end up in the emergency room for two to three days at a time. Larry was the first line of defense and I was there after.

Joan to Larry: You've actually equated taking care of Scott to "running a business." Tell us what you mean by that.

Larry: Scott's care became quite complicated to manage. I printed out caregiver schedules. He needed 24-hour care and we had six to eight nurses at a time and often had to swap out people who couldn't work certain days or certain nights. There were also personality conflicts—dealing with nurses who didn't like each other. If an aide couldn't come in, we would end up sleeping on the couch.

Joan: You have both said that you always wanted to make sure that you were "on the same page" as Scott regarding his end-of-life wishes.

Robert: Actually, Scott was really clear about his desire to remain in his home.

Larry: But there was a lot happening at once. Scott had an incredible will to live and a fear of dying and that actually made it really difficult. He was also deteriorating quickly, and the disease made it difficult for him to communicate with us. There was a lot of negotiating to do and he would "push back" on decisions, even if we had no other choice.

Joan: When Scott was no longer able to speak, you came up with a plan.

Robert: Scott went through a series of all kinds of efforts to communicate, from using his big toe, to eventually using his eyes to spell words. Larry had perfected a system of left, right, yes and no to actually spelling out words. It was like speaking in another language. You would sit in a room and watch Larry use a transparent sheet of letters to spell out sentences and Larry could actually understand what Scott was saying to him. It was frustrating for the rest of us who didn't master the technique, including my mom. But it really was quite remarkable.

Joan: You mention your mom. You've said that she really wanted to help but that she was also dealing with her own health issues.

Robert: Mom meant well but that was really the third rail. A mother's instinct never goes away. However I spent more time negotiating with my parents to let Larry be the primary caregiver of Scott. We had to make her accept that we were really in charge.

Joan: What was your biggest fear in caring for your brother?

Robert: The greatest fear was "what happens when Scott gets locked in." Scott had a young daughter and he wanted to live as long as possible for her. A turning point was when we pleaded with him to get a feeding tube and he resisted. Research clearly showed that this helps keep you ahead of the deterioration, but for Scott the idea of a tube was unbelievable.

Joan: When you become a caregiver for someone with a debilitating illness, you never know how long it's going to go on. You probably never dreamed that it would be all-consuming for 10 years, financially, emotionally, logistically.

Larry: We did talk about this when we had family conversations. And as the years went on, there were definitely moments where there was resentment and anger. It was very complicated to manage Scott's care, including the financial aspects. We gave Scott lots of love and care, but there is still the other human aspect of being frustrated. And then we had a tremendous amount of guilt. We were struggling with trying to make sure that we abided by his wishes but we were also trying not to let him suffer.

Robert: There were times when I thought Scott was being unreasonable; however then we would look at each other and say, "Look who's in what shoes?"

Joan: It was a long 10-year journey for you guys until Scott ultimately succumbed to the ALS. What advice would you give to others who are going through a similar experience?

Larry: Have a support group or have friends and family that you can lean on. It is overwhelming. Take care of yourself because if you can't take care of yourself, you can't take care of the patient. Things can happen very quickly and I think it's important to be as proactive as possible.

Robert: Make sure that you communicate early and often about what their wishes are for their care and their end of life.

Joan: In retrospect, is there anything you would have done differently? Anything that you wish you would have done?

Robert: Yes, I would have videotaped Scott a lot more. I wish we had captured Scott telling his daughter the story of his life. She was too young to realize what a special person he was. We all wish we had captured more of Scott while he was still in good health.

Joan: You guys are great role models to other families. We appreciate you sharing your story. You are truly inspiring.

Trash or Treasures

Every tooth in a man's head is more valuable than a diamond.
~Miguel de Cervantes, Don Quixote

Shortly after Brent was diagnosed with Alzheimer's, I awoke one morning and trudged down the steps as I tried to muster the energy to face a new day. I walked into Brent's room and found him weeping at his desk. Before him was a small clay figure of a dog missing an ear made by our granddaughter, Kalin, 17 years ago; a gray dinosaur eraser (once green) that his daughter, Midge, had given him more than 45 years ago; a photo of him and his son, Jay, on a boat in Brazil with their arms around each other and a look of adoration that few are able to obtain; a photo of him and me shortly after our wedding; a picture of our five grandchildren; and an ordinary plastic container that had been kept in our safe for 15 years to ensure its protection. He was carefully holding each piece as though it were the most precious item in the world.

"What are you doing?" I asked.

"I'm gathering up the items I want buried with me while I can still remember what I want," he solemnly responded.

"I promise, you'll be buried with them," I said, as the tears rolled down my cheeks.

• • •

Every day, I sit at my desk and stare at the safe. It's impossible to ignore considering it weighs more than 400 pounds and takes up all the legroom where I am sitting. I maneuver my legs astride the monstrosity to log onto my computer, pay bills, sew, read, or just think, in what I consider to be my sanctuary. As I hear the light trickle of the fountain that sits at the end of the couch, I inevitably begin the first of many attempts to open the safe; I am drawn to it like a moth to a flame. Left four, right three, left again, and then I cross my fingers as I slowly turn the knob to the right and hope for an audible "click." I grin as I grasp the handle and open the cavernous vault.

I look past the jewelry, passports, birth certificates, and legal documents. My eyes focus on a small blue plastic box containing Brent's partial dentures. I remove it from the safety of its home and gently cradle it in my hands. My body is filled with admiration, and I remember how unique, special, and unconventional my husband was. I smile and a warm glow fills me, as though I have been touched by the heavens and recall just how extraordinary and wonderful he was. We called him BIG, for his initials, and he was indeed BIG-ger than life.

Many have said, "Why didn't you throw his teeth away? That's disgusting!"

I simply respond, "My husband's wish was to be buried with his mother's teeth, so how can I throw his out?"

• • •

Fifteen years ago, after his mother passed away, I came home from cleaning out her room at the nursing home. I agonizingly made piles of trash and keepsakes. The first item in the trash pile was her dentures. Upon seeing this, my husband yelled, "What do you think you're doing? You can't throw those away!"

My rational response was: "Why not? It's not like she needs them. What are we supposed to do with them?"

Without hesitation, Brent said, "Put them in the safe so I can get buried with them."

I doubled over, laughing hysterically, and tears rolled down my cheeks as I tried to catch my breath. "I'm just glad she didn't have an IUD!" But I did as he requested and put them in the safe where they remained for 13 years.

The day after Brent passed away, I unlocked the safe and carefully bundled the precious items he had chosen to be buried with. I drove to the funeral home to make the final arrangements. Documents were signed, flowers chosen, and Jewish traditional preparations were made: the Chevra Kaddisha to cleanse and wrap him in a burial shroud, the Shemira that would sit with him the days preceding the funeral, and Shiva (which I adamantly refused to do). After all the decisions were made, Mr. Stein solemnly asked, "Is there anything else I can do for you?"

"There is one other thing," I responded. I placed on his desk the precious bundle: a rubber dinosaur trinket, a small clay figure of a dog's face minus an ear, a picture of him and his son, a picture of him and me, a picture of all five grandchildren, and the small blue plastic container.

As he scrutinized the items laid out before him, his eyes immediately went to the denture box and he said, "I will have the Chevra Kaddisha put his teeth in."

"That won't be necessary. These are his mother's teeth, and they're to be placed along with the other things next to his heart. His partial dentures are in the safe at home and will be buried with me. And I would like Frank Sinatra's 'My Way' played throughout the service."

At his funeral, hundreds of friends, some who went back more than 65 years, stood in line outside the funeral home in subzero temperatures to say goodbye to BIG. One remarked, "He was the original Fonz at our high school in the fifties before there ever was a Fonz on TV."

• • •

Fifteen years before Brent died, I couldn't fathom why keeping his mother's teeth was so important to him. But now I can. I am able to cradle the priceless blue box in my hands and feel blessed.

An ordinary plastic container holding his dentures would be trash to most, but to me they are the most valuable item in the safe. They are a constant reminder of just how special, and unconventional Brent Irl Greenberg was.

I am able to smile knowing that I could carry out BIG's final wishes—to die in my arms at home where he felt safe and loved, and, yes, to be buried with his mother's teeth.

~Robin Greenberg

Soul Food

A lake is the landscape's most beautiful and expressive feature. It is earth's eye; looking into which the beholder measures the depth of his own nature.
~Henry David Thoreau

My sister, Gale, peered out the living room window at the ducks and geese making their way from the lake to her garage door. Each and every morning and evening, Gale supplied cracked corn to them, and judging from the huge commotion they were now making, they were pretty upset she wasn't hoofing it out to feed them that instant.

Months earlier, Sis had been diagnosed with cancer. It had rapidly metastasized, and hospice was already set in place. I flew to Florida to care for her and the family.

The honking grew louder. I glanced once more at my sister's sweet face in the hospital bed in the corner of the living room. In spite of the incessant honking, her eyes were already drifting shut. I wiped away fresh tears, escaping to the garage to replenish the empty bowls of cracked corn. I planned on tackling the kitchen next, followed by the bathrooms. With so many people coming and going, there were countless chores to be done.

Plunging my hands into the warm, soapy water in the kitchen sink, I felt a warm hand touch my shoulder. I turned. Gale stood on wobbly legs, reaching out to embrace me.

"Do you know want I want you to do most?" she softly asked.

I swallowed the lump in my throat.

"Anything," I croaked, returning her weak hug.

"I want you to come into the living room and just hang out. All this doesn't matter," she whispered, sweeping the kitchen with one enormous gesture. "Just be with me."

I felt my hand lifting the plug, urging my worries and fears to accompany the water down the drain.

Sis clutched my hand in hers like she'd done a million times growing up. We both staggered into the living room with giggles, commenting on how her unsteadiness was most likely caused from the morphine and mine from sheer exhaustion.

In no time at all, we were snuggled under a patchwork quilt watching Sis's favorite Disney movie, *Ratatouille*, projected on the ceiling thanks to a projector Gale's daughter Michele furnished. It didn't matter that the bowl I now held out to my sister didn't contain fluffy popcorn. Instead, the remnants of any food Sis had been able to ingest that morning stared us in the face. Earlier, we'd shared several banana Popsicles. Sis had discovered they not only were tasty going down, but coming back up as well. We agreed that someone should make advertisers of the delicious frozen product aware of this fact.

When the movie ended, I helped my sister into the wheelchair that hospice had provided, pushing her around her beloved Lake Charm. The now satisfied ducks and geese gracefully floated across the shimmering water as an eagle soared overhead. Every now and then, a neighbor passing by would stop to give Gale a hug or ask how she was doing.

Safely indoors once again, Sis was too spent to enjoy a bath even though we were both sweaty and overheated from the Florida sun. Instead, we spritzed each other with cold water from a spray bottle while reminiscing of childhood days and racing through the lawn sprinkler. We giggled until our sides hurt, and then collapsed against soft pillows.

"Thank you," Sis murmured sleepily, her eyes already closed.

"I'm the one who needs to thank you, Angel Girl. I'll never forget this day as long as I live."

I tiptoed out the front door and onto the porch. The sun shot arrows of crimson, purple and pink into Lake Charm.

I'd set out to take such good care of my sister that day. How could I have known she'd been planning all along to take care of me?

"Thanks, Sis."

~Mary Z. Smith

95

The Clock Shoe

Memory is a complicated thing, a relative to truth, but not its twin.
~Barbara Kingsolver, Animal Dreams

Mother can't remember who I am,
talks in riddles, shifts place
and time mid-sentence.

Her body looks the same, her face
under a tent of tidy gray hair,
sweet, alert, yet wild-eyed.

Of the memories we shared
and used to laugh about
I have my half only.

She thinks she's in trouble
with her mother for staying out too late
with a girlfriend, both long dead.

Today when I visit Mother
she opens the door a crack.
She calls me aside to ask,

"Who is that man?
He's very nice, and I don't

want to hurt his feelings,"

as she points to my father,
"but I really must have him leave now."
They've been wed for fifty years.

I give her that simple Alzheimer's test, the task
of drawing a clock face with paper and pencil,
but she ponders, "Hmm, a clock?"

and stalls. "I could draw a violin."
A clock sits on the table in front of her
and she deftly draws a shoe. "A clock shoe,"

we laugh and begin a new set of memories
that will last her only for minutes.

~Sandra Berris

96

The Pink Balloon

Unable are the loved to die. For love is immortality.
~Emily Dickinson

The morning calls became my daily alarm clock. My wake-up messages alternated between "When are you coming over?" and "Why can't you come earlier?"

When my sister-in-law, Joy, had a stroke at age 60 and became almost totally paralyzed and compromised in her memory and cognitive abilities, my husband (her baby brother) and I suddenly and unexpectedly became her caregivers.

As recent empty nesters, we had just embarked upon an exciting new chapter in our own lives. With our kids grown and finally on their own, we had sold our house, downsized to a condo on the beach, and were looking forward to traveling and spending more leisure time together. Many of our plans included our two-and-a-half-year-old granddaughter, Ella, who was the newest love of our lives. We had a calendar of activities ahead of us, including play dates, sleepovers, and day trips to the Big Apple Circus and *Sesame Street Live*.

But, suddenly, our lives — along with all of those plans — came to a halt as we were thrust into a role for which we were totally unprepared.

Joy's husband, our brother-in-law, had died the year before, following a shocking diagnosis of an inoperable brain tumor. Never having had children, there was nobody on board to supervise nursing care, coordinate medications, handle finances, and assume responsibility for every aspect of Joy's care. That was, nobody except us.

Once we realized that we were the designated—and only—caregivers, we hit the ground running. We consulted with doctors, hired round-the-clock nurses, and ordered necessary equipment and supplies. We transferred all official papers into our names, put Joy's house on the market, and moved her to an apartment less than five minutes from ours—trying our best to make the transition as seamless as possible.

But the most demanding part of our new role was my sister-in-law's desperate need for company. Now confined to her bed for most of her day, she longed for companionship. And since my husband was still working and had less flexibility in his schedule, I was "it."

Daily visits to Joy became the first priority on my to-do list. Several hours a day, I sat by her bedside, focused on keeping her brain stimulated and her spirits intact. My time with her included doing crossword puzzles together, reading articles to her from the newspaper, discussing current events, reminiscing about the past, and learning details about the life of my sister-in-law that I never knew.

But there was another complication: my granddaughter. My very pregnant daughter, who was in the process of moving to a new apartment, had been depending on me to help her with babysitting. Torn between Joy and Ella, I faced the additional challenge of trying to coordinate a schedule that would incorporate the needs of a bedridden woman and an energetic toddler.

The first morning that I decided to bring Ella with me to visit Joy, I wasn't sure what to expect. As we stepped into Joy's bedroom, Ella spotted a big pink balloon attached to a flower arrangement that had just been delivered from well-wishing friends. Immediately fascinated, Ella started playing with the balloon.

As an expert in multitasking, I managed to play balloon roly-poly with Ella while chatting with Joy, who was delighted by watching the excitement of her two-and-a-half-year-old great-niece.

On our next visit together, I juggled my time between balloon hide-and-seek and conversation about old Frank Sinatra movies. And so it went. With each subsequent week, the routine grew more comfortable, as a continuing supply of pink balloons kept Ella's attention, and Joy was thrilled to have two of us for company.

But a few months after our visits became an integral part of our routine, Joy suddenly developed pneumonia. Shortly thereafter, she passed away. I worried about how to explain her death to Ella, who had begun to grow attached to her great-aunt and to the time the three of us spent together.

My daughter, who had heard all about Ella's visits with me, came up with the perfect solution. The next afternoon, she bought a pink helium balloon, and we ceremoniously sent it up into the sky to find Joy in heaven.

After that, Ella always associated pink balloons with her great-aunt, believing that every time she sent one up into the sky, it would find its way to Joy.

When Ella's sister, Hallie Jordyn, was born one month later, she was named in memory of her great-aunt. Shortly afterward, on a beautiful spring afternoon, while my husband and I were with Ella at a neighborhood playground, a pink balloon suddenly floated by us, hovering over the swings. There was no one else nearby, just one solitary, perfect pink balloon. As we all looked at one another in awe, I think we knew, somehow, that Joy was watching over us all... and smiling.

~Linda Saslow

97

The Promise

I believe in prayer. It's the best way we have to draw strength from heaven.
~Josephine Baker

The dreaded council had gathered. While gazing out the restaurant window, I nervously clanked the ice cubes in my tea with a spoon. We all knew why the family had assembled. It was about Grandpa.

My uncle looked at each of us with moist eyes. "We have some important and difficult decisions to make here today."

His words drifted away, as if someone were speaking to me in a dream. Certain key words were like the sharp prick of a needle: liver disease, diabetes, complications from exposure to ammonia... terminally ill. Then another: options.

Like a game of Russian roulette, we looked at each other to see who would say it. What were the alternatives?

Just a few years before, during my college days, I had worked in care homes and actively lobbied for residential rights for seniors and the disabled. Nobody at the table knew better than I how well or how poorly these facilities operated. Naturally, the high-priced ones were excellent, but what was affordable was generally inadequate. At any rate, my grandfather, who had more wisdom and integrity than anyone I had ever known, and was still blessed with a sound mind, deserved better than to be taken from his home of 50-odd years and relocated to an unfamiliar environment surrounded by people who couldn't even begin to appreciate him—the real him.

"We can hire a private nurse, but they're hard to come by in our little town, and I don't know how long we can afford to employ one," my uncle remarked.

An uncomfortable silence ensued.

"I'll do it. I'll take care of him!" I blurted out before thinking it through.

"I appreciate the offer, dear," said Dad, "but the job will be a lot harder than you realize."

In spite of the warnings, I insisted on being Grandpa's caregiver. Within a few days, I abandoned my job, live-in boyfriend, and hometown to move into Grandpa's vintage home.

The job wasn't easy, and there were times I was tempted to seek comfort through the various means that had failed me in the past—drinking or running away. But I resisted and stayed strong, knowing what Grandpa meant to me. And, secretly, I believed I could redeem myself for the denial phase I had endured when my mother had passed away a few years earlier.

The time passed more easily with Grandpa's hypnotic storytelling.

"He wasn't much of an outlaw in my opinion," Grandpa bluntly stated as he mulled over one of our family's ancestral stories. He shared what he knew about his great-great-uncle, Charles "Black Bart" Boles, the infamous Wells Fargo stagecoach bandit active in the late 19th century. Grandpa described him as a gentle soul with a passion for poetry, rather than the ferocious fugitive of his reputation.

With a droll sense of humor, he recounted his montage of memories, ranging from the hardship of being raised in a shack during the Great Depression to his success as an inventor.

But what my young, romantic heart loved most were stories of his honeymoon days, when he lived in a tent in the woods with his new bride.

"Bunny would cook breakfast on the campfire every morning before me and my brother Lee would set off to work on that lodge," he recounted.

As a special treat, I drove Grandpa up to Strawberry Lodge where he relished the old days and ran his hand over the fine masonry work that would be his legacy.

"This is my girlfriend," he teased, introducing me to his new friends at the lodge.

That trip to the lodge would be the last of many we had taken together.

Grandpa always made me laugh and lifted my spirits when I was down, but he soon needed cheering up himself. Once home, I attempted to reinstate a sense of importance. I asked Grandpa to show me how his ham radio and some of his inventions worked.

Even with faint sadness in his eyes, realizing he was no longer capable of doing what he once did, he beamed with pride as he shared his past. The combined smells of oil, rust, and machinery from his workshop are a fond memory, forever engraved in my mind.

As time passed, his condition worsened. My duties became physically and mentally challenging beyond my expectations. My face felt strangely contorted as I forced a smile, fighting back tears, struggling to lift him into his La-Z-Boy. Once, when he fell and hurt his hip, I couldn't forgive myself.

"Just put me in a home," he insisted.

"Grandpa, you taught me to never give up. I won't! I promise!"

I turned to prayer about 5,000 times a day for sanity and support.

"Let's go out for breakfast," he suggested each morning.

It was one of his favorite things to do.

But every time, with a lump in my throat, eyes stinging from suppressed tears, I had to gently decline and explain to him that he couldn't walk anymore, something he often forgot with maturing dementia.

Once I had him resting comfortably in his chair, consuming a bland, low-sodium, sugarless breakfast, I retreated to the bathroom to quietly detonate.

Nights were easier. Though Grandpa had always been more scientific than religious, he grew comforted by scripture and even took to prayer.

"Dear God, my granddaughter is going to say a little prayer now, so please listen to her," he sincerely implored.

Despite all the misfortunes, Grandpa always retained his marvelous sense of humor. There was a sweetness in him that made me laugh and cry.

"Ah, I peed all over myself," he joked after spilling peas during dinner one night.

Grandpa, who had always been my pillar of strength, was a brilliant and pragmatic man. To see him grow frightened of the inevitable was equally frightening for me, but I realized that what he needed now was my strength.

"Promise me you won't leave me alone," he asked one night.

"I promise," I assured him, squeezing his baby-soft hand.

His time was near, and the family, who had been remarkably supportive for all these months, had already said their goodbyes. As I sat in a cold, metal, fold-up chair beside his bed, I prayed I would wake should anything happen.

Soon after nodding off, I felt a light tap on my shoulder. I looked wildly around, but nobody was there. I was still holding Grandpa's hand when he took his last breath. A tremendous, unexplainable feeling of peace fluttered through me. He was at peace, too.

With a deep sigh, I looked at the clock. It was 12:01, the exact time that my mother had passed five years earlier.

"Perhaps she was the angel who woke me," I mused.

With a deep breath, I realized that my work with Grandpa was done. He left with comfort and dignity, and I, though broken down, had grown, healed, and learned to appreciate life. The invaluable time I spent with this dear man had made me stronger. It embroidered a path of focus, strength and encouragement, instilling the promising belief that anything I dreamed to do... was possible.

~Mitzi L. Boles

98

More than a Mom

For many are called, but few are chosen.
~Matthew 22:14 KJV

In many ways, I thought that being a mom qualified me for the title of "caregiver." Doing laundry, preparing meals, and administering Tylenol as needed filled my days. However, it wasn't until our youngest of four sons was diagnosed with brain cancer that I truly understood the role of a family caregiver. At first, many aspects of life remained the same. Nick's condition was treated mostly in hospital settings, and my role seemed limited to providing transportation, rearranging the schedules of our other children, and encouraging Nick as he faced a roller coaster of good news and bad news.

Keeping Nick's spirits up became my passion. Searching for new games, puzzles, and books to keep Nick's mind occupied while he lay in a hospital bed consumed my energy. Reaching out to friends and family through a website I built for Nick released much of my stress as well as enabled me to share the highs and lows of Nick's battle.

At first, I was able to keep my career as a teacher. Thankfully, many co-workers donated their sick days to me so that I could be with Nick without losing my income or benefits. When Nick's journey entered its second year, though, I chose to take a leave of absence and devote my life solely to helping Nick. Slowly, cancer began to alter Nick's health in noticeable ways. He lost the ability to use his left arm, so our focus became helping him function with as much independence as possible. I'll never forget the joy we experienced when one of our older sons came home from college, dug out the Nintendo system, and discovered that Nick could play a few games using only his right hand! A surge of hope and laughter temporarily filled the walls of our home. As Nick's primary caregiver, I felt a huge sense of relief knowing that Nick was happy in that season of altered physical capabilities.

Several months passed, and Nick's legs weakened to the point of needing a wheelchair. Wanting to keep Nick's spirits up, we rearranged furniture and had a friend help my husband build a ramp so that Nick could come and go into our backyard as often as he liked. One day, someone surprised us and showed up with an electric wheelchair that had belonged to her mom. Vividly etched into my heart is the grin on Nick's face as he took off across our yard at full speed! He loved going all the way to the fence and then stopping at the very last second so that he could hear me scream.

Nick's health weighed heavily on my mind from the moment I woke up until the last second before I fell asleep. Balancing his needs with the everyday needs of our other children became a challenge. Situations that seemed huge to Nick's siblings (homework, friend issues, etc.) seemed trivial to me in light of Nick's condition. This often led to feelings of jealousy in their hearts toward Nick. Realizing the seriousness of Nick's health, I found myself angry many times when I saw jealousy in the eyes of our other kids. My anger combined with their jealousy and then compounded by the anxiety we were all under every day led to many heated conversations when we were not around Nick. Guilt began to sit heavily on my shoulders as I juggled the roles of caregiver, wife, and mom. Most days, I felt like a failure at all three.

The endless flow of meals from our church family, cards from friends and family, and gifts for Nick served to keep our family afloat in a sea that seemed filled with constant tidal waves of sadness and tension. I thought often of caregivers who might not have such support, and it broke my heart. I was thankful for every pie, every roast, every card, and every gift. Somehow, it seemed odd to be able to say "thank you" to God at such a difficult time, but honestly, there were no other words to show my gratitude. Caregivers cannot keep caring and giving without the love and support of friends and family.

The medicines Nick was required to take daily surpassed the contents of even my grandparents' medicine cabinet. Because tumors kept returning after radiation, chemotherapy, and multiple surgeries, we turned to alternative supplements, and I found myself on a journey into a land I never knew existed. When the medical world gave up on Nick, I couldn't. Somehow, I learned of an Amish herbalist three hours from home, and my mom and I set out on a journey to find his tiny office in the woods of Indiana. I smile as I recall this adventure with Nick and my mom. Although I believe Nick thought we had lost our minds, he joined in for the experience with his predictable, fun-loving spirit and enormous grin!

As his pain intensified and his condition worsened, we returned to traditional doctors for assistance and care. Even though our hearts never accepted the news that Nick was dying, our minds were beginning to wrap themselves around the reality that cancer was taking over Nick's frail 13-year-old body. As a mom, my heart was breaking. But as a caregiver (and only by the grace of God), I stayed strong. Accepting medical equipment from a friend so that Nick could shower and use the restroom safely upset me on a maternal level, but strengthened me as a caregiver. I wanted to know that Nick was safe, no matter how much my heart ached every time I walked into the restroom and was reminded that our house had become more like a hospital than a home.

The last week of Nick's life, our oldest son was home for Thanksgiving break. As a nursing student, Erich stepped in to help take care of many of Nick's medical needs. While we had been blessed by the help of many nurses from our church, I cannot put into words the burden that was lifted when Erich arrived and stayed by Nick's side 24/7. Watching my oldest son gently care for my youngest son brought tears to my eyes daily.

As our entire family gathered around Nick to say "goodbye," I wept deeply. Hearing Nick hum as he left this earth and went to heaven was the most painful moment of my life. As a mom, I felt devastated. As a caregiver, I felt lost. In my immediate grief, I told my husband I wanted to begin a foundation in Nick's memory. We began the Nicholas Yancy Nischan Foundation in order to carry on Nick's legacy and touch the lives of others who are hurting.

My arms still ache to scratch Nick's back. My eyes still long for the sight of Nick's grin. But deep inside I know that he is in the hands of a caregiver beyond compare—one who not only cares, but who also heals completely. Nick now runs on streets of gold, medicine-free, with two strong hands. I consider it a privilege to have been chosen to be both his mom and his caregiver.

~Tammy A. Nischan

99

Changing My Expectations

The best things in life are unexpected—because there were no expectations.
~Eli Khamarov, Surviving on Planet Reebok

To mark the occasion of my mother's 75th birthday, I drove 30 miles north of Springfield to visit her in Lincoln. I had been making this same dutiful trip for nearly nine years, and it amazed me to contemplate just how much time had passed since being forced to involuntarily place my mother in a healthcare facility.

I arrived at the nursing home as the residents were finishing their midday meal and quickly located my mother at the round table in the farthest corner of the dining room. This section was dedicated to the elderly requiring the most help to eat their meals, and additional staff monitored the table and responded to the extensive needs of this dining party. After introducing myself, I offered to take over feeding my mother her remaining lunch. As I alternated slowly between spoonfuls of all-pureed food, I had ample time to assess my mother's overall physical appearance. Although my visits had dwindled considerably in the past several years, she still appeared the same, perhaps only a bit thinner.

As usual, when not resting in her bed, Mom was sitting in her reclining geriatric chair, the medical equivalent of a La-Z-Boy on wheels. Her body movements were constantly monitored by the personal safety alarm affixed to the chair and also pinned to the top of her right shoulder. She was wearing a large bib to catch the runny food as it dribbled down her wrinkled face. Completely dependent on others for her meals now, she opened her mouth slowly to chew and swallow small spoonfuls, as if eating was a difficult task.

Mom's arms were wrapped tightly around her body, her legs were deeply bent at the knees and pulled up to her right side, and her fingers were clenched into deformed fists. This twisted pose, resembling a protective fetal position, was possible because the footrest of her geriatric chair was extended. For no apparent reason, she abruptly raised her left arm and held it up high in the air, as if requesting permission to talk. But no question would escape her lips because Mom had not spoken for the past three years. My attempts to lower her arm by applying gentle downward pressure failed, and Mom continued to keep her left arm raised in the air.

As I continued to study Mom's physical appearance, I was saddened to realize that none of her former friends would recognize her now. My mother looked nothing like the beautiful woman who had entered this nursing home almost nine years ago and had disproportionately aged over 20 years in that time. She was dressed in standard attire—baggy gray sweatpants and a loose-fitting, button-up shirt—both allowing for easy dressing and laundering. Her undergarments consisted of a comfortable stretchy white undershirt and an adult diaper, necessary for many years now due to her incontinence. Her neatly cuffed crew socks were perfectly white because Mom could no longer walk and hadn't had the desire or strength to attempt it in the past three years.

My inspection ended when Mom declared lunch was over by suddenly refusing to open her mouth any longer. After wiping the remaining food from Mom's face, I wheeled her from the dining room into the empty family room located just past the nurses' station. Meanwhile, my mother still stubbornly held her left arm extended in the air, although it was sagging lower now as she grew tired.

This was my favorite part of visiting, and I pulled out my cosmetic supplies and got straight to work by first brushing her hair in a misguided attempt to make it lie better. Next, I gently cut and filed her jagged fingernails; her nails were always in desperate need of tender, loving care. Then I slathered Vaseline on her chapped lips and slowly massaged vanilla-scented body lotion on her neck, shoulders, arms, and hands. I was never certain if Mom liked this routine because she never objected or showed signs of enjoyment, but it always made me feel useful in some small way.

Over the past 13 years, I have watched helplessly, like a passive member of a captive audience viewing a tragic Shakespearian play, as a cruel and heartless thief slowly and painstakingly stole everything from my mother: personality, job, independence, home, possessions, money, cognition, memory, mental health, dignity, quality of life, and finally her physical health. Mom is currently left with only one card left to play in this deadly Alzheimer's game: her extraordinary will to live. This last recognizable trace of what used to be my mother, coupled with the excellent and compassionate care she receives at the nursing home and the ongoing love of her children, continue to keep my mother alive.

It would seem unfathomable for most, but my visits have finally become a pleasant experience after a great deal of soul searching. I had struggled for years watching my mother decline, painfully witnessing her waste away without the ability to help. I came to see her at the nursing home with high hopes of sustaining the special connection between the two of us as mother and daughter, desperately trying to preserve the close bond that existed between us before she became ill. But it wasn't possible any longer, leaving me frustrated, bitterly disappointed, and reluctant to return because it was too difficult to accept that our relationship, as I had known it, was gone forever.

As her illness progressed and merciful time allowed me to ultimately accept her fate, I was finally able to let go of our previous relationship. I learned not to expect anything from my mother: not to watch for a smile of recognition, not to anticipate any intimate discussion, not to hear her speak my name, or even to speak at all. Shedding all those unrealistic and selfish desires set me free at last.

Without expectations, I learned to enjoy merely spending time with her. I found happiness just holding her hand, brushing her hair, reading to her or wheeling her outside to feel the sunshine on her face.

Mom's 75th birthday was drawing to a close, another bittersweet celebration mixed with happiness at seeing Mom reach another year in her life and sadness from witnessing what little quality of life remained. I couldn't help but wonder how many more birthdays Mom would see as I prepared to leave. Kissing my mother goodbye, I prayed that I might also share her determination and strength for the untold future that lay before us.

~Kathleen H. Wheeler

The Long Goodbye

Man's feelings are always purest and most glowing
in the hour of meeting and of farewell.
~Jean Paul Richter

I listened to Nathan's anguished whisper, tears rolling down his cheeks. "Please take me home." Easing down beside him, I grasped his hand, trying to ignore the fear that clutched my heart... but I knew. There aren't many secrets between partners of 52 years. Slumped against wadded sheets, his face ashen, hopeless, his hands and arms bruised from IVs, he meant, "Take me home and let me die in peace." Six hospital admissions in four months, and he was exhausted, resigned.

The doctor agreed. "And besides that, he hates me," he added. That was true.

Later, alone in the darkened ICU waiting room, my mind wandered back to that hot August evening when Nathan and I had promised "... in sickness and in health... 'til death us do part." We blithely mumbled, "I do." I sank lower in the chair, sobbing quietly when the words to a favorite hymn about the breath of God filling the body with new life came to mind.

I could not cure Nathan's chronic obstructive pulmonary disease (COPD), but I could pray for God's healing breath. I hummed the soothing melody, and the verses offered peace at last. He was in God's hands—as he had always been.

On that cold December day, I enrolled Nathan with hospice and brought him home, knowing that our time together might be measured in hours, two weeks at the most. I watched in stony silence as the master bedroom and bath were transformed into a crowded semblance of a hospital room. Equipment lined the walls, was stored under the hospital bed, beside it, stashed in the closet, and in every drawer of the bathroom cabinets. It didn't matter to Nathan. He was home. I wandered around in a fog trying to keep track of all the schedules.

After two weeks, I could see hope in Nathan's eyes. Hospice showed us exercises to strengthen his body and to conserve his available oxygen. I'd urge, "Let's try four more." Mentally, I set small goals: get out of bed, walk around the room, go to work at the computer.

I hated the wheelchair until I realized it was only a tool, a way out of the room. He could relax by the fireplace, his favorite spot to sit. His feet propped on the hearth enjoying a good movie, he'd comment, "Sometimes, I don't feel sick at all." My heart warmed that he remembered what it felt like to be well.

I would sit beside him and just touch him to let him know that regardless of how the disease destroyed his body, he was still the same person to me.

Dreary winter days dwindled by, and spring sunshine created shadows through the trees. The next challenge was to go outside. It would require stronger legs to navigate steps. I dragged out my four-inch aerobic step, put it between the walker legs and said, "It's up, up, down, down. Let's get ready to go outside." It worked.

It's hard to give care 24/7. Stress is overpowering. Exhaustion, sleepless nights, missed calls for help, guilt from not doing enough or from hovering too much. The delicate balance changes every day, and it's never perfect. Caregiving is not one-sided. Like so many other times during our years together, Nathan and I ministered to each other.

I carted in the medicines and breathing treatments four times a day, and he taught me how to change the spark plugs and battery on the lawn mower. I tried to be the chef and create inviting meals. In return, he showed me how to replace a faulty light switch without being electrocuted. When I announced, "It's Wednesday. My name is Jean, and I'm your nurse for today," he rolled his eyes while formulating a reply.

"I need to show you how to use the air compressor so that you can inflate the tire on the wheelbarrow." Not too exciting. One day after exercising, he remarked in surprise, "Look, I've got muscles again," showing off his biceps.

Unfortunately, there were episodes in between when hospice would caution, "He may not come out of it." He had already surpassed anybody's expectations. The right-side heart failure and advanced COPD made recovery less successful. Each morning, I would peek around the corner into his room, fearful of what I was going to see—Nathan sleeping or propped up in bed struggling to breathe.

I planned our 53rd wedding anniversary, sure that it would be the last. Both our rings needed repair. "I love my rings, and I want to wear them again." He smiled because the set had been his choice.

Friends visited, but nothing raised Nathan's spirits like pizza and beer lunches with old college buddies. His eyes brightened, and laughter filled the house at the outlandish stories of marching band trips and dance gigs. "I hope they never get tired of coming," he said.

For 16 months, Nathan's care focused on his quality of life while the quantity of his days slipped away. It was his decision to be at home in the house he built, surrounded by the flowerbeds he worked and relaxing on the patio he bricked. He could enjoy the deer that wandered out of the woods, nibbling on the nuts and vines. It thrilled him to watch a doe tiptoe close to the house and snatch every hosta leaf in the garden.

In his last hours, Nathan lay comfortably in bed, cradled by soft pillows. The morning sun warmed his room. I soothed his body with a fragrant lotion to let him know that he was not alone. Standing close by, I placed my cheek next to his, and whispered, "I love you," and added a kiss on the warm, moist lips that I had loved so long.

I soon realized that his breathing had stopped, and he had

quietly gone to his eternal sleep. No longer struggling to breathe, his face showed a peace that I had not seen in months. The long good-bye was over. God had granted my last prayer from the old hymn, "And give him peace."

~Jean Webb

Listen with Your Heart

The most precious gift we can offer anyone is our attention.
~Thich Nhat Hanh

You know how you remember that one moment in your life that changed everything? What you were doing when President Kennedy was shot or when man first walked on the moon? I'm dating myself, but that's the way I'll always remember the moment I found out my mom was dying of cancer.

I was attending Crime Bake, a mystery writers' conference in Boston, where I had a total fan girl moment after interviewing the brilliant author, Sue Grafton. Exhausted but happy, I flew to Florida to meet my mom, Rita, in the new home she had purchased as a family vacation home for her giant brood. It was a gorgeous sunny day, with birds chirping, lawn mowers groaning, and kids squealing in their swimming pools. A very normal day for many, and then my world collapsed to the tune of "Viva Las Vegas," the ringtone alerting me to a call from my mom. But it wasn't my mother on the phone. Instead, my sister had the very unpleasant task of being the bearer of bad news. After going to the doctor with a cold and cough that just wouldn't go away, Mom was diagnosed with stage IV lung cancer.

I'm pretty sure my brain just stopped working at the word "cancer," although I remember hearing "terminal," "six months," and "no hope." Mom wouldn't be joining me in Florida after all, and I just knew that I had to get on that next flight home. After blubbering my way through the airline conversation, tossing stuff in my luggage and waiting endlessly for the taxi, I still couldn't wrap my mind around what was happening.

Walking into Mom's house, reality quickly set in as somberness and tears permeated the room. Since she had opted out of medical care that offered no real hope, we knew home hospice was what we needed to do. Along with my eight brothers and sisters, a schedule was devised where at least two of us would be there at all times. When you add in the rest of the family, the house was never empty, and Mom got to see everyone for a final visit.

Being single, I moved in to begin a journey of the best and worst six months of my life. I thank God every day I didn't have to go it alone, and that Mom had everything so organized. All the final decisions were made. She had already arranged her own funeral and paid all her bills. Mom never wanted to be a burden to anyone.

Now all we had to do was care for her, a woman who was used to doing for others and not having them cater to her every need. And, oh, how she hated feeling so helpless. She despised needing assistance to take a shower, go to the bathroom, and even change the channel on the television.

Still, in the beginning, it was pretty easy. Make some soup, sandwiches, egg salad. Give her Tylenol when she wasn't feeling so good. But, eventually she needed a walker. One time, she needed to get to the bathroom in a hurry, so she tried to do it without the walker. My brother and sister were right there and chastised her for it, worried that she might fall. It was the first time I ever heard her use the "f word." Her frustration and humiliation were felt by us all, but it only made us more patient and sympathetic.

Toward the end, she could only tolerate watching endless episodes of *The Golden Girls* on television. While I always enjoyed the show, we now found ourselves giggling at things the writers probably hadn't thought would be funny, like the dated outfits. If their shoulder pads got any bigger, they'd all look like linebackers for a football team. But it provided us with much-needed laughter and brought back many memories.

It was during this phase of caring for my mother that she

managed to give a lasting gift of precious memories to me and every-one else in the family. You'd think after 50 years, I'd know everything there is to know about my own mother. But I found out I knew very little. With her strength waning, we began going through old pictures, and she started telling me stories. Being the middle child in a pack of 14 kids, she led quite the life, and while I knew the basics, I'd never made time to find out the specifics.

It turns out she went to a one-room schoolhouse where every girl wanted to be a nun and every boy a priest. She loved school and was the editor of the school paper. Her favorite drink was Coke, and she dreamed of coming to the big city to work as a secretary. She was very fashionable and loved red lipstick. I was shocked to find out she could do a split and was very athletic (things that aren't in my genes). When she met my dad, it was love at first sight.

I knew, of course, that their union produced nine children, 23 grandchildren, and 22 great-grandchildren. But I was surprised when I asked her if she would change anything in her life. Without hesitation, she said, "Not a thing." She felt blessed to have made it 80 years and felt that with her children she was leaving a living legacy.

In reality, I was the blessed one. By having those six months, I grew to know my mom more than I had in all the previous years. Our bond was stronger than ever. I now had memories and a family history I could pass along to my children and grandchildren. I do regret the years I wasted being too busy in my own life to take the time to stop and ask questions and really listen to the answers. It was a disservice to both of us, but like most young people, I was convinced that the world revolved around me. So, even in the end, she was teaching me things, like how to really listen. Looking back, I've come to realize that throughout this time, she gave me one more precious gift—a renewed, strengthened relationship with my sib-lings that persists to this day.

I never liked the song, "Cat's in the Cradle," and now I really know why. It's not only about not being there physically for your kids, but not being there physically and mentally for your parents as they age. I can't get back the years that I missed, but I can go on knowing that those last six months were God's gift to me.

Being a caregiver is more than just dispensing medications. It's talking and listening and helping and anticipating. It's being there because you want to, not because you have to. I never realized what exactly went into being a caregiver, but now I have the utmost respect and reverence for those who endure every day. I also know that if I had the choice, I'd do it all again in a heartbeat.

~Barbara Vey

Meet Our Contributors

Alexis Abramson, Ph.D. is a champion for the dignity and independence of those over 50. She has been featured in many national publications, including *TIME*, *Forbes*, *The Wall Street Journal*, *Entrepreneur*, and *People* and she has appeared frequently as an on-air expert gerontologist on *Today*, CNN, CBS, MSNBC and numerous other media outlets. Dr. Abramson is the author of *The Caregivers Survival Handbook*, a guide to help caregivers balance the responsibilities of caring for others and for themselves. Find out more at www.alexisabramson.com.

Sandy Adams has been writing, speaking to women's groups, and teaching marriage seminars for over 20 years. She and her husband of 39 years reside in Georgetown, TX. She has one son and four grandchildren. Sandy's passion is in finding and sharing the beauty and joy of each new day.

Monica A. Andermann lives on Long Island with her husband Bill and their cat Charley. In addition to frequent credits in the *Chicken Soup for the Soul* series, her work has been included in such publications as *Sasee*, *The Secret Place*, and *Woman's World*.

James Ashley and his wife Rowena have a 17-year-old son. James has had an exciting career, which has taken him to many parts of the world. He is a Vietnam veteran. James loves meeting new people and exploring their cultures. For the past four years, he has operated care homes for the elderly, which has been the most rewarding experience of his life.

Sharon Babineau is a decorated Canadian soldier, hockey player, and inspirational speaker. She has facilitated seminars, support groups and workshops for over a decade. She plans to write a book about her journey to share the lessons she has learned with others. E-mail her at sharon@mindbreak.ca.

Hector Badeau received a bachelor's degree from New England College. He and his wife Susan have raised 22 children; 20 adopted from foster care, most with disabilities. He has devoted his life to caregiving. He enjoys camping, sports and church activities. E-mail him at hectorbadeau@yahoo.com.

Sandra Berris was co-founder and editor of *Whetstone Literary Magazine*, 1982-2000. Her degrees include a B.S. from the University of Nebraska and an M.A. in education from Stanford University. Her work has appeared in several little magazines including *Prairie Schooner*, *The Midwest Quarterly*, and *Willow Review*.

Laura Boldin-Fournier has degrees from Arizona State University and C.W. Post College. She worked for many years as a teacher and a librarian in New York. Today Laura is a freelance writer living in Florida. Her hobbies are reading, writing, and traveling.

Mitzi Boles (Brabb) lives in central Arizona with her husband and two young children. She holds a bachelor's degree in journalism from California State University, Sacramento, and runs a wildlife sanctuary. Aside from animal rescue, she enjoys writing articles and children's books about wildlife. Please visit her website at wondersofthewild. org.

Jan Bono wrote a humorous personal experience newspaper column for over 10 years, garnering 11 state awards. She has penned several humorous short-story collections, a dozen one-act plays and a mystery dinner play, all produced, and a novel currently awaiting publication. Check out her work at www.JanBonoBooks.com.

Laura Bradford loves sharing stories about the hope and the help that have come her way as she lives to serve others. Still a caregiver, she oversees the needs of her mother-in-law and is always on call for grandparent duties. In her spare time, she enjoys praying, long walks, and gardening.

Robert J. Brake, Ph.D. is a retired college teacher and freelance writer who loves lifelong learning, animals, great one-liners, great characters, and being the center of attention. E-mail him at oobear@centurytel.net.

Judy Brown lives in Holland, MI. She has worked for Evergreen Commons, a senior center, and currently works and volunteers for Holland Rescue Mission. She enjoys writing, both academic and inspirational, and plans to continue this endeavor.

Jane Brzozowski lives and writes at the base of the Uncanoonuc Mountains of Goffstown, NH. She is happy to once again be in the same *Chicken Soup for the Soul* edition as her sister, Lava Mueller. This time, they are featured in each other's stories!

Barbara Carpenter maintains the blog becblog.com, and a site where episodes of an on-going drama appear: bectales.com. This is her fifth contribution to the *Chicken Soup for the Soul* series. She is passionate about her two children, four grandchildren, one great-grandson and her husband of 52 years. Life is good.

Adam Cass is a personal trainer who learned the lessons of parenthood and patience from Mother. He is the proud father of Sophia and Ava and will ensure that they know who Grandma was and how much she loved them. Adam wants to thank his brother Lewis Cass for being the engine in the caregiver wheel.

David Cass is a professional tarot card reader, interpreter of crystals and a corporate trainer. Mom's life and death inspired him to become a harp therapist and to use harp music for healing. David wants to thank his brother Lewis Cass for keeping him on track and focused and being the tireless leader of the caregiver team.

Cindy Charlton is a professional speaker and author bringing her message of hope and inspiration to people of all ages. She writes personal essays on her life as a survivor, and is a contributing columnist for *inMotion* magazine. She considers raising her two boys the greatest blessing in her life.

Emily Chase speaks at conferences and retreats across the country. She is the author of six books, including *Help! My Family's Messed Up* (Kregel, 2008). Her newest book, *Standing Tall After Falling Short* will be released by WingSpread early in 2012. Visit her at emilychase.com.

Terri Cooper, a former nurse, is now a magazine columnist and has published numerous articles, devotionals and anthology stories. She spends her days not only treasuring time with her parents but also enjoying her new granddaughter, and thanks God for all of them.

After teaching for 39 years, **Anne Crawley** is now retired and living in Pennsylvania. Although she misses teaching, she is active with tutoring, reading, swimming, visiting her two daughters and spending time with her mother. Hopefully, retirement will bring time to work on her writing. E-mail her at armezzanij@aol.com.

Maryanne Curran is a lifelong resident of Massachusetts where she enjoys traveling, writing, walking, and spending time with her family. E-mail her at maryannecurran@verizon.net.

When **Dianne Daniels** isn't shopping with her grandmother, she is busy working as an author, speaker, and parent coach. She wrote *Mothering Like The Father: Following God's Example In Parenting Young Children*, and has contributed to several compilation books, including *Chicken Soup for the Soul: New Moms*. Visit Dianne at www.MotheringLikeTheFather.com.

Lori Davidson is a human resources professional in central Maine. She lives on a small farm with her husband John and teenage daughters Hayley and Claudia. Lori's story is dedicated to the memory of her father James (Jimmy) Lefferts. E-mail Lori at lorisd115@gmail.com.

Peggie Devan is a Registered Nurse with a Bachelor of Science degree in psychology/sociology. She resides in Sarasota, FL, and is the caregiver for her 93-year-old mother. She cared for her father until his death in 2005. Peggie enjoys reading, embroidery and music. Her poetry can be found at jbstillwater.com.

Michele Dillingham graduated from California State University Sacramento with a Political Science degree. Michele has been a mortgage loan consultant for over 20 years. For the past 15 years she has written a weekly column in the *Sacramento Bee* on lending. Michele loves writing and painting. E-mail her at michelechicken@yahoo.com.

Lucille Engro DiPaolo resides in Plymouth Meeting, PA. She has been published in *Chicken Soup for the Soul: Celebrating Brothers & Sisters*. Lucille has completed many adventures on her bucket list including parasailing and ziplining.

Danielle M. Dryke is a program evaluator and researcher with an M.S. degree in international development from the University of Amsterdam. She has lived in Mali, Lebanon, The Netherlands, Denmark, and her native Minnesota. Danielle enjoys salsa dancing, socializing and retreating to ARC Retreat Center to write her memoir.

Although **Janet Perez Eckles** lost her sight, she gained insight to serve as an international speaker, writer, columnist and author of a #1 book on Amazon: *Simply Salsa: Dancing Without Fear at God's Fiesta*, Judson Press, August 2011. From her home in Florida she imparts inspiration at www.inspirationforyou.com.

Best known for her award-winning role as Ann Kelsey on NBC's *L.A.*

Law, **Jill Eikenberry** has had a long and distinguished career on stage, screen and television. Currently she can be seen in the film, *Young Adult*, playing the mother of Charlize Theron.

Nancy Engler lives in Arizona with her two daughters and two dogs. Some of her children's literature has been published in *Boys' Quest* and *Children's Playmate Magazine*. Her nonfiction stories have been published in *The Ultimate Teacher* and *Chicken Soup for the New Mom's Soul*. Nancy draws in her free time.

Joy Feldman, a retired executive secretary, vigorously works out. She studies and practices organic gardening and the violin, writes poetry and articles. Her award-winning biographies and poetry have been published in local newspapers. She enjoys sharing her garden's bounty, writing, museums, live theater and her family. E-mail her at Joyfeldman@verizon.net.

Jean Ferratier, a previous *Chicken Soup for the Soul* contributor, has a passion for sharing stories. She is an Archetypal Consultant, helping people link their synchronous moments to their life purpose. Jean's book is called *Reading Symbolic Signs: How to Connect the Dots of Your Spiritual Life*. E-mail her at jferratier@gmail.com.

Anna Fitzgerald received her Bachelor of Arts degree, with honors, and Master of Arts degree from the National University of Ireland, Maynooth in 2011. Anna enjoys reading, writing and traveling. She writes a blog at annasbananasaboutbooks.wordpress.com. She is planning a career in publishing. E-mail her at pearl4@eircom.net.

Rosemary Francis lives in Kilmarnock, VA, a very historical area, where she enjoys visiting old plantation homes. Traveling is a passion, especially to see grandchildren. At home, she enjoys writing, gardening and singing. She has been published in *Aquila*, a British children's magazine, and in the *Chicken Soup for the Soul* series.

Leeza Gibbons is the co-host of *America Now*, the nightly syndicated TV news magazine, and *My Generation* (on PBS stations). For 17 years she also has hosted and produced the nationally syndicated radio program *Hollywood Confidential*. But while Leeza has three decades in front of the camera, a star on the Hollywood Walk of Fame, and 27 Daytime Emmy Nominations (she won three), she is most proud of being mom to Lexi, Troy and Nathan and wife of Steven. Leeza honors her mother's legacy with The Leeza Gibbons Memory Foundation and its signature program Leeza's Place, offering free services for family caregivers. Visit www.leezasplace.org.

Michael Gingerich lives in Hershey, PA, with his wife Kathy and son Matthew. He is also the father of two other sons Adam and David, and a new granddaughter. He is an author, counselor and pastor. Michael can be reached by e-mail at michael.gingerich@hotmail.com.

Pam Giordano received her Bachelor of Science degree at Georgian Court University. She is a retired elementary school teacher whose hobbies include writing and painting. She edits the newsletter at Traditions of America at Hanover, an active senior community in Bethlehem, PA. E-mail her at pam.giordano@gmail.com.

Robin Greenberg resides in St. Louis. Her life's purpose was caring for her husband who was stricken with dementia, then Alzheimer's. With his last breath, she became one. Now she is learning to live separately, searching for her light. E-mail her at robgreenberg@att.net.

Bill Halderson received a Bachelor of Arts degree from California State Polytechnic University, and a Master of Arts degree in government from Claremont Graduate University many long years ago. Bill is retired from a career as a corporate manager and trainer. He lives and writes in Cookeville, TN. E-mail him at billandmonica1943@frontiernet.net.

Erika Hoffman writes chronically! Her novel, *Runaway Faith*, is scheduled for release in 2012. Her dad, who lives with her, turned 92 in December 2011!

Nancy Hoffstein graduated from New York University in 1983. She currently works as an accountant and enjoys writing as a hobby. E-mail her at njh.kaplan@gmail.com.

Thom Hunter is the director of BridgeBack Ministries, based in Norman, OK. Thom's books include *Who Told You You Were Naked?*, *Surviving Sexual Brokenness: What Grace Can Do*, and *Those Not-So-Still Small Voices*.

Beverly Isenberg lives in Northern California. When George, her husband of 60 years, was diagnosed with Alzheimer's disease she became his primary caregiver and blogged about her experiences providing love and care to him. Still writing, she tries to find humor in most situations. E-mail her at Bev358@gmail.com.

Barbara Joan lives in upstate New York and enjoys reading, writing and painting. She is the proud mother of three grown children, a daughter and twin sons. She is the grandmother of three beautiful grandsons: a four-year-old and 15-month-old identical twins.

Jolie Kanat is an award-winning essayist with a master's degree in the humanities. Published in eight anthologies, she is a substitute essayist for the *San Francisco Chronicle*, a contributor to NPR's *Perspectives*, the author of a full-length nonfiction book, greeting cards, and songs for Time Warner. E-mail her at jolieokay@gmail.com.

April Knight has just completed a romance novel: *Sweet Dreams, 65 Bedtime Stories for Big Girls*. She writes a column called "Crying Wind" for the *Indian Life* newspaper. She is a professional artist and her paintings can be viewed on www.cryingwind.com.

Mary Knight has enjoyed a career as a professional writer for over 30 years.

She is currently working on an MFA degree from Spalding University and will soon complete her first young adult novel, entitled *What's Left Unsaid*. She lives in Lexington, KY, with her husband and two cats.

Ruth Knox has been putting words to paper from the time she could first hold a pencil; it brings her as much joy today as it did then. Now living in Idaho, Ruth is once more a newlywed. She also loves camping, biking, hiking, and painting. E-mail her at ruthknox@live.com.

Janey Konigsberg lives in Rye Brook, NY with her husband Don. They are very active grandparents to their 12 grandchildren. Janey received a Bachelor's degree in English from Adelphi University. She was a caregiver for her elderly mom, Rosie, who passed away just before her 100th birthday.

Tom Lagana is coauthor of *Chicken Soup for the Prisoner's Soul, Chicken Soup for the Volunteer's Soul, Serving Productive Time, The Quick and Easy Guide to Project Management,* and *Serving Time, Serving Others.* Contact him at P.O. Box 7816, Wilmington, DE 19803 or e-mail TomLagana@yahoo.com. Learn more at www.TomLagana.com.

Ginny Layton received her undergraduate degree from Auburn University and her Master of Arts degree from Boston University in 1995. A pastor's wife, she enjoys making music with her three boys in Mississippi. Ginny plans to write many more inspiring stories about life with her eldest son. E-mail her at ginn3music@gmail.com.

Over the years **Lynne Leite** has been an employee, college graduate, business owner, and homemaker. She is now embracing and pursuing the dream she believes God called her to since childhood—to be a storyteller through her speaking and writing. You can learn more about Lynne at www.CurlyGirl4God.com.

Tiffany Mannino is a sixth grade teacher and breast cancer survivor living in Bucks County, PA. Tiffany loves to feed her artistic spirit by traveling abroad, writing, decorating, dancing, and laughing. She also has a story published in *Chicken Soup for the Soul: New Moms*. E-mail her at tlorindesigns@gmail.com.

Debbie Matters is the founder and principal training facilitator of Your Communication Matters Inc., a training and development company based in Toronto, Ontario. She was pleased to release her first book *If I Ran This Place... Communication for Results* in March 2011. E-mail her at debbie@ycmatters.com.

Ann McArthur started telling stories before she could write her name. In her teens, she entertained at slumber parties, spinning adventure tales featuring her friends as the smart, brave heroines. Now she writes for adults. Look for her first literary inspirational novel, *Choking on a Camel*.

Jeri McBryde lives in a small southern town outside of Memphis, TN. She has retired from the library system and spends her days reading and writing. She loves crocheting and chocolate. Her family is the center of her life.

Retired as CEO of a fairgrounds and event center in Northern California, **Delois McGrew** makes her home in northwest Arkansas. She divides her time between her distantly located family members, volunteer work, her own writing, active participation in writing organizations, and as an acquisitions editor for High Hill Press.

Cara McLauchlan is a writer, wife and homeschooling mom from North Carolina. She enjoys writing stories about the beauty of life's ordinary moments. To read more, visit her blog "Joy Goggles" at www.joygoggles.blogspot.com or e-mail her at cara@crankymommies.com.

Cecilia Egger McNeal is an avid adventurer. A rancher's daughter from Colorado, she relocated to Alaska, living a subsistence life. Then this mother of eight created a ranch/ retreat in the northeastern woods of the Midwest. Now traveling to Africa to aid women, she resides in Montana. E-mail her at cowgirlsmom@hotmail.com.

Michelle Close Mills' poetry and short stories have appeared in many anthologies including several in the *Chicken Soup for the Soul* series. Michelle resides in Largo, FL, with her wonderful husband Ralph, two great kids, two ornery kitties, and three cockatiels. Learn more at www.authorsden.com/michelleclosemills.

Janet Miracle is a retired teacher and librarian. She lives in Kentucky with her husband Carson. She received a bachelor's degree from the University of Maryland and master's degrees from Eastern Kentucky University. The mother of three grown children and two grandchildren, Janet enjoys gardening, traveling, and listening to music.

Yvette Moreau works part-time as a secretary and full-time as a wife, mother and grandmother. She enjoys knitting as much as writing and uses both to bring comfort and hope to others. She plans to continue writing and to teach knitting classes in the future. E-mail her at yvettemoreau4@gmail.com.

Lava Mueller lives in Vermont with her husband and two children. She is fortunate to be a frequent contributor to the *Chicken Soup for the Soul* series. Lava is especially excited to be in this book because her sister, Jane Brzozowski (who Lava references in her story, "Can I Do This?") also has a story in this book. E-mail Lava at lavamueller@yahoo.com.

Tammy A. Nischan is a mother, wife, high school teacher, and freelance writer living in Kentucky with her family. Helping fellow Christians on the road of grief is Tammy's passion. Blog writing and photography are her favorite pastimes. Visit her anytime at My Heart His Words (www.tammynischan.blogspot.com).

Robert Nussbaum is a lawyer by day, and a writer in the very early morning hours. This is his third piece published in a *Chicken Soup for the Soul* anthology. He thanks his family, and especially Richie, his in-house editor, for direction and support in his "second career."

Galen Pearl is the pen name of a Southern girl transplanted to the Pacific Northwest. Recently retired from teaching law, she blogs and leads retreats and classes based on her program to develop habits to grow a joyful spirit. She enjoys her five kids and two grandchildren, taekwondo, the mountains, and mahjong.

Janet O. Penn is the president of Janet Penn Consulting, LLC (JPC), an Internet business consultancy; prior to founding JPC Janet worked in the publishing and web development industries. She chairs her synagogue's social action committee and is deeply involved in community outreach. Contact her at janpen@att.net.

Ava Pennington is an author, speaker, and Bible teacher. She has published numerous magazine articles and contributed to 22 anthologies, including 16 *Chicken Soup for the Soul* books. She has also authored *One Year Alone with God: 366 Devotions on the Names of God* (Revell, 2010). Learn more at www.AvaWrites.com.

Saralee Perel is honored to be a multiple contributor to the *Chicken Soup for the Soul* series. She is an award-winning columnist. Her book, *The Dog Who Walked Me*, is about her dog who became her caregiver after Saralee's spinal cord injury and her cat who kept her sane. E-mail her at sperel@saraleeperel.com or www.saraleeperel.com.

Wendy Poole is a part-time instructor at a community college in Toronto, Ontario. She has a Bachelor of Arts degree and an Early Childhood Education diploma, with high honors, from York University/Seneca College. She enjoys traveling, writing, and spending time with her family and dog, Mishka.

Robyn Pring has a B.A. in Theater and English from Marymount Manhattan College. She owns and operates Robyn's Exquisite Journeys, a home-based luxury travel company. Her fascination with foreign cultures has led her to visit 65 countries so far. She also enjoys Broadway, ballroom dancing and sharing travel essays in online forums.

N.R. is a young Kenyan woman currently working in the Kenyan corporate world. She only discovered her passion for writing in May 2011, and is now putting together a collection of short stories based on true events in her life. E-mail her at lucid.dreamer.ke@gmail.com.

D.R. Ransdell gives a big thanks to the staff at St. Joseph's Home in Springfield, IL, where her grandmother is a current resident. Please visit D.R.'s website at www.dr-ransdell.com.

Founding director of a non-profit agency serving residents in care facilities, **Carol McAdoo Rehme** is a 25-year volunteer and advocate for the frail elderly. During her lifetime, she has found herself as both caregiver and care recipient. A veteran editor and author, she publishes prolifically in the inspirational arena.

Ann Robertson's years as an educator in English, art, and Bible mostly served to educate her. Still learning, she loves traveling with her husband, whether it's to exotic lands or simply across theirs. Additionally, her active role as Nonny keeps her life grand. Learn more at annelizabethrobertson.com.

Carolyn Roy-Bornstein's essays have appeared in many journals and anthologies including *JAMA*, *The Writer*, *Brain, Child*, *Literary Mama*, *Kaleidoscope*, *Archives of Pediatrics & Adolescent Medicine*, *The Examined Life* and Chicken Soup for the Soul. Her new memoir *Crash!* will be published by Globe Pequot Press October 2012. Read more at www.carolynroybornstein.com.

Linda Saslow is a freelance writer and journalist. She has published three books and was a reporter for *The New York Times* for more than 20 years. She continues to write for several publications and non-profit organizations, while also enjoying running, yoga, volunteerism and spending precious time with her two granddaughters.

Loretta Schoen grew up in Sao Paolo, Brazil and Rome, Italy and now resides in South Florida with her husband, two cats and two dogs. She enjoys traveling, working with abused animals, and spending time with her grandson Aiden. She is currently writing medical stories to inspire and empower patients.

George Schoengood received his AB from Brooklyn College, his MPA as well as Ed.D from New York University. He taught at Hunter College and Herbert H. Lehman of the City University of New York. At 91 years old, he enjoys discussing current events and playing the harmonica. He doesn't use e-mail but you can write to his son, Matthew Schoengood, at mschoengood@gmail.com.

Dr. Samuel Schwartz lives and practices in Rye Brook, NY. He is devoted to the practice of chiropractic, rehabilitation and nutrition. Sam loves his work and caring for his family and many patients. As the saying goes: "thus, he has never worked a day in his life." E-mail him at samdi143@aol.com.

Rick Semple is now a professional caregiver for a special needs gentleman and enjoys an active schedule of sports activities with him. Rick also enjoys being a husband, the father of two grown children and a busy toddler, and the grandfather of two. E-mail him at rsemple@comcast.net.

Larry Shaps works for Apple Inc., helping schools make the most of technology. He also enjoys riding his vintage Triumph motorcycle, playing acoustic guitar, and running along the Hudson River near his home in New York City's Greenwich Village.

Dr. Robert I. Shaps is the Superintendent of Schools in Mamaroneck, NY. Dr. Shaps received his B.A. in English from Hobart College, his Masters in Teaching and Learning from Harvard University, a Certificate of Advanced Graduate Studies in Educational Administration from the University of New Hampshire, and his Doctorate of Education in Educational Leadership from the University of Pennsylvania. He resides in Yonkers with his wife Kathleen and his son Ari. He has four children and one grandson.

As the bestselling author of 16 books, including *Passages*, **Gail Sheehy** has rocked the culture with her work. In her book *Passages in Caregiving: Turning Chaos Into Confidence*, she tells her inspiring story of caring for her husband through years of cancer and describes stories of families who we can relate to. To learn more about Gail Sheehy's books, please visit gailsheehy.com.

Deborah Shouse is a writer, speaker, editor and creativity catalyst. Deborah is donating all proceeds from her book, *Love in the Land of Dementia: Finding Hope in the Caregiver's Journey*, to Alzheimer's programs and research. So far, she has raised more than $80,000. Visit her website at www.TheCreativityConnection.com.

David Michael Smith of Delaware loves spending his free time with his wife Geri and children Rebekah Joy and Matthew. Occasionally he finds time to write. "The Garden" will be David's fourth story published in the *Chicken Soup for the Soul* books. He continues to give God alone the credit. E-mail him at davidandgeri@hotmail.com.

Mary Z. Smith is a regular contributor to Chicken Soup for the Soul. When she isn't busy penning praises to God in publications such as Chicken Soup for the Soul books, *Guideposts* and *Angels on Earth*, she enjoys walking in the quaint little town of Newton Falls, Ohio where she now resides, enjoying visits from her grown children and two small grandchildren.

B.J. Taylor continues the family tradition at the hotel suites to this day. She is an award-winning author whose work has appeared in *Guideposts*, two-dozen *Chicken Soup for the Soul* books, and numerous magazines and newspapers. Learn more at www.bjtayloronline.com and check out her dog blog at www.bjtaylorblog.wordpress.com.

A veteran stage, film and television actor, **Michael Tucker** is perhaps best known for his role as Stuart Markowitz in the hit series, *L.A. Law*. He now splits his time between acting and writing. His first book, *I Never Forget a Meal: An Indulgent Reminiscence*, was published by Little Brown & Co. *Living in a Foreign Language* and *Family Meals* were published by Grove/Atlantic. And his debut novel, *After Annie*, is published by The Overlook Press and will debut in March.

Penelope Vazquez moved to Los Angeles in 2002 to become a professional dancer. She has toured with artists around the world. She lives a fulfilled life as a mother and wife. She enjoys teaching dance to kids and continues to fulfill her passion as a professional dancer by doing local gigs every now and then.

Barbara Vey is the popular "Beyond Her Book" blogger and contributing editor for *Publishers Weekly*. When not reading, she attends national conferences for authors and readers. A huge fan of the Milwaukee Brewers and Green Bay Packers, Barbara is also an avid *Amazing Race* fan. E-mail her at barbaravey@gmail.com.

Carolyn Wade has lived and gardened on three continents. Now back home in the Pacific Northwest, she enjoys reading, writing, gardening, travel, and time with her husband, children, grandchildren and friends.

Beverly F. Walker lives in Tennessee and cares for her husband who has cancer. She enjoys writing and has stories in many *Chicken Soup for the Soul* books. Her interests also include photography, scrapbooking pictures of grandchildren, and offering comfort through her computer to other parents who have lost a child.

Samantha Ducloux Waltz is an award-winning freelance writer in Portland, OR. Her stories have appeared in *Chicken Soup for the Soul* and numerous other anthologies, as well as *Redbook* and *The Christian Science Monitor*. She has also written fiction and nonfiction under the name Samellyn Wood. Learn more at www.pathsofthought.com.

Barbara Briggs Ward is the author of the award-winning Christmas story entitled *The Reindeer Keeper*. Barbara's been published in *Highlights for Children, McCall's, Ladies' Home Journal*, and *Chicken Soup for the Soul: Christmas Magic*. Learn more at www.thereindeerkeeper.com.

Jean Webb graduated college with a music degree. She is a former aerobics instructor and worked in an office where patients were fitted with custom-made artificial eyes. She has been published in two other *Chicken Soup for the Soul* books and loves the writing process.

Kathleen H. Wheeler is a marketing communications professional living in central Illinois with her husband and two daughters. Passionate about writing and music, Kathleen is working towards the publication of her first book about renewed family relationships after an extreme caregiving odyssey with a musical twist. E-mail her at KathleenHWheeler@comcast.net.

Kim Winters earned her MFA degree in writing for children and young adults from Vermont College in 2005. When she's not wearing her caregiver's hat, Kim leads writers' workshops for teens, and is finishing edits on her first young adult novel, *Keeper's Mark*. E-mail Kim at kwinters16@sbcglobal.net.

Amy Wyatt is a wife, mother, speaker, and writer, living in Dacula, GA, with her husband Greg and their children Spencer and Mary Lyndsey. Amy travels the country representing Epilepsy Advocate and founded Signs of Life, a ministry encouraging others to live more abundantly in Christ. E-mail her at amypwyatt@gmail.com.

Susan Yanguas holds a Bachelor of Arts degree in romance linguistics from Cornell University. She has authored two novels, and her essays have been published in *Urbanite Magazine*. Her parents, especially her father, are her inspiration.

Jeanne Zornes has written hundreds of articles and seven Christian-living books, including *When I Prayed for Patience...* (Kregel). She holds a master's degree from Wheaton College. She and her husband, a retired teacher, live in Washington State and have a young adult son and daughter. She blogs at jeannezornes.blogspot.com.

Janet Zuber was a nurse for 43 years, during which time she cared for Adaline. She has since retired and cared for other elderly relatives. Her daughter, Heather Zuber-Harshman wrote the story on Janet's behalf. Heather spends her time writing short stories, devotionals, a novel, and blog posts at heatherharshman.wordpress.com.

Meet Our Authors

Joan Lunden truly exemplifies today's modern working woman. A member of the sandwich generation, Lunden is a mother of seven including two sets of twins 7 and 9 and is also a caregiver to her 93-year-old mother. She hosts RLTV's *Taking Care with Joan Lunden*, a series dedicated to caregivers, for which she won a 2010 Gracie award and she is the spokesperson for the nation's largest senior referral agency, A Place for Mom.

An award-winning television journalist, Lunden was host of *Good Morning America* for nearly two decades, making her the longest running host ever on early morning television.

Her other books include: *Joan Lunden's Healthy Cooking*; *Joan Lunden's Healthy Living*; *Growing Up Healthy*; *A Bend In The Road Is Not The End Of The Road*; *Wake-Up Calls*; and *Good Morning, I'm Joan Lunden*. Joan also wrote the foreword for *Chicken Soup for the Soul: Thanks Mom*.

More recently Joan has become an entrepreneur. She helps women have beautiful healthy skin with her Murad skin care line *Resurgence*. She and her husband invented a child safety device, Kinderkord, which they launched in 2008. Joan's line of home décor, Joan Lunden Home, is sold on QVC, as is her new line of TWIZT cookware and SMART&SIMPLE kitchen appliances.

Five years ago Lunden created Camp Reveille, a unique retreat in southern Maine where women can re-energize, jumpstart their fitness, and renew their spirits to achieve a healthier balance in their lives. (www.CampReveille.com)

For more information you can visit Joan Lunden's Healthy Living website, JoanLunden.com, for health, wellness, and lifestyle tips, family information and parenting advice.

Amy Newmark is Chicken Soup for the Soul's publisher and editor-in-chief, after a 30-year career as a writer, speaker, financial analyst, and business executive in the worlds of finance and telecommunications. Amy is a *magna cum laude* graduate of Harvard College, where she majored in Portuguese, minored in French, and traveled extensively. She and her husband have four grown children.

After a long career writing books on telecommunications, voluminous financial reports, business plans, and corporate press releases, Chicken Soup for the Soul is a breath of fresh air for Amy. She has fallen in love with Chicken Soup for the Soul and its life-changing books, and really enjoys putting these books together for Chicken Soup's wonderful readers. She has co-authored more than four dozen *Chicken Soup for the Soul* books and has edited another three dozen.

You can reach Amy with any questions or comments through webmaster@chickensoupforthesoul.com and you can follow her on Twitter @amynewmark.

Featured on
JoanLunden.com

I have created an online community with my website **JoanLunden.com** where I provide information to help make women's lives and the lives of their families easier, happier and healthier. From healthcare to skincare, safety to style, **www.JoanLunden.com** has quickly become a go-to site for women across the country.

A PLACE FOR MOM

Do you need to find the perfect place for a loved one to live? Are you looking for in-home care? Do you have a family member struggling with Alzheimer's? I highly recommend using a senior advocate or elder referral service to help you navigate this journey. **A Place for Mom,** the nation's largest senior living referral service, provides families with one-on-one guidance free of charge. The senior living advisors at **A Place for Mom** are kind and knowledgeable, and easy to talk to about any senior care situation. Learn more at **www.APlaceforMom.com**.

A WAY TO STAY HEALTHY: TWIZT COOKWARE

Check out my **TWIZT** cookware, a new line of healthy nonstick cookware available at **QVC.com**. You can ensure that you are preparing healthy meals for your family by cooking on the TWIZT line of ceramic nonstick cookware. Learn more about **TWIZT**, my **SMART&SIMPLE** products and **JOAN LUNDEN HOME** at **www.JoanLunden.com**.

A WAY TO HAVE BEAUTIFUL SKIN:
RESURGENCE BY MURAD SKIN CARE

Five years ago Dr. Howard Murad introduced me to **Resurgence** skin care. **Resurgence** is designed to target the signs of hormonally aging skin and help restore balanced, healthy and glowing skin. I love how my skin looks and feels, I love my **Resurgence**, and I know you will too! Order **Resurgence** skin care for yourself today at **www. JoanLunden.com**.

A PLACE TO GET AWAY: CAMP REVEILLE

Are you a caregiver in need of a break? I created **Camp Reveille** as a haven where women of all ages can take a break from their busy lives to take care of themselves, relax, renew their sense of play, and be re-energized. Camp Reveille's idyllic location on Long Lake in southern Maine offers an active waterfront and beach, where you can swim, sail, canoe and water-ski. Women can enjoy tennis and a myriad of fitness classes including yoga, Pilates, Tai Chi, Zumba, and mind/body classes such as meditation and breathing for stress reduction. Traditional camp activities such as archery, arts and crafts, and a 50-foot climbing wall are some of the most popular activities. Sign up now at **www.CampReveille.com** to join me as I host this four day/three night getaway every August.

Follow Joan Lunden Online:
http://twitter.com/JoanLunden; @joanlunden
http://www.facebook.com/JoanLundenFanPage
http://www.youtube.com/user/JoanLunden
http://blog.joanlunden.com

Thank You

We owe huge thanks to all of our contributors. You poured your hearts and souls into the thousands of stories and poems that you shared with us. We appreciate your willingness to open up your lives to our readers and share your own experiences as family caregivers or as the recipients of that care. Your advice and experience will help hundreds of thousands of people just like you.

We could only publish a small percentage of the stories that were submitted, but we read every single one and even the ones that do not appear in the book had an influence on us and on the final manuscript. Our editor Susan Heim read every submission to this book and put together the first draft of this manuscript with great attention to the issues that were most important to me and to Chicken Soup for the Soul publisher (and my co-author) Amy Newmark. Assistant publisher D'ette Corona worked with all the contributors, obtaining their approvals for our edits and the quotations we carefully chose to begin each story. Editors Barbara LoMonaco and Kristiana Glavin proofread the manuscript and made sure the book went to the printer on time.

My long-time colleague and friend Elise Silvestri and my daughter Lindsay Krauss, also now a colleague, were invaluable to me in obtaining, transcribing and editing the interviews and special stories provided by many wonderful, sharing friends and associates.

I also want to thank all my children and my husband Jeff for their patience while I worked on this book, especially during our winter holiday break! And of course, my thanks go to my mentor and inspiration, my mother Gladyce, whose picture graces the back cover of this book, and who makes every day that I am a family caregiver a special day.

~Joan Lunden

Share with Us

We all have had Chicken Soup for the Soul moments in our lives. If you would like to share your story or poem with millions of people around the world, go to chickensoup.com and click on "Submit Your Story." You may be able to help another reader, and become a published author at the same time. Some of our past contributors have launched writing and speaking careers from the publication of their stories in our books!

Our submission volume has been increasing steadily—the quality and quantity of your submissions has been fabulous. We only accept story submissions via our website. They are no longer accepted via mail or fax.

To contact us regarding other matters, please send us an e-mail through webmaster@chickensoupforthesoul.com, or fax or write us at:

Chicken Soup for the Soul
P.O. Box 700
Cos Cob, CT 06807-0700
Fax: 203-861-7194

One more note from your friends at Chicken Soup for the Soul: Occasionally, we receive an unsolicited book manuscript from one of our readers, and we would like to respectfully inform you that we do not accept unsolicited manuscripts and we must discard the ones that appear.

www.chickensoup.com